PUBLICIZING AND PROMOTING PROGRAMS

THE McGRAW-HILL SERIES IN THE MANAGEMENT AND ADMINISTRATION
OF CONTINUING EDUCATION

Consulting Editor
Rosalind K. Loring, Dean
College of Continuing Education
University of Southern California

Apps: PROBLEMS IN CONTINUING EDUCATION
Cooper: ETHICS FOR EDUCATING THE LIFELONG LEARNER
Farlow: PUBLICIZING AND PROMOTING PROGRAMS
Lenz: CREATIVE PROGRAMMING AND MARKETING IN CONTINUING EDUCATION

PUBLICIZING AND PROMOTING PROGRAMS

HELEN FARLOW

University of Illinois

McGRAW-HILL BOOK COMPANY

New York   St. Louis   San Francisco   Auckland   Bogotá   Düsseldorf
Johannesburg   London   Madrid   Mexico   Montreal   New Delhi   Panama
Paris   São Paulo   Singapore   Sydney   Tokyo   Toronto

Library of Congress Cataloging in Publication Data

Farlow, Helen.
    Publicizing and promoting programs.

    (The McGraw-Hill series in the management and
administration of continuing education)
    Bibliography: p.
    Includes index.
    1.   College publicity—United States.
2.   Adult education—United States.   I.   Title.
II.   Series.
LB2331.63.F37   659.2'8'3781   79-10918
ISBN 0-07-019947-7

1234567890DODO7832109

This book was set in Optima Medium by Black Dot, Inc.
The editors were Robert G. Manley and M. Susan Norton;
the designer was Anne Canevari Green;
the production supervisor was Richard A. Ausburn.
R. R. Donnelley & Sons Company was printer and binder.

"What we must do—much *more* than people in other kinds of educational activity—is to call attention to ourselves, to dramatize our work. This, simply enough, is what promoting continuing education means: using advertising, publicity, direct mail, personal contact to make people aware of us so that they do what we want them to do—enroll in classes, visit cultural centers, participate as citizens in community life."

Milton R. Stern, Dean
University Extension
University of California, Berkeley

CONTENTS

ACKNOWLEDGMENTS

One of the several pleasures in writing this book has been my enjoyment of the generous cooperation I received from each of the several people whom I asked for (and from whom I received) permission to use materials or quotes. These include:

Marilyn Barnett, Fairmont Hotel, New Orleans
Larry Bramblett, University of Georgia
Lowell Eklund, Oakland University
Nancy Greene, Indiana University–Purdue University at Indianapolis
Gayle Hendrickson, University of Minnesota
Virginia Lawler, State Department of Labor, North Carolina
Marjorie Leamnson Stonehill, Indiana University–Purdue University at Indianapolis
Philip Lesly, the Philip Lesly Company
Philip Nowlen, University of Chicago
Larry Stewart, Radio Station WDWS

There were others, recruited through the brute exercise of nepotism, drafted but able consultants in particular areas of specialization:

Darrell Blue, Director of Production, WCIA-TV
Larry Farlow, Photographer, Illinois State Natural
    History Survey

And most especially, there were three colleagues who served as preliminary readers, making suggestions and comments on the first-draft manuscript, all thoughtfully conceived and deeply appreciated:

Harold J. Alford, Rochester Institute of Technology
Jerold W. Apps, University of Wisconsin–Madison
Milton R. Stern, University of California, Berkeley

Helen Farlow

A DIALOGUE BETWEEN YOU AND THE AUTHOR
(WITH A VOICE FROM THE REAR)

Help!

What's the matter with you?

I'm involved in this program.

What's wrong with that? Lots of people are involved in programs. You've probably done it before. If you haven't, there are scads of old hands at this kind of thing who will help you or give you advice.

Yes, but there's the publicity.

What about the publicity?

I have to handle it. I not only am involved with this program, I have to take care of the publicity. I have to tell the people about the program and invite—no, incite—them to take part. I have to, well, attract registrations.

That's not hard, whether you are in full charge or just one of a publicity-promotion staff or committee. You can do it.

I don't know how!

Don't worry. I'll show you. After all, whether your program is a symposium, a workshop, a course, or a sequence of courses, a conference or institute—they're all publicized pretty much alike. They are all continuing education programs.

Even if they're not sponsored by educational institutions?

Often, particularly if they're not sponsored by institutions which call themselves "educational" or which are not educational in the strictest sense of their major mission.

Like what?

Oh, like agencies, businesses, organizations, libraries, churches, Y's. . . . There can be all kinds and combinations of sponsors. If the program is addressed to the out-of-school adult and is on a postsecondary or even postgraduate level, it is a continuing education program.

(Voice from the rear: "Did you forget basic adult education?")

Not at all. But how can it be "continuing education" if the adult doesn't have a basic education? You can't continue something you don't have in the first place.

How are *you* going to help me?
Help!

I wish you'd stop with that "help!" stuff. It ruins my incentive, if you know what I mean. I am going to tell you about a guidebook.

A guidebook? What good will a guidebook do me? I can't stop and read it. Not in that jungle out there.

Dummy, that isn't a jungle. At most, it's a thicket. There are paths to follow, and nice people (and some not so nice), and surefire maps, and little platforms you can climb up on at regular intervals to check your progress and survey the terrain.

Lions and Tigers and Bears?

No Lions and Tigers and Bears. OK. Some stinging scorpions and a few swamps and bogs and morasses, granted. But no Lions and Tigers and Bears. If you follow the paths and check the map at every turn and keep at it early and late, it'll be a breeze—and even easier next time. You see, I wrote this book. . . .

A book?

Yes, and it's called Publicizing and Promoting Programs. It's to help people like you.

It's a guidebook?

Yes, and a map, and a checklist, and it points out those little platforms where you climb up to assess your progress, and there are clues on how to skirt around the puddles, and traps and snares for . . . well, the scorpions.

No Lions and Tigers and Bears?

Only a few.

I'll try it. Where's that book?

This is it.

(Voice from the rear: "Help!")

INTRODUCTION

ABOUT THIS BOOK

There are several books out on what currently is being called the "marketing" of programs. More are in the works.

This examination of ways to provide information and promotion for continuing education to the end of generating registrations and enrollments is wholesome and sometimes useful.

In this book, you will find such terms as "publicity," "promotion," "public relations," and even "p.r." used instead of the more popular term "marketing."

This is due to a personal and perhaps trivial preference; the reader who wishes to do so may substitute "marketing" whenever it seems appropriate.

This exposition was conceived as a handbook, even a workbook, and it is our hope that—despite the size required to tell the readers what they need to know about publicizing and promoting continuing education programs—it will remain a practical, down-to-earth guidebook, easy to read, easy to use.

The book will be of particular help to people in community colleges and school systems—people who often must publicize the programs they develop and/or administer or are given jobs with publicizing and promotional responsibilities while they yet are without professional media or publicity experience.

It should be useful, also, in major higher continuing education where promotion is coupled with program development duties.

And it exists outside institutions of higher learning. It is evident that this kind of book also can be of help to other sponsors of public discussion, workshop, and similar programs which are (in fact if not in name) continuing education activities—programs sponsored by civic, religious, social, fraternal, and commercial organizations, including agencies, foundations, and institutions.

Publicizing and Promoting Programs is a guidebook. It is organized sequentially, one step leading to the next.

If the amateurs, professionals, or in-between practitioners in continuing education publicity will follow the Timeframes and Checklists in this book, they will find it to be a specific, exact, and logical guide to carrying out promotion and publicity on a project from its earliest beginnings through its postperformance evaluations.

Thus, the book is separated not into chapters but into "phases"—phases of operation and activity in publicity and promotion.

After this "Introduction," you will find Phase I, "Gearing Up." This portion of the book will be your guide in doing things early and getting them out of the way—the very earliest parts of the preparation. Because almost everything can be done and *should* be done in advance, it will be the most important part of this volume.

Phase II will stress "Carrying Through"—a guide, again, to carrying through the actual publicity-promotion of your program or other continuing education activity.

And then you come to the climax of all this activity—Phase III, "D day." This outlines and, again, guides you through the day or days when the program takes place—or, at the very least, the day or days when it begins. You will find—perhaps to your surprise—that the basic pattern for surviving D day with success is quite constant, whether your project is a program, a workshop, a symposium, a conference, an institute, or a formal short- or long-term class.

So now it's over, and you can relax?

Not yet. We have Phase IV, "Mop Up."

This is your assessment of the highs and lows in the publicity-promotion effort for that particular project. And it will be useful. No publicity-promotion effort is complete without it. It will establish the record which you, as a competitor in what can be a most exciting arena, have scored with the initial effort in which you used this book as a guide. Taking score is not difficult to do, and it will enable you to improve on that score next time out, with an awareness of where you were successful and of where you will wish to change tactics and techniques.

Because, as Phase IV will insist, "There always is a next time."

Well, now you can relax, and relaxation may be made more felicitous than it might otherwise be because here we gather, for easy access, a Phase V, "Et Cetera."

Gathered in this part of the book are inclusions, calendars, and Checklists for year-round publicity efforts; references; and an annotated bibliography—a gathering of the sources and pragmatic ideas which you will use not only in this particular guided tour of duty but also as other, more or less sophisticated occasions arise which need and deserve your publicity effort. Think of it as the hall closet—all the things you want to keep on hand but which have no other place will be crowded into Phase V, "Et Cetera."

TONE OF VOICE

This book will be preachy. If your enthusiasm doesn't soar off the top of the charts, if you have a ho-hum attitude, this book was not meant for you. If you aren't a missionary at heart, you didn't belong in continuing education in the first place.

There will be successes, if you follow the guidebook carefully, and there may be failures. But you cannot help but learn skills and strategies which will serve you well, now and in the future. Even if you go this route as practitioner of promotion only once, the techniques you have practiced that one time will be useful in program development and in helping use and focus the publicity efforts of others.

As you read and use this guidebook, you will find many apparent repetitions. If they are repetitions, that is deliberate. For example, you will note that advance planning and preparation are emphasized, over and over, in different or even in the same contexts. You will see Checklists which sometimes repeat items on other Checklists. Because of the nature of your preparatory effort, this again is necessary, for in publicity and promotion nothing must be allowed to fall between the chairs. And you will see Timeframes that sometimes seem to be—and are—an echo, stronger or weaker as the circumstances warrant, of earlier Timeframes.

Why do we repeat ourselves? Reader, we do not intend for you to fail, or to minimize your success, simply because we did not tell you and we did not remind you and we did not instruct you to pause and review and react. This is not only a guidebook; it is a guidebook which attempts to tie strings around your finger.

Some of the things we will require of you until they become the second nature of any publicity effort you may make are (not in any particular order):

1. Be ethical.
2. Be mannerly. Good manners breed goodwill.
3. Be accurate.
4. Preplan and practice complete advance preparation.
5. Learn the constant use of analysis, Timeframes, Checklists, Inventories, coding for tracking and evaluation.
6. Be specific in your use of the proper techniques and patterns for the preparation of *usable* publicity materials. There are correct and incorrect ways of preparing materials. Learn how to do it right and why it has to be done just that way.

DEFINING THE TERMS

Admittedly, I am equating the "marketing" of continuing education with huckster-ism and the hard sell. I am not alone.

Milton R. Stern of the University of California, Berkeley, once remarked that the omnipresent term "marketing" lost some of its credibility for him when he turned to a reference and found the notation "See billboards."

I must allow, however, that the term "marketing" is held in repute by many educators in continuing education for whom I have great respect, although this book seldom uses this popular term, "marketing," to describe its processes and goals.

Lowel Eklund of Oakland University, Rochester, Michigan, has put the market-ing idea as it concerns continuing education into graceful words:

> *Our target, very simply, is the arm of consumerism—service to the client and his needs. We must be client-oriented and dedicated. We have a great calling. The job of bringing intellectual enlightenment and economic improvement is one calling for professional competence and missionary zeal as we exploit and encourage the improvability, if not the perfectability, of man. If, as Camus said, "Man is the only animal who refuses to be what he is," we are the principal purveyors of the means by which this process is effected—continuing educa-tion.*

Promotion, publicity, public relations—the outreach communications ele-ments—constitute the third phase in a marketing package which is made up of:

1. Identifying prospective clients, and putting the client and the client's needs and wishes first at all times
2. Devising and developing activities to meet those needs and desires
3. Promoting and publicizing the prospective activities so that those who can make use of the activities can learn about and take part in them
4. Carrying out the activities to the benefit of the participants
5. Assessing the completed project for evaluation and future direction

Publicity . . .
Promotion . . .
Public relations . . .
These are the terms regularly used by people who do publicity for a living.

And they are among the facts of life for practitioners—professional or otherwise—in continuing education.

So let us state some basic definitions.

Many people—even people who should know better—think publicity, promo-tion, and public relations are the same thing.

They aren't the same thing at all, any more than brothers and sisters are the same people. Yet there are elements of kinship and, in fact, sometimes the three function in much the same way and with much the same result.

Publicity is a comparatively unadorned statement of the facts and nothing but the facts. It involves getting information out to the general public or to target publics about what you are and what you are doing.

Promotion is bringing in the bodies. When we speak of "promotion" in the case of continuing education, we are talking about stratagems and strategies which are aimed at generating enrollments or registrations.

Public relations is a blanket word for efforts and activities which establish or enhance the "halo effects"—ways of presenting your institution and its programs which result in goodwill on the part of others. Someone defined it as "living right—and seeing that others know you *are* living that way."

Publicity, most simply, is letting people—the right people, those you wish and need to reach—know what's going on. This can be a one-shot effort, or it can be a sustained campaign, an ongoing thrust. When it is practiced on a continuing basis, it builds the profile of what you are doing; it provides those you hope to impress with a spectrum of your activities; and, in aggregate, it justifies your existence.

Promotion is the term for the effort or cluster of efforts which you mount when the goal is not only to gain recognition for whatever you have available (in this case, an outreach project) but also to stimulate action from others so that they will take advantage of the availability of your program (and, in this case, will attend).

Public relations, although sometimes misused, is an honest term meaning just exactly what it says—activities which enhance a person's or a unit's relationships with and image in the minds of those who make up its public.

Used correctly and in its historic and legitimate sense of providing accurate information to a public or publics, the term "public relations" can be uttered and written without apology.

Public relations can in some ways overlap its siblings, publicity and promotion. To abandon the "family" figure, we may see that publicity and promotion are, in fact, integral parts of public relations.

In the strictest sense, publicity implies working through the media, while public relations is much less specific. Anything that helps promote good feelings on the parts of others in regard to your activities and programs is basically good public relations. A program can be mounted which will benefit both the registrants and the institution, yet a single discourteous or inept official or faculty member can turn the whole thing sour—i.e., bad public relations. On the other hand, a flimsy program can be accepted and even praised if the officials or faculty who represent your institution do so with warmth and capability.

When focusing on publicizing a program, public relations might include providing special helps to the media in ways not necessarily related to the outreach activity you are promoting; or it might be anything else which helps provide a warm climate for the work you are doing.

It thus involves not only letting people know about activities, as is true with straight publicity, and not only combining publicity with promotion in a mix intended to get people's positive involvement and participation in those activities, but also the less tangible components which make up goodwill.

As you read this book, you will see references to the family which we have called promotion, public relations, and publicity. You will also see the frequent use of an abbreviation—p.r.

Granted that "p.r.," as a term, is slanguage or jargon. Purists will argue that "p.r." is a simple abbreviation for "public relations." This is true. However, the language long before our time already was corrupted to the point where "p.r." was used as an umbrella term, and that is how it is used here, for it is too late to undo the damage.

For the whole publicity/promotion/public relations mix, good p.r., including good p.r. which is related to outreach or continuing education activities, is a job for professionals. There are people who think, "Anybody can do p.r." Not true. They are like those who say, "Anyone who can read can cook." Also not true. The former turn out reams of unusable news releases which end up in the round file. The latter, of course, turn out inedible messes.

This book will not attempt to compress a degree in journalism, a number of years in the media, and wide and generous experience in educational p.r. into a single volume.

What it will do is, simply, help you perform well in a field of endeavor which is not completely familiar to you, and do it as easily, efficiently, and effectively as possible.

THE MYTH OF THE BETTER MOUSETRAP

WHY PUBLICIZE?

You can have the best continuing education program in the world—serving an honest need, solid yet imaginative, superbly staffed—but if people do not know about it, they can't profit by it.

Letting them know about it, and doing so in a way that underscores its applicability to their needs or wishes, is the job for publicity and promotion.

Look facts in the face. People are not going to beat a path to your door. Your light will not shine in the wilderness.

There is no such thing as a better mousetrap.

Let us take an example, using two fictitious universities in the same state as the sponsors of similar continuing education programs.

Both Upstate and Downstate Universities have planned programs, addressed to the opinion leaders of the state as well as to research specialists and members of the manufacturing community, on an identical topic—interpretation of the Toxic Substances Act.

There is great confusion about interpretation of this act, and direction has been sought by the chemical industry, by biologists, and by thinking people in general.

Upstate's program has been magnificently promoted—brochures, letters of invitation, selective telephone calls, articles in the commercial and the trade press, appearances by steering committee members on talk shows, and the use of other public service broadcast units.

Downstate's steering committee members have been more complacent. This is a marvelous program with headline speakers, they tell each other. It is needed. People want it. All we need do is send out an announcement. We'll have standing room only. We'll be turning people away.

You know what happened. Downstate's program bombed. Upstate's was a signal success.

PUBLICITY: A COMPETITIVE SPORT

Continuing education, like politics, is an art of the possible. Publicity is what makes it possible.

Publicity is a sport—a competitive sport!

Exercising the art of publicity can be fascinating. As you grow more adept through diligent practice, you constantly will be trying to beat your own record.

The first item to realize is the competitive aspect of any publicity which is directed principally toward using the news media to attract enrollments and registrations.

Every release you send out, every interview you attempt to schedule, every phone call you make to a news desk is a competitive effort.

White space is limited.

Air time is limited.

You may think that the size of today's newspaper or magazine or journal and the news time of broadcast media are elastic. You may think that print and air space is predicated on the amount of news or appropriate feature material available that day.

You are wrong.

In general, print white space—the space available for articles of all kinds—is determined by the numbers of advertising inches which have been sold for the issue scheduled that day, week, or month—depending on the kind of print vehicle being used. There are very few exceptions to this rule.

And in general, broadcast time is strictly circumscribed by the station's format, with a set number of minutes and hours dedicated to public service broadcasting.

There is no such thing as two-way stretch in print space and air time.

Thus, every time you put out a release or schedule a press conference or use whatever tools and tactics you have at your disposal (or which you can invent or scrounge), you are in competition.

With whom?

With everyone—but *everyone!*—who wants to get on the air or into print at that particular time. With everything that is happening in the world that month, week, day, or hour which may be as worthy for selection for time or space as your program. With everything that is enough more interesting or exciting than your program that it may gobble up that scarce air time or white space.

For this reason, as will be underscored later, the materials you provide for the media must be *accurate, to the point, prepared to hold copyreading and rewriting to a minimum, and presented with honesty, courtesy, flair, and a demonstrated understanding of such immutables as deadlines and space and staff limitations.*

Memorize that statement. Paste it on your typewriter. Set it to music and sing it in the shower.

Publicizing and promoting continuing education programs is an art whose time has come.

As sponsors of continuing education activities proliferate, and as the competitive aspects of attracting users to such activities multiply, the need for virtuoso performance of the art also grows.

The fact is that even among the largest, most complex, and most prestigious institutions and organizations carrying on various kinds of continuing education for adults, there are only a small number which have professional full-time *continuing education* publicity-promotion people or departments.

How many can you identify?

Very few.

The National University Extension Association (NUEA), the major organization of universities most actively engaged in a spectrum of continuing education activities, has a small but active Information Services Division.

Its membership tallies about fifty.

Although they are both interested and involved, most of these fifty people are only peripherally publicists and promoters.

Some primarily are program development people who do their own publicity on a fairly sophisticated level. Others are specialists in some particular subdivision of publicity, but they are not professionally qualified or active in any but a small corner of the field, such as graphics or paid advertising.

Quite a few can be characterized as "learners." They want and possibly need to know more about continuing education publicity-promotion practice and ploys. They come to meetings to pick up what smatterings of expertise they can. And, of course, they are more than welcome.

Yet the NUEA is the organization of the 280-plus major American institutions most actively engaged in a variety of efforts in the field of continuing and adult education and public service.

In most of the major institutions in this organization, the coordinator, project director, or steering committee has—somehow—to grind out the publicity. The same usually holds true when the continuing education sponsors are agencies or organizations not formally organized primarily as institutions of higher learning. In other cases, the publicity problem is turned over to a general institutional publicity office where the practitioners—able as they may be in their own niches and working within the parameters of their own backgrounds—are not trained or experienced, philosophically or professionally, in the special skills and strategies necessary to get out the word and bring in the bodies.

Do-it-yourself and improvisation, then, too often are the name of the game in publicizing and promoting continuing education. This is a shame and sometimes a disaster. Effective publicity definitely is not the amateur hour.

PHASE I

GEARING UP

PRELIMINARIES

Aristotle, already quoting a proverb, said it best:

*Well begun is half done.**

The successful publicity-promotion campaign is one in which, by gearing up, the entire job can be "well begun" and much more than "half done" far in advance of the activity being publicized.

It is one in which the person in charge of the p.r. area of the activity keeps *full*

---

*Note: To those who argue that Aristotle did not make this statement in these exact words—peace. There is no contest.

What he did say (in translation) was:

"The beginning, as the proverb says, is half the whole."—Aristotle

And what some others said:

"Begin, and then the work will be completed."—Goethe

"Didium facti qui caepit habet." ("He who has begun has the work half done.")—Horace

"Great is the art of beginning, but greater the art is of ending."—Longfellow

Et cetera.

control of all that goes on in the p.r. effort; in which the effort is *completely* organized for efficient operation; and in which every possible task will have been performed and every possible bit of material will have been *prepared well ahead* and kept ready to slip into use at the appropriate moment.

THE GEARING-UP PROCESS

As you gear up in your campaign, you will be:

1. Establishing your role in the organizational structure of the project
2. Analyzing the project for its p.r. potential, analyzing the p.r. pluses you have at hand, and analyzing the outreach elements you may use
3. Contributing your very special p.r. skills and insights to the development of the project
4. Realistically determining the "magic mix" of publicity—the combination of elements most likely to get you the public response you want for your program or event
5. Operating on an "early bird" basis and demanding similar advance preparation from coworkers and vendors (printers and other suppliers)

The gearing-up period—the span of time between the "Go" signal and the 6-week countdown immediately preceding the event—is when you do the advance work necessary for your publicity-promotion effort.

Why a 6-week countdown? The figure may seem arbitrary, but long experience by practitioners proves it to be an effective timespan for the concentrated promotion effort.

During this period, all materials of whatever kinds should be prepared; your preliminary approaches to the news media should be made; your people-pleaser ducks should be lined up in a row.

This is "get ready" time, and if you use it profitably, the countdown and D day should be downhill all the way.

START WHERE YOU ARE

A good rule for any endeavor which requires the coupling of creativity with major effort is—*Start where you are.*

Fantasizing can be great fun. Wouldn't it be great if? . . . Sure it would. But you are going to operate much more competently, more thoroughly, and with a maximum of efficiency if you look facts in the eye and make the most of what you have available.

To be able to start where you are, it is useful first to determine exactly where you are at the moment.

What do you have available to you?

Going for you?

At hand?

In order to help you marshal your forces—for that is exactly what you do during the gearing-up period—the information and advice presented in this part of *Publicizing and Promoting* will include sets of guidelines, criteria, and Checklists.

The pages on which these three kinds of lists are found must be your "bible." Learn them by heart. Have them copied and mounted on cardboard for instant reference. Post them on your bulletin board. They can make the difference between a classy job and a tacky one.

Follow them continually and explicitly, for guidelines—rules of proceeding and of relating to others—are vital. The activities and attitudes covered by the guidelines mark the professionals who move by them and reveal the amateurism of those who do not.

GUIDELINES FOR PRACTITIONERS

The guidelines which follow are grouped as to areas of emphasis.

Guidelines for Practitioners in Publicizing Continuing Education Programs

Involvement
1. Be involved.
2. Be audience-oriented.
3. Be specific in relationships with associates.
4. Be realistic.
5. Keep control.

Pizzazz
6. Be inventive.
7. Be imaginative.
8. Be audacious.

Professionalism
9. Be the early bird.
10. Be prepared. (Remember what you learned in scouting?)
11. Be organized.
12. Be thorough.
13. Be accurate.
14. Use Inventories.

15. Use Checklists.
16. Use Timeframes.
17. Use deadlines.
18. Set priorities.
19. Use codes.
20. Keep good records.
21. Use good taste.

The guidelines are admittedly redundant. They overlap. They are intended to overlap. They are intended to touch all bases—to be so complete that, if they are followed to the letter, nothing will be omitted which can contribute to the conduct of your publicity-promotion campaign.

Involvement

There is a very good reason why *involvement* is put at the head of the list of guidelines.

As the publicity-promotion honcho—the person at whose desk the buck will stop in this entire part of the effort—*you must deal yourself* in early during the planning period.

We will call the promotion-publicity staff or committee simply your task force—to save words.

There is no way that you, with your task force, can do a good job of promotion for a program which was well along in the planning-development stages before you were asked (or allowed) to sit in on the steering committee meetings and conversations.

It is to be hoped that you have the clout to refuse—absolutely!—to do the Band-Aid bit if the program planning already is well along toward final formation.

The Band-Aid bit? This is my term for the project-saving emergency action that p.r. people too often are called upon to take when it is too late to give a project the full treatment it deserves and needs.

It is true that often the p.r. team is able, through heroic measures, to "save" an ailing project, but the resulting feat of salvage usually is not worth the extremes of time, effort, and begging for favors which it requires.

The publicity-promotion head, by whatever title that person is called—chair, director, coordinator, any of a dozen others—can be one of the best-qualified resource people a program development staff or a project steering committee can have.

This person can enhance the program through knowledge of people pullers, participants, and ploys that will attract the desired audience.

Given the necessary time and support in terms of help and money, the publicity-promotion person can organize and mount a campaign which will make the program planners' dreams come true.

And he or she can perform the valuable role of keeping realism in the publicity mix and of playing the devil's advocate, whenever that abrasive but sometimes necessary stance must be assumed for the ultimate good of the project.

INITIAL CONCERNS: TIME AND BUDGET

A principal reason why you must insist on "deal me in early—or forget it!" is based on allocations of money and of time.

The steering committee must be put under authoritative pressure to (1) give the p.r. person some money, however little, with which to operate and (2) give the p.r. person as much time as possible (a year-ahead alert is not too early).

For p.r., even at its least elaborate, costs money.

It costs to hire extra help and assign on-staff help to the project on a released-time basis or on overtime. Released time, of course, means that staff members are relieved of usual duties in order to take on your project, but they are not paid anything extra.

Paper costs money.

Printing costs money.

Graphics cost money.

Postage costs money.

Gasoline costs money.

Photographs, posters, flyers, and other p.r. instruments, as listed throughout this book, cost money.

P.r., even at its least elaborate, takes time.

As the Timeframe on pages 124–125 indicates, preparation for a major program takes a minimum of 6 weeks, and this is 6 weeks *after* all arrangements have been made, schedule and speakers locked in, and all systems *go*.

Time is required to prepare special media mailing lists. (See pages 98–101.)

Time is required to meet printers' deadlines . . . journal and magazine deadlines . . . graphic artists' deadlines . . . broadcast deadlines.

Time is—most simply—required if you are to be the "early bird" who makes a successful promotion effort become just that—a success.

In 99 occasions out of 100, the particular program you are publicizing is not your only job. It is a set of chores which has to be fitted in among other efforts; it is in fact only one piece of the complicated jigsaw puzzle which is your total career responsibility.

So an advantage in being involved early on is that you will have a breathing space in which to survey the major responsibilities and priorities of your schedule during the next 6 months or so—particularly during the 6-week countdown toward the project's D day—and with these responsibilities and priorities in mind, *make time* to give this particular project the attention it must receive. (See pages 149–151 for a "detailed guide" for wrapping a steering committee around your typewriter.)

ATTRACTING AUDIENCES

Ivory towers still exist, even in this day of evening schools, downtown campuses, and computerized educational delivery systems. So another reason for being dealt into any project at the moment of its first anticipatory breath is so that you can keep the dwellers of the ivory towers in touch with the realities of the world which holds the publics they hope to address.

Whether you are working in an academic setting or one inhabited by workers in social, civic, nonprofit, or business organizations or agencies, you may find to your dismay that researchers, scholars, and theoreticians have limited ideas and instincts about what will attract participation in programs by people outside those ivy-wreathed walls, whether the ivy actually exists or is a figment of a professorial or professional imagination.

An educator's—or a committee's—enchantment with a topic is not a very good reason for putting on a program with it as the theme, although such enthusiasm is a plus in any activity.

Specialists in program development put great stock in needs assessment and in targeting audiences, but these are not exact sciences. Needs assessment ofttimes involves the use of questionnaires or other kinds of written or oral instruments. Yet it is a truism that people who answer questionnaires usually are accommodating folk who are apt to tell you what they think you want to hear.

So the happy fact that of 2,119 people registered in a variety of evening classes at your institution, 211 said they would be interested in a seminar on Saul Bellow and the American novel, doesn't really mean a thing. They were just being nice about it. Would 20 of them enroll? Maybe, maybe not.

But let us assume that a needs assessment has been made, whether it be by seat-of-the-pants hunch, an evaluation instrument, or the enthusiasm of the sponsors. Objective, subjective? At this point, what's the difference! The project is under way, and you—the p.r. person—can be of utmost use to the staff or steering committee.

Properly and completely involved and consulted, the publicist should be able to advise the planners as to which of several prospective program presenters—people who may, on paper, have equal qualifications to fill a certain slot in the agenda—can help bring in the bodies.

It can be important for your program staff or committee to realize that there are individuals, particularly in academe, who have very high recognition quotients among their peers, but whose names and talents are not familiar even to informed members of the general public.

In the same discipline or area of expertise, there are other men and women who somehow are drawing cards, perhaps through chance or perhaps through a certain flair or visible accomplishment which raises them above the rest in the eyes of the public.

If I am going to try to attract people to a public discussion program, for example, it helps a lot if somewhere on the program there is a Barry Commoner or a James Michener; a James Reston or a Henry Ford; and oh! what bliss it would be to get a Walter Cronkite! A United States senator—*any* United States senator—is a boon to the p.r. practitioner.

Now let's think a little smaller. Governors draw well; so does the state or national president of an organization, particularly if your program is addressed to members of that organization; so do writers of important (or, at least, popular) books. There could be a very meaningful list of people-puller categories, a list which would be as long as this entire book. Perhaps some really bright program development person one day will write that book.

But for the purposes of program p.r., one test is fairly simple. Let us take it for granted that you are reasonably well read and see a certain number of newspapers and nonprofessional periodicals regularly. Now, if the person being sought as a program ornament is not in your area of professional interest, *but you do recognize the name*, chances are that other people who aren't in the luminary's field also will recognize him or her and be tempted to attend your program.

Name recognition is not the only test. The same kind of pulling power can be assumed if you recognize the person's stature when you hear him or her described in a single phrase:

"You know, he's the one who discovered. . . ." "She's the one who wrote. . . ." ". . . the president of. . . ." "The spokesperson for. . . ." ". . . the star (or producer) who. . . ." Any instant-plus-one recognition of this sort, predicated on the prospective speaker's portfolio, office, or accomplishment, is valid.

There are other people pullers which you, as the p.r. head, can suggest to the staff or steering committee as criteria which they should consider in attempting to generate enrollments or registrations in their project.

Program Pluses

As the p.r. practitioner, you may also wish to bring to your steering committee or planning committee's attention the fact that professionals in the field have evolved some ground rules to help them structure programs which will attract audiences or enrollments.

Director Philip M. Nowlen of the University of Chicago's Center for Continuing

Education is one of the few people in the field today who are primarily program developers but who also have the skills to publicize the programs they originate and coordinate.

Nowlen developed a Checklist of seven "P's" for use in creating programs with built-in appeal. I have added an eighth "P" ("People," which Nowlen's list touches upon, but with little detail).

His "P" pluses are the stuff an effective publicity-promotion campaign can be built upon.

It is your responsibility, as the p.r. person, to get your steering committee to incorporate as many of these "P" factors as possible into the project you are working on. The more the better.

Nowlen calls his seven "P's" "an approach to psychographic as contrasted with demographic data." He defines the term "psychographic data" as "psychological factors—beyond the demographic—which influence 'point of purchase' decision-making." In lay terms, these are factors which turn people on to the extent that they hasten to take part in your project or enroll in your class. Similar lists are used elsewhere, but Nowlen's is among the best.

Checklist of Psychographic "P" Factors

Purchaser—This is the individual (or group) responsible for initiating the "purchase," and is not necessarily the individual who eventually will sit in your classroom or auditorium.

The purchaser could be a spouse, parent, boss, or board of trustees.

Product—This is the need you are actually filling. You must know this for effective marketing. The clientele can be buying anything from status to job skills to economic self-defense (a businessman who buys a course not out of hope he'll learn something, but out of fear that his competitor *might*).

Price—This affects the "credibility" of the product. Most of us try to put on programs at the lowest possible cost plus a reasonable profit. However, this is often a mistake, depending on the market segment for which the program is designed. An example is a $35 law course which a university offers. That same course could be offered for $345, and marketed to senior partners of the most prestigious law firms in Chicago. Instead of a cheap brochure, hand-addressed engraved invitations would be sent to those senior partners. To a man making $200 a day ($48,000/year) a $35 program just looks too cheap to be any good.

Place—Proximity of market to conference location can be a liability or an asset, depending on the market segment. If money is not a big problem, the purchaser can be buying a nice trip as well as an educational experience.

Presentation—This is the total "feel" of the experience. A high school or community college has a different "feel" than does a prestigious university. A good acquaintance with your market segment and its psychographics will tell you what "feel" to promote. Also important are such things as the room setup. If the students see themselves as the equals (or betters!) of the presenter (in *whatever* significant way) the setup should reflect this.

Process—This is the entire means (or any part of the means) by which the content is delivered to the student. If the process is attractive enough, it can be a major factor in a purchase decision; conversely, if it is sufficiently unattractive, this may outweigh the rest of an otherwise good program in the mind of a potential student. An example of process is the Book of the Month Club's policy of sending a book every month to members, unless specifically instructed not to do so. It takes a conscious decision on the part of a member to avoid buying a book, and many people like this process. An unusually easy registration process, allowing telephone registrations, use of credit cards, etc., can increase the number of students.

Premiums—These are the "extras" that the student gets by buying the program. They can be an entree to campus cultural activities (art films, concerts), access to athletic facilities, etc. For example, New York University found the number of registrants and "no-shows" both increasing. They investigated and learned that it was cheaper to buy a course at N.Y.U. and get access to the university's tennis courts than to join a tennis club.

People—We have referred to the pull which can come from inclusion on your program of a speaker who is so well known that people in the general public—or people in his or her specific professional disciplinary area of renown—will want to hear him or her. Speaking from personal bias, I probably would not attend a conference on future world directions unless the likes of a Galbraith or a Heilbroner were to be on the platform, and I might not attend an opera unless promoted to do so because Beverly Sills was the prima donna.

Why Programs Fail

Every experienced program development specialist and, certainly, every p.r. person has seen this disaster: A program, although planned in high spirits and absolute confidence to meet a supposed need or to satisfy the educational or cultural desires of a constituency, just never gets off the ground.

Two examples: A lengthy needs assessment, supported by numerous personal interviews with the opinion leaders of a middle-sized city, revealed a major problem in that city—poor communications among the disparate population segments. This led, in turn, to the mounting of a discussion series aimed at attaining a community of understanding among these segments.

Too bad. All that advance work! All those hopes soaring in the upper atmosphere!

Because what happened is this: Almost nobody signed up. The program took place on schedule, all right, and in the lively discussion and argument it engendered can be called a success.

But the only reason it even got off the ground was that a longtime educational administrator in that city went out on the streets and into the neighborhoods and agencies to buttonhole people and browbeat his friendly associates in all the ranks of town to attend the meetings. It was a captive audience.

The series will not be repeated.

Another program, a conference dealing with an overlooked facet of work discrimination, was planned on a major campus. The program was to meet an obvious need: It would supply previously unavailable but much needed information.

Since the program was addressed to a business-industry-government audience and only peripherally to academic administrators, and since the high-caliber speakers being brought in from all corners of the country commanded sizable speakers' fees, the registration fee was not small.

An announcement was sent out with a return coupon for further information. Several hundred "send me more information" coupons were returned to the campus.

The prospective program had to be canceled through *lack of registrations.*

Why, when it looked like a sure winner, and since it was a program both wanted and needed?

A sampling of those who had said "send me more information" and yet who did not enroll were queried. The survey revealed three reasons for not attending, in about equal proportions from those who replied.

The program fees were too high.

The program missed its target audience (business-industry-government) and would have been attended principally by impecunious educators—counselors, placement people, affirmative action officers.

It was to have been held in May, at a time when travel and in-service training dollars have been spent, since most educational institutions begin their fiscal year July 1. The timing was bad in another way as well. It was scheduled to begin on the evening of a Sunday which, that year, also was Mother's Day. Anyone who came from a distance would have had to spend that special day traveling to the conference—what kind of a callous child, even a child of 35 to 55 years of age, would do that to a Mommy?

All the needs assessment in the world won't help if you let your staff or committee do something dumb like scheduling a program on Mother's Day—unless, in fact, it is a concert or other event honoring dear old Mom.

A major rule in publicizing continuing education programs is to have something to offer which is clearly defined—and to have a distinctly identified audience to whom it will appeal.

The first time you hear a committee member say, "This is what *we* plan to do," or "This is what *they need*," or anything like either of those, interpose from the standpoint of the p.r. person.

"Yes," you interrupt. "But what do *they* want? What do *they* see as their need? I am supposed to attract participants or enrollments. To whom am I addressing my publicity and promotion? To the person? To that person's boss?"

REALISTIC EXPECTATIONS

You are there, sitting with that steering committee or that staff, *to take hold of their ankles and pull them down to reality*, to put their feet on the ground. This is an important part of the p.r. function. As a person with closer contact with the real world, through the media, through your assessment of programs, you will find this to be true—whether they like it or not, whether *you* like it or not.

A committee, or even a staff or a p.r. task force, which senses an opportunity for a spectacular publicity push can get out of hand as easily—and as dangerously, as far as your overall goals are concerned—as cattle on a dusty drive who suddenly smell fresh water.

As the p.r. person on the job (whether you do this full time or are semiexperienced, a volunteer, or an out-and-out amateur), one of your major responsibilities will be to keep the committee's expectations down to a reasonable pitch.

If they have a nice, workable project in mind, aimed at maybe an audience of 100 members of the general public or of a group of specified publics, or if the project is intended principally for members of an organization, that is, a "captive audience," there is no rational reason for the p.r. effort to become a Barnum and Bailey extravaganza.

If you are dealing with such a program—one that probably can be nicely handled with three releases plus an early alert and some brochures—don't let the committee hear a whisper from you (or anyone else) about such exotic p.r. delicacies as press conferences, press kits, interviews, talk shows, and the like.

Gilbert and Sullivan's *Mikado* said it thus: "Make the punishment fit the crime." A continuing education project is no crime, or it shouldn't be. But if you can paraphrase that sentence into "Let the p.r. effort fit the program we are publicizing," you'll be on level ground.

It's not only that the nice little project does not *need* the full-scale effort. It also is that overkill may spoil not only this project but also others which may emanate from your organization or institution. You must not arouse false expectations—as to either the extravagance of the effort or its results. Neither should you invite the press to a picnic when they were led (falsely) to expect cherries jubilee.

Do not hesitate to pull out all the stops when the occasion warrants; but do not overplay the publicity when a well-thought-out, well-executed, yet modest p.r. backup will more than satisfy the need.

If you are a publicist worth your salt, you will be working on a continuing basis with friends in the media. If you are sincere, they will be your real friends and not people cultivated for the sake of favors they eventually may be able to deliver. It is unfair, in a p.r. push, to impose on people's good nature when their support is *not* needed. Your media friends are both people and professionals, and they will not forget—nor should they.

You will find some sample p.r. mixes for various sizes and kinds of projects in this book. However, the matter is so important that "Be realistic"—especially in keeping your committee-sponsor-staff expectations within bounds—has been placed high among your guidelines.

KEEPING CONTROL

The Canadian humorist Stephen Leacock used a fine, descriptive phrase when he once described an addlebrained soul as leaping on his steed and "riding madly off in all directions." This is exactly what can happen to an otherwise sound publicity push when the lines of responsibility have not been clearly defined.

There must be one person who is in charge, who:

1. Coordinates all materials
2. Sets and enforces all Timeframes, all deadlines, all release dates, all patterns of action
3. Screens all copy and graphics
4. Both dictates and arbitrates

That person is you.

Someone has to know every detail of what's going on at any given time. Someone has to see that the mailings go out. Someone has to ensure that there is not excessive double-teaming going on where media contacts and services are concerned. This someone must be able to speak with authority to the publicity task force and to the steering committee and to the senior staff, telling them exactly how the campaign is being planned, how it is progressing, and who is doing what.

There must be a leader, a chief officer, an administrator for the publicity-promotion effort.

There is only one way to operate, and its ingredients are:

Advance organization.
Constant use of Checklists of responsibilities.

Disciplined use of schedules and other components of your Timeframes. (Your calendar of promotional activities is called a Timeframe. See examples on pages 124–125 and 230.)

The key word is *control!*

As the p.r. head, you must—repeat *must*—be in full control at all times, with both directional and veto powers. As you ask your task force members to sign themselves up for specific duties (page 148), you will notice that they are asked to provide "assistance."

This control ensures that the attitude of your volunteer help (or of those drafted people who are your associates but who are unaccustomed to this kind of duty) is to *assist* you and not dabble or take independent action. Why? Because such going "madly off in all directions" can foul up the overall promotion-publicity plan.

Let us again state the major caution we touched upon in discussing the guidelines for realistic approaches:

Scale your effort to the scope and stature of the activity being planned. Do not attempt to pull out all the stops for every program; those of moderate scope and importance will not need—or deserve or attain, even if you try your hardest—all the media attention implied in the larger-scale Timeframes.

Indeed, such a huge effort may contribute to a condition of diminishing returns. If you attempt to give your promotion-publicity the big dash and do the whole bit every time, you soon will wear out the welcome in media circles for both yourself *and* your institution, organization, or agency.

A LOOK IN THE MIRROR: WHAT ARE YOUR ASSETS?

Being faced with the unaccustomed duty of publicizing a program can be scary, even if the lions and tigers really don't exist.

Don't panic.

Look in the mirror.

For starters, inventory your assets. It will make you feel better, and confidence breeds competence. It will also enable you to find the gaps in your inventory and fill them in before the big push begins.

Examine the Checklist beginning on page 26; you can probably add other assets to it.

The lists that follow represent a fairly full stock. Check off the assets you have now. Decide which ones you're going to add right away. And ponder those that are going to be hard to get.

Let's go.

It is not necessary to comment on each of the twenty-four items in the inventory of blessings. Some are amplified elsewhere. Others can stand on their own without further discussion.

COUNT YOUR BLESSINGS: AN INVENTORY

Have now	Will have	Must work at

This is not revival rhetoric, but your greatest assets may be the *intangibles:*
1. Goodwill—you only miss it when it's gone!
2. Ethical standards and behavior, which translate into honesty, integrity, courtesy, and fair play
3. Accuracy—habitual triple-checking, triple-proofing
4. Dependability
5. Dedication: Anyone working in continuing education must be a missionary at heart
6. Enthusiasm, which (happily) is contagious
7. The friendly regard of people in the commercial print and broadcast media
8. The ability, desire, and patience to work well with people
9. *Control* of the publicity element of the activity—in fact as well as name

Your more tangible assets can include:
1. The services of a professional publicity person
2. A staff photographer and/or photo lab
3. A staff artist and/or graphics person
4. Personal and/or staff time which can be allocated without shortchanging other responsibilities
5. Other kinds of help—students, volunteer workers, steering committee or planning committee members, publicity pros and semipros at cosponsoring or cooperative institutions or agencies
6. Access to a duplicating service or print shop
   Services available:
   a. Printing, duplicating of other sorts
   b. Folding
   c. Stapling
   d. Binding
   e. Collating
   f. Stuffing envelopes
   g. Preparing envelopes (pasting on preaddressed mailing labels, etc.)
7. Access to a mailing center, which may offer the services above except duplicating, and which may also do ZIP-Coding and sorting
8. A realistic amount of money for such "luxuries" as duplicating, postage, and help
9. Access to a copying machine (fine for small numbers of reproductions)
   If the machine has special features (such as being able to duplicate addressed mailing labels so that you can have a number of sets at hand), this is a plus

Have now	Will have	Must work at		
			10.	In-house access to the printed page or the airways (your newsletter, house organ, or bulletin, and those of your associates and cosponsors; a regular radio or TV spot, the broadcast of a related activity, in rare cases a sponsorship role in local radio or TV)
			11.	Special pages, sections, and programs related to education or your area of activity, to which you have ready access
			12.	Access to an automatic typewriter
			13.	A good reference library of your own
			14.	Access to more specialized reference materials
			15.	Access to demographic studies or—much better—the counsel of a professional demographer

You will find that you or others can operate quite well with almost any combination of the tangible assets when these are complemented with a lot of hard work, preparation, and at least a little budget support.

But you cannot, under any circumstances, operate without the intangibles listed above. Working well with people is a must which you'll find underlined time and time again in this book. Control of your programs' publicity element has been mentioned before, and it will be mentioned again. It is stressed throughout this book.

But has anyone talked with you about ethics?

ETHICS

Ethics are crucially important to those who work in education-related p.r. This is one area in which you can't make exceptions based on preferences and personalities. You've got to play it straight, right down the middle of the path.

What do I mean—ethics in promoting programs?

Just what I say. You have got to treat all media outlets equally, as a matter of professional courtesy and as just plain good practice.

If you want to be cold-blooded about it, you can look at it this way: The little, insignificant publiciation or station you really don't need this time around may be in a position of key importance the next time—it may get bought up by a giant conglomerate, or it may appeal particularly to some segment of the population whom you've never heard of but may hear of, loud and strong, next time you're called upon to publicize a program.

There are lots of snide little ways you can stack the deck in favor of a preferred media outlet if you choose to do so: You can schedule a press conference for a time which conflicts with the less-loved outlet's deadlines. You can leak a feature—who has to know it comes from you?—to a favorite outlet. You can tip off one news desk about another news desk's perhaps more imaginative plan for coverage.

Don't do these things.

Don't do any of them ever.

They will come back to haunt you.

In dealing with the media, the Golden Rule is a good one to keep in mind: Treat others as you'd like to be treated if you were in their shoes.

Here is what I would consider ethical behavior in dealing with the media:

1. All *official* releases and materials—news and feature releases, suggestions for coverage, facts sheets, and so on—go out to everyone at exactly the same time and in exactly the same form. Everything to everybody—same time, same format. Got it?

2. But we live in a system of free enterprise. An energetic and enthusiastic newsperson may want to give your program additional coverage, whether in advance or at the time of the event. You can't give this person the official materials ahead of time, even if they are printed, assembled, and ready—sitting in that box over in the corner of your office.

   What you *can* do is help this enterprising reporter get exclusive feature stories in his or her area of interest. Stories which are not echoes (or harbingers) of the hard news coverage which will follow. OK?

   Or let's say that the background material you give the press suggests several possible news or feature angles. If one news desk seeks to follow them up and others do not, swell. That's the cue for you to help that outlet's reporter with the suggested story—although not to the extent of squeezing out the competing newspeople from the straight coverage they have indicated that they prefer.

3. Do not, of course, carry your evenhandedness to ridiculous lengths. If one paper, say, does not have a person who covers the religious news and another paper does, you would not make a huge pitch for the first paper to follow up on the religious implications of your program. What you *would* do is provide the first paper's news desk (the one without a religion writer) with all the materials—including the suggestions for coverage of the religious angle—marked simply "FYI" (for your information).

ACCURACY

Let's also look briefly at a matter which crops up again and again when we talk about publicity and promotion: accuracy.

Inventiveness and imagination are swell and may be the qualities which will distinguish your project from many others in the way it is presented in brochures or to the media. They may in fact get you mileage they couldn't get otherwise.

But there is something more important than imagination, and that is *accuracy.*

Nothing in the world—nothing—will destroy your credibility and that of your project and your institution faster and more completely than inaccuracy.

"Can't I make one little mistake?"

No.

Every fact in every release; every fact stated in your brochure and in any phone call, conversation, memo, or visit to the media; every item on every agenda—all *must be absolutely accurate.*

Don't exaggerate, and don't promise what you're not sure you can deliver. Asked by a member of the press for the identity of your major speaker, don't reply "the Vice President of the United States" unless you have his acceptance of your invitation to speak on your program *in writing.* A verbal assurance or commitment from an aide, no matter how exalted in the ranks, or from a friend, no matter how close, is not enough.

Say, instead, "We have invited the Vice President of the United States, but we haven't yet received a formal acceptance. If the Vice President's schedule will not allow him to come, we will have a different speaker of stature—you can depend on that." And then, as the p.r. person on the steering committee or staff, be certain the press *can* depend on that.

That is a rather lofty example, but the point applies to even the most modest program. Asked the same question about a local project, don't say that the president of the chamber of commerce is going to speak unless you absolutely know that he or she will and have it in writing. Give the press the same kind of answer as is suggested above.

A noted editor has a motto which is drilled into his staff:

"Get it. Get it first. *But get it right.*" That's not a bad motto for you.

Situations sometimes arise when a fellow committee or staff member says, "Let me have my secretary find those figures for you," or "My graduate assistant can take a run out to the library and look that up."

This should make you terribly, terribly uneasy. It should give you a case of the galloping jitters.

I want to *see* where it says that 279 prospective transfers from community colleges were turned away from the Big U last term. I want to *see* where it says that such and such an institution has had thirty-one Nobel laureates on its faculty since 1920. I am not going to put those words—or any others which I can't check—into a release coming from my institution or into the mouth of one of our administrators. I am not going to put them on a facts sheet or into a press kit or in any other handout materials until I have *verified them myself.*

When something from my typewriter or office hits a news desk, I want them to be able to take it for granted that every fact and figure has been researched and verified.

Anything you send out should be proofed at least twice, and if it is anything of distinction or delicacy, it should be proofed three times. Triple-check. Triple-proof. Be dependable. Build that reputation for being right.

Earlier, it was stated that you can't make mistakes. Not even one. Nevertheless, sometimes you are going to goof. There is no way that you can operate in the field of publicity-promotion and *not* goof sometimes. When you do goof, mop up after yourself as quickly as possible—tell the folks and let 'em know. Right away. With apologies. And then get back again to being right.

We've mentioned dependability as an adjunct to accuracy. But there is another side to dependability, and that has to do with scheduling.

One of the things you may give those in the news outlets, on an early approach, is an advance schedule of releases and events. Make certain you stick to that schedule.

If you say you are going to have a release to them by 8 A.M. Tuesday, have it there. If you say that Senator Hendry is going to arrive at 9 A.M. for a press conference, have him there, even if you have to drag him out of bed to be there.

If something has to be changed, be sure to carry 'round a *complete new* schedule, not just a correction of the previous one. Make sure the new schedule is dated; make sure it is flashy in appearance (to get their eye); and make sure that it *tells them to discard* the earlier schedule. If you are in their office, you may be able to take it from their file and tear it up. Do that if you can.

 **A tricky point is in promising the delivery of a notable's speech or paper. Try not to promise the media that you will deliver a speech copy at a certain time unless you have the speech in your hot little hand when you are doing the promising. Tell them, instead, that they will have it within an hour after you get it.**

A FACTS SHEET

We now come to your preparation of a facts sheet about the project to be promoted. This may seem like a needless chore—mere busywork.

Believe me, it is not.

Put down on paper what you want to do and how you want to do it. You will be glad you did.

A facts sheet is useful in many ways. It can be a help when you approach the news media. It can be a Checklist as you write copy for brochures, for posters, even for letters of invitation. You will give copies to the project's directors and steering committee (and will they be impressed!), and you certainly will use it as you progress from square A to square B and on down to D day, working with your fellow publicists.

The questions you will answer on your facts sheet are the same which will be answered, later on, when you begin to prepare your news releases—i.e., Who? What? When? Where? Why? and How?

If you are announcing an extramural class schedule, or a schedule of on-campus or on-site evening or special-hour (such as Saturday morning or late afternoon) credit or special-interest courses, your facts sheet will look more like the sample on pages 32–35, except that yours would probably list more courses, since the course listing in the sample has been drastically abridged.

The caution regarding the replacement of a facts sheet with one which has been updated also applies to press kits and information kits (which will be discussed on pages 186–199. Be certain that the old ones, if they are in an editor's or a news director's or a reporter's hands, are confiscated and destroyed. Also be certain that all the new materials are prominently *dated* and that they do not look exactly like the earlier ones. Change the color; change anything you can to make them stand out as new and as being substituted. If you write copy in which new facts—contradicting earlier information—have been included, assert this in a note stapled to the later release.

DIVIDE AND CONQUER: MAKING THE JOB MANAGEABLE

The facts sheet which you have developed, following the pattern on pages 32–35, provides a simple framework for considering your program's promotion effort as a cluster of components.

Looking at the entire promotion process, behemoth-big, can scare you to death. Looking at it a bit or an element at a time is reassuring and cuts it down to obviously manageable proportions.

You undoubtedly will use a brochure or other direct mail piece as one of your publicity-promotion tools, for it is a fact that many institutions and organizations rely principally on direct mail to attract audiences and enrollments from the adult public. Properly used, as outlined on pages 68–81 direct mail can be extremely effective as a recruiting tool. Don't ever knock it. However, program sponsors who lean on this tool exclusively—or nearly so—and who ignore or underplay the use of the *news media* may be overlooking their best bet.

Almost everyone reads newspapers and listens to radio-TV, right? So why not give the white space and air time the big dash, as most successful publicists do?

Some of us feel very strongly that education is news, and when we talk about programs or courses for the public, that's what we are talking about. Continuing

Press Contact: Josie Marcus, Room 114, College Hall,
College Park, IL 12876 217/333-0517

FACTS SHEET

1. The kind of project (conference, class, etc.)

2. Its title and theme

3. The cosponsors

4. Location(s) where the activity will be held

5. Date it will be held (or begin)

6. Number of sessions or classes, dates and
times

7. Registration regulations

8. Fee, if one is charged (and specify what it covers)

9. Registration limits (cancellation level and date,
cutoff level)

10. Target audience(s) _____

11. Speakers, instructors, panelists, moderators

(specify) _____

_____

12. Special features, added attractions,

possible liabilities _____

_____

_____

(ATTACHMENTS—A roster of the steering committee [with
assignments], a roster of your p.r. task force [with
assignments], and a schedule of the activity, even if
only a rough is available at the moment.)

August 16
For Immediate Release

Contact: Josie Marcus
Associate Director, Communications
Office: 333-0517
Home: 299-7678

FACTS SHEET—FALL COURSES, CONTINUING
EDUCATION FEATURE STORY POSSIBILITIES

WHAT   150 Continuing Education courses for
adults. Noncredit courses, vocational development, personal enrichment, or just
plain fun. Thirty new courses this fall.

WHEN   Fall. Ranging from 1-day to 12-week
courses. Beginning dates vary; most
courses begin between Sept. 15-Oct. 15.

WHERE   Most courses held at Stanton campus.
Twenty-two courses offered at Morton in a
new program to take education where the
people are.

WHY   More than 12,000 adults attended continuing
education courses last year.

SPECIFICS Below are brief descriptions of fall
courses with feature story possibilities,
listed in four categories: General Interest, Home Improvement, Business, and Wom-
en's Courses. For more details, contact
Josie Marcus (333-0517).

Complete schedule of courses attached.

GENERAL INTEREST COURSES

THE AGE OF UNCERTAINTY (Schedule, p. 4) College
courses via television continue with Galbraith's "Age
of Uncertainty" and a course for teachers, "Dealing
with Classroom Problems," both offered for college
credit. An interview with students or instructor
could reveal whether learning by TV is as valuable as
learning in a classroom.

BEYOND UNIVERSITY WALLS (Schedule, p. 4) Education is
moving out of the classroom and traditional settings.
This series of six classes is our attempt to involve
community institutions in college-level education,
symptomatic of the general trend.

A WORKSHOP IN INFORMAL CHILDREN'S DRAMA (Schedule,
p. 5) "Let's pretend. . . ." What child has never
played make-believe? The psychological implications
of make-believe and the value of structured children's
drama would make an interesting article. Dr. Betty
Maxwell of our Theatre Department is an authority on
the subject.

CHINESE LANGUAGE AND CULTURE (Schedule, p. 5) Our
Sinologist, Connie Lee, can provide excellent background on China from her residence there and study of
the nation.

BEGINNING GRAPHIC DESIGN (Schedule, p. 5) How graphics
affects us every day—TV, advertising, publications,
home and building decoration, etc.—will be discussed
by locally well-known artist, Elaine Hollingsworth,
and would make an interesting article or interview.

ART OF GOOD CONVERSATION (Schedule, p. 6) People like
to talk to each other, yet almost everyone believes
he/she does it poorly. Either of our instructors,
radio commentator Jim Pollicita (WXLW) or Dr. Hollis
Pryor, lawyer and speech professor at Butler, is full
of good ideas on how to improve readers'/listeners'
skills as conversationalists.

METERS, LITERS, AND GRAMS (Schedule, p. 7) Metrics are coming. The kids are learning it in school; Mom and Dad will have to learn. How metrics will change our lives and how the average person can make the transition easily are two topics to be covered by our instructor, Ellis Schwager.

FOR MEN ONLY (Schedule, p. 9) The "battle of the sexes" is always an interesting topic—and here's a new approach to it. How can men relate successfully to the new liberated woman? Psychologist Seymour Levey has some interesting ideas on what is happening to men in the '70s and how they can cope.

HOME IMPROVEMENT

ENERGY AND DOLLAR SAVINGS FOR HOMEOWNERS (Schedule, p. 7) A timely topic as we move closer to higher heating costs. There are many things the homeowner can do to save energy besides installing insulation, according to our instructor, consulting engineer Charles Craft. He'll be glad to share "how-to" tips.

FOR WOMEN

ALTERNATIVE CONCEPTS OF POWER (Schedule, p. 9) Dr. Ruth Rank can provide an interesting interview on what power is, why some people have it and others don't, and how women can develop it, which would make a good feature on "What You Should Know to Get Ahead."

BUSINESS

STRESS MANAGEMENT (Schedule, p. 8) How to handle stress and convert it into a positive force is a topic with much appeal these days. Instructor Kristin Holmberg can provide a good interview.

education! As news, it rates a share of white space and air time. Because news about educational opportunities and programs may not be exactly earthshattering, the share may not be big, but there it is, and don't let an opportunity slip away.

Many agencies, groups, and institutions which put on and publicize programs shy away from use of the media for two reasons:

First, they feel insecure. They don't know how to approach the media. Second, they feel rebuffed. The story or public-service announcement they sent out with such high hopes didn't make it into print or on the air. The article they put out didn't draw the audience or enrollment that they had hoped for.

Sadly enough, they are right on both counts.

Material which is not prepared in a professional manner doesn't have a hoot of a chance of getting used. Newsrooms are understaffed. Their people can't take the time and trouble to rework your little masterpiece into a usable form.

This need no longer be a problem because by following the tips on pages 57–64, you will be able to turn out professionally prepared news releases and public-service announcements that will attract the eye and meet the needs of print editors and broadcasters.

WHAT IS NEWS?

In applying "divide and conquer" tactics to the promotion job, we first will look at the program's possibilities as a news vehicle—a happening which merits (free) white space in the print media and air time on the broadcast channels.

It may help if we look rather closely at *news itself*.

A top-level assignment editor on a major national paper describes news as "something that shouldn't have happened in the first place."

That is a pretty cynical attitude.

However, *news* may best be defined simply as *something that interests many people today*.

In a basic denominator, news can be the back-fence announcement that a neighbor and the wife of another neighbor have run off together, or "Did you know that the Kelly kid has been accepted at Stanford?"

The publicist must zero in, however, on definite outreach approaches and vehicles. So, to your local news outlets, both print and broadcast, news is:

Something that will affect the community in rather direct ways

Something that involves local people

Something unusual which will happen in the community by the bringing in of "name" participants and/or special events of interest

 When a local news outlet has its own constituency or bias—that is, if it addresses itself principally to only one or only a few segments of the community—its news factors must include one or more applicable elements. The information you provide should include and stress any news components which appeal to the special interests of this group or groups. In other words, the news factors should speak directly to the interests or needs of an outlet's particular constituency—labor, women, an ethnic group, a social group, or whatever.

And if the news involves or can feature one or more instantly identifiable persons taking part in the project you are promoting, its value will be enhanced, especially if they are knowledgeable, articulate, and maybe a little controversial.

There are several kinds of news which a publicist needs to be aware of and know how to use to advantage.

Spot News

Spot news is news which happens without instigation and cannot be influenced by a publicist.

Examples of spot news: an accident, an earthquake, the birth of quintuplets, the outcome of an election or football game.

Manufactured News

Manufactured news is made up—or otherwise given a helping hand—by someone in the media or by a publicist.

The ways to create news are literally without number. Created or manufactured news may be as dignified (or undignified) as a Presidential press conference or the annual report from General Motors. It may be as hokey as a barrel race over Niagara Falls or a wedding on the back of a float at the county fair.

News Features

News features are the interesting sidebar facets of the news quotient of your activity.

Most news features are manufactured news in that you *reach* for them—i.e., they are not central to the information you need to present to your prospective registrant.

They do not necessarily bear directly on the who, what, where, why, and how of the program but are peripheral to these basics.

If Senator Rumpus is going to keynote your important public discussion program, the *news identification* for your thinking audience probably is that he is a member of the Senate Foreign Relations Committee and its acknowledged expert on emerging fiscal policy in the Iron Curtain bloc. The news *feature* may be that his twin sister is county clerk.

The first fact could generate participants. The second is a fillip of interest which may give you (as publicist) another opportunity to bring the activity to public notice through the media, but it would not *in itself* be a program plus.

The Checklist below touches on each of the three kinds of news. It is far from being comprehensive, but it will do for starters.

News: What It Is and How to Make It

When Is It News?

It is news when it contains one or more of the major ingredients of human interest, namely:

When it is new, a first, a last, a biggest, a most expensive, a worst in *x* number of years (e.g., plane crash), a fastest, an oldest.

When it is unusual.

When it has to do with famous persons.

When it is directly important to great numbers of people—e.g., information about impending changes in the state or federal income tax.

When it involves conflict—e.g., battles, divorces, athletic contests.

When it involves mystery, crime, or scandal.

When it reveals a secret.

When it reveals future plans, trends, or prospects (encouraging or threatening).

When it is funny.

When it is romantic or sexy.

When it is appealing—e.g., babies, animals—and touches your heart.

When it strikes or concerns home (your neighborhood, your family, your friends, your job).

Ways to Make News

Tie in with news events of the day. (For example, if there are headlines about a water shortage in your town, this is the time to announce your water conservation conference some months away.)

Tie in with another publicist.

Tie in with a newspaper or other medium on a mutual project.

Conduct a poll or survey.

Issue a report.

Arrange an interview with a celebrity.

Bring in a celebrity from elsewhere.

Take part in a controversy.

Make an analysis or prediction.

Arrange for, write, cover a speech.

Form a committee and announce the names of the members.

Hold an election.

Announce an appointment.

Celebrate an anniversary.

Issue a summary of facts.

Tie in with a holiday.

Tie in with a well-known "week" or "day."

Adopt a program of work.

Make a statement on a subject of interest.

Make a trip.

Make an award.

Hold a contest.

Pass a resolution.

Appear before public bodies.

Stage a special event.

Write a letter.

Release a letter you have received.

Adapt national reports and surveys locally. (If a federal report states that nationally 51.9 percent of high school graduates went on to college, use this as a starting point for a release on the number from your area who are attending college.)

Entertain.

Stage a debate.

Organize a promotion.

Fete an institution, such as the Bill of Rights.

Inspect a project.

Organize a tour.

Develop a community calendar or program.

Issue a protest.

Issue praise.

Issue and diagnose statistics.

Stage a demonstration.

Stage a "gag."

Make a picture. (This may accompany many of the foregoing.)

Quite a smorgasbord of ideas and guidelines?

I agree.

But like a smorgasbord, it offers something for everyone. Any program or other activity which your group, agency, or institution can conceivably sponsor can be defined as news in one or another of these aspects.

"News Language": Some Definitions

Terms with which you may not be familiar are grouped in the "Glossary." However, in order to eliminate a lot of thumbing back and forth, here are some definitions of terms which may crop up as you supply the news media with information about your project.

A *news release* or *press release* is an article that is professionally written (or written in a professional style) and which can be used *as is* by the people in the newsroom to which it is addressed. It can go to both print and broadcast newsrooms in the same form, although it is wise to write as tight as you can—that is, use as few words as possible—when you write for the air. (However, do not be disturbed if your releases are rewritten; rewriting of general releases is a practice on many news desks.)

A *public-service announcement* (PSA) is a brief statement about your program or activity for use on the air. The key word is "brief."

A *calendar notice* is the print equivalent of a PSA.

 The style of calendar notices (unlike that of PSAs) varies widely from newspaper to newspaper, from magazine to magazine, and from journal to journal. Study your outlets for style. Some columns are grouped under topics—e.g., "Meetings," "Entertainment," "Sports." Others are grouped by day. Do an autopsy on the style used in the paper or other publication you are addressing, and follow it to the letter.

The three approaches listed above are basic to your effort. Here are some others which are often used, even in promoting a small, community-based program:

The placing of *feature stories* and ideas (including the setting up of *interviews*).

Unless you are a professional news writer, the stories are best written and scripted by other people—the real pros. However, you can and should provide your local or area newspeople with all sorts of ideas—maybe through verbal contact, maybe by submitting an idea sheet during a visit to the newsroom or as an adjunct to a news release.

Columns and comments. You can submit feature ideas to columnists (print) and commentators (radio and TV broadcast).

Photographs and photo ideas (print) and suggestions for *filming* (TV). Photographs are still pictures taken with a camera. Film implies motion.

Special-interest programs or enclosures or editions. Submit ideas, articles, and features for special pages, sections, programs, or series, and seasonal programs, sections, or enclosures.

Editorials. The editorial page and the "editorials on the air" (increasingly common) reflect the opinions of the publication's and station's management on affairs of concern to themselves and/or the public.

Letters to the editor. A letter may be written by an individual or on behalf of a group and sent to an editor or a station manager. Letters appear in the editorial or "this is my opinion" part of a publication or a station's programming.

Fillers. An editor can throw in one or two short sentences to fill up little spaces at the bottom of columns. They seldom are used by the broadcast people.

Interviews. An interview provides an excellent way to get the word out in advance of your program. In general, an interview is a one-to-one conversation between a reporter and a prominent person about a matter of interest or concern.

Group interviews. In a group interview, as the words imply, two or more people from as many separate newsrooms interview the prominent person at the same time.

Talk shows. These are radio or TV shows on which a host or an interviewer talks to someone. For our purposes, that someone is a spokesperson for or a sponsor of a program or activity; the talk is about his or her area of interest or about the specific activity being planned or under way.

One kind of talk show is a short spot– 4 minutes and 10 seconds if unsponsored, about 3 minutes and 10 seconds if sponsored. It usually is a sort of "live" community calendar, announcing an event or a cause, and giving a phone number. It is a brief one-to-one interview, usually with the same host each day. It is apt to be scheduled as a local insertion in the morning network news programs.

A second kind of talk show is a half-hour *discussion*, with varying hosts on most community-based broadcast outlets. One, or two, or even three guests discuss a matter suitable for comment and (when they are plumping for a program rather than a cause) can do some good advance promotion as they go along. You'll usually find discussion programs scheduled on Sundays, during daytime hours, or in morning or noontime slots on weekdays.

The third kind is the *phone-in* question-answer program. It, too, usually varies as to host. The guests from your project may be one or several in number, and several usually is best when a controversial subject is being aired, because they can take breathers from fielding the questions which are phoned in. This, again, can be a Sunday feature, or—as frequently is the case—it can be scheduled in the late evening after the nightly news.

Letters to the editor (or news director) often are splendid ways to call additional attention to your project or to thank the people at the news outlet itself or the community at large for support of the project once it is completed.

Given limitations of space and air time, most outlets use only the most interesting or provocative letters to the editor. Keep yours brief and to the point; avoid slander, libel, and pornography (or simply bad taste, according to the mores of the locality and the readership or audience). The writer's full name and address should be signed; anonymous contributions are frowned upon by the responsible press.

Fillers should be submitted in a group with a 3-em dash (---) separating them. Some editors use the term "10-heads" instead of "fillers" because they are likely to put a 10-point heading on them, like this : BODY FOUND, or PROGRAM PLANNED.

APPROACHES TO THE MEDIA

In your initial approaches to the news media, your instructions again are "do your homework." Attempt to learn exactly which people you will want to tell about your activity.

As soon as you begin gearing up for promotion, the publicist (you) should go to see, call, or write the people in the newsrooms, both print and broadcast.

Let them know who you are, what you are doing, and how. Keep them informed about what is going on throughout the duration of the program, but avoid becoming a nuisance.

The welcome you receive may well depend upon what time of day you visit the paper or the station.

Never go to the office of a weekly newspaper on the day before press day or on press day itself. How do you know when the paper goes to press? Look in your state press association's rate book and directory, or simply call up and ask.

Never go to or call the office of an afternoon daily newspaper between 10 A.M. and 1 P.M. (After 2 P.M. is better; the people have had time to get some lunch.) From 10 to 1 they will be fighting a deadline, and they have no time for callers unless by some unlikely and historic chance you are coming in with the really great story of the year ("I just saw the Governor murder the chancellor of the university in a quarrel over the affections of the woman president of the First National Bank.").

Never go to the office of a radio or TV station (unless you've got a hot item) from 1 hour before broadcast time until after the newscast itself. (And if the newscast is at 12 noon or at 6 P.M., give the people a chance to get something to eat before you barge in on them.) Fairly early in the day is good at most stations.

Find out to whom at the newspaper or station you should be addressing your releases (and your explanations and invitations). It is not very bright to take up the sports editor's time if your project is on money management for women. If you've a feature in mind, talk with the features editor. If you want an editorial, talk to whomever writes the editorials.

If you're not sure whom to talk with, ask somebody—ideally the assignments editor.

When you are dealing with metropolitan newspapers and broadcast outlets, it often is difficult to get in to see the people you'd like to talk with. So it is not a bad idea (in fact it is a very good one) to arrange your initial visit in advance, by phone or by note or both.

1. If you are going into a strange newsroom absolutely cold—a stranger to one and all—start with a phone call. Ask the editor or news director (if the outlet is a small one) or whoever answers the phone on the news desk (if the outlet is good-sized or large) whom you should see about the particular type of coverage or advance notice you are interested in.

Often—in fact, usually—the reporter who will cover (and even who will talk with you) is not the assignments editor. The news editor or news director or anchor person may not make the assignments. Try to identify the right person in advance.

2. You now have someone's name. The next thing you do is to write that person a short note, telling him or her who you are and what you will want to talk about, and enclose a facts sheet (see pages 33–35) for background information. The facts sheet always should include the basic information (who, what, why, when, how) and any other details which might be helpful to the coverage. You end that note with a sentence like this:

    "I will call you Tuesday morning (the 26th) to set up a definite appointment."

3. On the 26th—avoiding the same deadlines you would if you were visiting a newsroom—you will call your contact and set up the appointment.

4. And you'll keep that appointment. News departments of any size are protected from the casual walk-in visitor by guards and doorkeepers. They will take your card or a note you will have prepared ahead of time and either phone it in or take it in to the person you want to see. Getting an OK, they'll either give you directions or show you in; in many shops, the person you are going to see will come out to the hall to greet you.

You won't have to hang around the newsrooms* after that initial visit, until you hand-carry the press kits and other materials around when the countdown starts. Not if you make the necessary prearrangements and are prepared for the interview.

Thus, you will have in hand, ready to give the reporter or newscaster:

1. Another copy of the facts sheet.
2. A copy of your initial release—the bare-bones one which gives basic facts. (They can be embroidered upon in later releases.)
3. A schedule of future releases. Tell the reporter or newscaster when he or she will get a press kit and a ticket.
4. As part of that schedule, or on another sheet, a listing of some feature and sidebar ideas to spark up the precoverage.
5. Any *professional* and applicable photographs immediately available.

If any goodies are involved—parties or the like—make mention verbally or in a little notice included with the handouts.

It doesn't hurt to put the handouts in a little folder or an envelope. Be sure *all* materials you leave carry the name, address, and phone number of the press contact person for the program (usually yourself).

A PUBLICIST'S GOAL: WHITE SPACE AND AIR TIME

It would be very nice, indeed, if everyone engaged in publicizing and promoting continuing education could have an ample inventory of publicity tools within immediate reach. But, except for a few huge-budget continuing education operations in metropolitan settings and/or with national impact, such riches seldom are at

---

*In some (very few, in my experience) small communities or suburbs, the editors and news directors like to have people hand-carry material to them on even a weekly basis. Either they are lonely, like the Maytag repairman, or they think it is good community relations. *I* think either the U.S. mail or hand delivery, but with the delivery only going to the receptionist or to whoever's sitting at the news desk that moment, does just as well—if, big *if*, all materials are properly addressed and identified. Unless, of course, late-breaking hard news is involved.

hand. You—like most of the rest of us—are limited in your publicity-promotion efforts by the outlets and strategies which can be used in your community or area.

Let's call the outlets and strategies available to you for publicity-promotion the *tool kit.*

For people with grandiose publicity dreams, the limitations of a local or regional tool kit can be a disappointing factor. Those with negative outlooks and philosophies, on the other hand, will use the limited tool kit as an excuse to slack off on the job.

The realist rolls up his or her sleeves and gets at it, making the most of whatever is in the tool kit that can be put to good use.

DO YOUR HOMEWORK—
TAKE AN INVENTORY OF YOUR PUBLICITY-PROMOTION OUTLETS

First, the realist takes an inventory, acknowledging that he or she must do a lot more than identify the easiest outlets for promotion-publicity materials.

In taking inventory of available outlets for the tool kit, look for instruments and ploys you can use to publicize programs. Analyze the media *in your area* to discover their particular emphases and interests. Look closely at articles and broadcasts by individual staff members—writers, reporters, editors, columnists, newscasters, talk show hosts.

Becoming thoroughly familiar with the contents of your tool kit will enable you, once the 6-week countdown period has come, to practice marksmanship in your promotional efforts and materials—concentrating on the people and the outlets which will give the best return for both time and money.

It is imperative, then, that you know exactly what is available in your community, area, or state in the way of news outlets which will get your message to the adult public and thus help you generate registrations or enrollments.

A Checklist of publicity outlets is provided below. It can be used to prepare a master inventory—your tool kit. Some things we will mention are publicity-promotion outlets and how to use them; how to get white space and air time through first-line and backup approaches; and people pullers.

The Tool Kit:
Publicity-Promotion Outlets and How to Use Them

Print

A.   Daily, weekly, and biweekly newspapers, including associations of papers (alias "the chain gang")

B. Special-readership newspapers, including:

The ethnic press
The religious press
The underground press
The labor press
Campus publications
Shoppers and other throwaway ad sheets that also contain articles, calendars, notices, etc.

C. Other special-audience publications, national or regional:

Magazines
Journals
Occupational-professional publications, including newsletters

D. Other general-interest (unrestricted readership) print outlets:

General magazines
Wire services
News and feature syndicates
Regional bureaus of national publications
Correspondents and stringers
Supplements
Comic-book formats (that is, an informational/promotional booklet with a story line and cartoon characters—like a comic book!)

E. Local, immediate-area, and statewide print outlets with their own targets:

House organs
Newsletters
    In-house
    Agency
    Vocational
    Club
    Organizational
    Associational
    Industrial
    Business

Church
Special-interest
Hobby or avocational
City guides and calendars

Broadcast
Even though there is a visual difference between television and radio, both types of broadcast media can be approached and serviced alike. The major difference is not in which of the two types of broadcast media you are hoping to use; it is in the size of the market which a given station covers.

You will find these broadcast market areas well defined in the annual *Broadcasting Yearbook* (see the "Basic Bookshelf," pages 96–100):

A. Community radio-TV (general listenership-viewership)
B. Special-audience radio-TV
C. Metropolitan radio-TV

By size of station and its listener-viewer population, you will analyze, approach, and service the broadcast media as follows:

1. Hosted talk shows
2. Call-in shows
3. Interviews
4. Locally produced special-interest programs (home, school, sports, books, hobbies and crafts, gardening, farms, etc.)
5. Locally produced variety shows
6. Editorials on the air
7. Public-service announcements (PSAs)
8. Original public-service programming

Getting Air Time

Getting white space in newspapers and other print media is one thing. This topic is fully treated in the section "Approaches to the Media" (pages 42–44). Getting air time is another. There are two major differences:

1. White space sometimes can be stretched. Always depending upon the advertising being carried for that day, which in almost all cases determines the size of the news hole, more pages can be added to a day's run. However, stretching white

space is a rare circumstance. Air time cannot be stretched. There are only so many seconds, minutes, and hours in any broadcast day.

2. Newspapers and other print outlets do not have any *legal* obligation to serve the public interest.

Newspapers are not licensed. They do not have to answer to the public except as their contents fall within the bounds of good taste and accuracy, avoid libel and slander, adhere to copyright regulations, and avoid wordings or inferences which might make them liable to suit. Anyone who has the money and really wants to do so can start a newspaper—or a magazine or journal, for that matter. And the publisher-editor does not have to use your material or handouts, even if you buy an ad in the sheet.

Radio and television stations are different. They are licensed. They have to justify their retention of their licenses. And they are obligated by regulation to spend a percentage of their air time in public-service programming. This does not mean that they have to use *your* (i.e., any particular person's) material. It is just that they have to use the regulated amount of air time in some sort of public-service production of their selection.

All radio and TV stations have to make application to the FCC (Federal Communications Commission) every 3 years for operating licenses. In that application they have to make what is called a "promise of performance." That essentially is a statement of programming intentions.

At the time of their next application they have to show a "proof of performance."

Obviously, the two should be similar.

The promise of performance is based on what the FCC calls "affirmative ascertainment." This means that station ownership and management personnel must go out into the service region and interview "community leaders" to see what they feel are the most significant problem areas that exist at the time. This information is added to viewer comments received by the station in the mail and by way of phone calls.

The information gained through the ascertainment process is usually run through a computer and filtered in various ways. The result usually is a list of ten or twelve key problems or issues which people have identified. These items are usually general enough to cover most areas of public service—i.e., the economy, government, education, etc.

All this information must be kept in the station's public file. This file is available at any time for inspection by members of the public.

If you want to have access to a station for its public-service material, it might be a good idea to visit the station and check the public file to determine what areas the station has ascertained to be potential areas of service.

It might be helpful to read the license application and base the request for access on some specific item in that document.

Then send to the station a formal request to have access to serve this particular need. The station's license application is *part of the public file* and is available for review.

It goes without saying that stations are apt to be protective of their prerogative to make their own programming decisions. And they are a bit uncomfortable about the requirement to maintain the public file. The fear is that someone with adversary intentions, or some real nut, will come in and find a loophole somewhere and make them do all sorts of things that they had no intention of doing. Of course, this fear does work to the advantage of the people seeking time. Tread carefully, though, when you make inquiries of a station based on its public file. You are likely to be viewed with some suspicion when you ask for access to the public file.

USES AND MECHANICS OF PUBLICIZING AND PROMOTION ON THE AIR

Most local stations have very few places in their open schedules for public-service programming of any kind. They are, however, usually committed to some method of presenting short messages of the "Community Calendar" type, and these notices are given to them in the form of *public-service announcements* (PSAs).

The notices used by local stations within the "Community Calendar" slot are mostly of the church bazaar type. They are put on the air in the extreme fringe times (such as late at night and very early in the morning), where commercial sales of time are difficult or impossible.

Occasionally, you will find stations that schedule PSAs as a block in a slightly better time slot—during a movie matinee, for example.

It usually is possible to get your PSA on the air by mailing it in to the public-service director or the program director.

 **When you don't know whom to address at a station by name, in any connection dealing with your program or activity, mail your PSA, news release, or feature suggestion to the station manager, or call the manager at the station with information and inquiries.**

In some metropolitan areas, PSAs are sent in on rather stylized forms, with seconds and number of words listed. (See pages 58–59.) In smaller areas, put your short message on a *postcard* and mail it in. Handling postcards is easier for an announcer than shuffling around and possibly dropping a bunch of pieces of paper of different sizes. The announcer armed with postcard PSAs can simply go through them as if delivering a lecture from notes.

Timing the PSAs' arrival at the station also is important. In most communities, sending them a week or two before you want them used is a good rule of thumb.

 **In metropolitan areas, try to get PSAs in at least *2 months* before you want them used.**

The station is likely to provide only the most basic copywriting service.

This copy is likely to be read over a *slide* or *simple art card*. Local stations will tell you what size of slide or card they can use. In preparing such material, you might offer your organization's art or photo services if you have them. If not, you might want to consider *an offer* to spend a few dollars to help the station produce the material to run in your spot. It costs something to make artwork and slides. Most stations would like to hear you make the offer to pay, even if they refuse the offer (see also pages 117–121) and do it for free.

In obtaining air time for programs other than those which include PSAs, it will pay you to listen to and watch local shows and acquire some knowledge of which on-air personalities to approach because of their evidenced interest in your type of activity.

As you listen and view, over a period of time, categorize your area stations, using labels of your own, such as news emphasis, country music, hard rock, mixed format. Most local community stations fall under the latter rubric.

Sometimes interesting and profitable use can be made of the kinds of knowledge about outlets which you will be collecting. One educational outpost reported that in trying to attract high school seniors and recent graduates to lower-level evening classes, they abandoned the general and news stations and concentrated their broadcast efforts on the hard-rock stations to which the young adults turned their dials. The results were phenomenal.

On-air interviews offer you an additional opportunity to get broadcast programming which will help promote your continuing education activity. Interviews often are produced under the direction of the news department. A call to the station manager (or a question put to the manager during a visit to his or her office) usually will verify this fact.

If the station's news department *is* involved in its on-air interviews, it usually is a good idea to develop a personal line of communication with the news director or some other key person in that department, especially the assignments editor. (Increasingly, the medium-to-large stations do have assignments editors who are different persons than the news directors.)

Programming which falls into the interview-family category holds some promise for those publicizing and promoting community-based activities. But don't expect too much. The most you are likely to get is a simple interview or panel discussion. Only programs in the larger markets are likely to commit much of a budget to interview programming. The station management is likely to listen to your supplications for an interview or panel discussion, though, because they have the equipment and the bus is running—another "passenger" won't cost any extra gas. That is, they already are in operation, and the additional program component you propose will fit into their regular schedule without any more financing or staff.

Again, the only factor which limits interview programming is available air time. These days, even the fringe times are often sold—to religious groups, to country music organizations, etc.

You remember that stations will still have some time for public service—even if they don't like to admit it—because they usually have made a promise to the FCC in their license application (see pages 48–49).

Some stations invite the public's interest and participation in programming; others seem to hoard their public-service programming time with very little leeway for contributions of material or ideas from those outside their select circle.

Television Channel 2 in Detroit does a top-flight job of informing the public of a group's opportunities for notice on that station and of services and programs in which participation is accepted.

A little three-fold (six-paneled) giveaway brochure is advertised at frequent intervals over the station. Called *It's Easy to Tell Your Story on TV2*, it outlines five different ways that individuals, organizations, and institutions can get their message on the channel.

TV2's cover message tells its viewers:

"Your project, message, event or opinion must be non-profit. It should interest a significant share of a very large audience. Direct funds appeals generally are not appropriate. But within these flexible limits TV2 is committed to free and uncomplicated access to the air by the community we are privileged to serve."

This sort of public outreach instrument is becoming increasingly available from major stations. More stations—with a view to a good public image—probably will follow.

When you line up an interview, *you will be expected to bring the person to be interviewed to the station.* It would require a rare interview prospect, indeed, to bring the television-radio people out into the hinterlands to interview your spokesperson.

Some sponsors of continuing education activities—usually the ivory tower types on the steering committee—want to save wear and tear on a speaker or distinguished or newsworthy visitor by scheduling a group interview—that is, an interview much smaller and less structured than a press conference, but with representatives of several media outlets included at the same session.

Group interviews save effort for the prominent person, but this is the only advantage they have. Most publicists (myself included) avoid them assiduously.

Why? Because they breed bad feelings, that's why.

Take a typical group interview. You have, perhaps, three reporters and a prominent person. Two of the reporters were given the assignment at the last minute, and the third knew about it long enough ahead of time (or perhaps was a little better at being a reporter than the other two) and did a little background check on the prominent person—enough so that he or she had a couple of good and provocative questions up a sleeve. If the prepped-up reporter has to pull those questions in the group interview, the other two reporters also will hear the answers—they will be coasting on the prepared reporter's advance work and brainpower. The result will be that the prepared reporter (the best of the lot—right?—and a person to cultivate) will not like you or your project very well.

So if enough newsroom assignments editors show interest in an interview to make a group interview seem appropriate, skirt by it and go right into a full-scale press conference (see pages 180–186). Moves better, elicits more coverage, and keeps the folks (*all* the folks) a whole lot happier.

Somehow, a formal press conference with more structure than a group interview seems to stimulate more discussion and prompt better preparation on the parts of those who attend it than does a group interview.

 **Some hints about other kinds of interview programming. Because they usually are scheduled in moribund time slots, phone-in types of programs rarely draw much of an audience. Your project will have a good chance if it deals with something which is (or should be) of interest to a large segment of the general public—for example, Heart Week, getting out the vote, the right to privacy, better education for our children. Despite the fact that phone-in programs are sometimes comparatively ineffective, do not ignore this means of getting your message across. At the University of California, Berkeley, last year, such programs generated more than 3,000 phone calls.**

Another obvious opportunity for appearance on radio or TV is in *news programming.* In most operations you will have to have either a hard news event or something which offers good feature material. A natural is a big-name guest who can be interviewed. This is the sort of thing where you should plan a press conference and let the TV and radio stations know about it as far in advance as possible. If it is a really big name, most TV stations will send a camera crew and reporter for both the conference and interviews. *Don't forget to leave time for these interviews* in the schedule the steering committee sets up for the notable in question.

All stations like to have something which is exclusive.

An interview is that "something."

Arrangements should be made through the news director or the assignments editor. As is always the case, a personal contact in the newsroom is a help. Give a reporter a call and tell him or her about it. Sometimes a friendly reporter can get to the assignments editor for you.

However, be certain that an interview offered in a TV-competitive area either is offered to all stations or is so clearly something that only one station or one host-newscaster would be interested in that other stations and their hosts-newscasters would not feel put out or ignored.

 **Keep in regular contact with a station's news department, even though you may not have anything for them at the moment. Telephone in items of interest. Hand-carry releases. See the people socially. It helps to stay in touch.**

Once in a while, a really interesting item will appeal to a station as a topic for a special program or series. I suggest that *exceptional* items be taken to the station manager or the program director. But it really depends on your best personal contact.

Remember that stations are constantly approached by people and organizations that have "great" stuff for them. Very little of it can ever hope to make it to the folks at home. If you are turned down, keep going back. Persistence often works.

In all these areas, remember that there is a difference between getting time on a station and having something to say, and saying it effectively.

Because TV is primarily visual, give some thought to what visual material you could provide to add interest to your interviews. Demonstrations, displays, and special costumes are examples.

TV Mechanics

The ratio of length to width of a TV screen is about 3 × 4. This means that many pictures taken for newspapers or other media are in the wrong proportions. You might want to produce something specifically in 3 × 4 proportion.

Thirty-five-mm slides work very well, provided that they are horizontal. If you offer slides, be sure that they are shot so that the essential material in each picture doesn't come too close to the edges. There usually is a little loss around the edges of slides. At the most it won't likely exceed one-sixth on each edge or two-thirds overall. The station production manager, art director, or chief photographer can advise on visuals.

If you have graphic art available, it is best to show it to someone in the station production department and get an opinion. Very high contrast stuff often doesn't work very well. Too much white in a picture is usually worse than too much black. The television system has some trouble with line art which is too "busy." Lots of very fine lines don't translate very well to television. They often cause a moiré pattern—the kind of swimming, floating pattern that makes you a little seasick to watch.

Almost all stations can broadcast 16-mm motion-picture film. Many can now handle super 8, and the largest stations can show 35-mm motion pictures.

Unless your available film is professionally produced or particularly unique, avoid it. If film is necessary, the station can produce it for you. Home movies tend to look like home movies.

Most stations—radio as well as TV—will accept professionally produced *audio* to be included in the production of public-service material. Quarter-inch audio tape that runs either 7½ inches per second or, preferably, 15 inches per second (ips) can be used. This should be full-track recording only. Half-track or four-track recorders won't work unless the top has been bulk-erased prior to recording to ensure that there isn't other material on the other tracks. If in doubt, check with the station.

They will probably be able to use audio tape cassettes but would prefer ¼-inch reel-to-reel tapes. Use large hub reels if available. This helps ensure that the tape will play at the proper speed—essential if music is involved. There is nothing worse than music that plays just a little slow or that runs at uneven speed.

Dressing for the Cameras

The old adage "clothes don't make the man" may have been true for its time, but on color television the right clothes can really help your image.

Advancing techniques have already made obsolete many of the former guidelines for effective appearance on color television. The following recommendations for wearing apparel will help you look your best on color television.

Suggestions for Women

HATS   Not too many women wear hats on television these days, but if you or your spokeswoman plan to wear one, you or she should avoid hats with wide brims. They create sharp face shadows from overhead lights. Plain colors are best.

DRESSES   Stay away from white or very light-colored dresses, suits, and blouses.

They make the face look dark. They also make you look fatter. Solid colors are the most effective on color television.

Avoid small patterns, checks, and stripes. They look "busy" on the screen. Black, navy blue, and royal blue materials also should be avoided. They all look black and lose detail on the screen. Medium-range colors are recommended.

JEWELRY   Generally speaking, jewelry may be worn. However, you'll be smart to avoid large and extremely bright jewlery, which tends to flare and distort the picture. To be certain, check jewelry on camera before air time.

GLOVES   It is unlikely that you or your program's representative will wear gloves unless you are using a picture taken outdoors in winter. If gloves are used, oyster white, ecru, tan, or pastel colors produce best results. Avoid pure white (as in dresses, hats, and blouses).

SHOES   White or light-colored shoes make your feet look big. Wear darker colors.

MAKEUP   Properly blended makeup in natural tones should be applied *to all exposed skin areas*. This is especially important for hands which, without makeup, present a strong contrasting tone next to other exposed skin areas. Lipstick should be a clear red tone, and it should be applied lightly; avoid dark reds which may contain blue pigment. Eye shadow may be used sparingly. Makeup should be checked on camera before air time.

Suggestions for Men

SUITS   Medium-tone gray, blue, brown, or mixed colors are preferable. Avoid suits with stripes, checks, or small patterns. If black or dark blue suits are worn, avoid light-colored accessories.

SHIRTS   Gray shirts look the best. Avoid pure white shirts (they make the face look dark). Off-white shirts or pastel colors may be worn.

NECKTIES   Muted colors are suggested. Avoid checks or very small patterns which "swim" on camera.

HANDKERCHIEFS   Avoid pure white breast-pocket handkerchiefs. Muted colors and off-white are recommended.

MAKEUP   Most men need some kind of makeup if they are to appear on television. This may range from a suntan shade of powder to reduce shine to television pan-stick makeup to cover beard shadow, sunburn, strong skin coloration, blemishes, etc. It is essential *that all exposed skin areas, including the hands and ears*, be covered. Makeup should be checked on camera before air time.

PUBLIC BROADCASTING

TV stations which are designated as "public broadcasting" or "educational broadcasting" carry very little locally produced material.

Their evening hours are taken up principally by programs which are syndicated or which the PBS network now offers in program service much like that of the commercial networks. This programming comes down a network line like CBS or NBC. Many of these stations are installing satellite receivers to get this programming.

The materials arriving at PBS stations by syndication or, increasingly, via this network include the fine BBC serials and other offerings of that ilk. Symphony, opera, and ballet are popular.

They also include some news analysis, some series on problems and concerns, with guest experts.

Many PBS stations also feature one or more classes, sometimes in combination with newspaper articles, sometimes in combination with correspondence courses and even with an occasional meeting with an instructor.

Such courses usually are offered for credit to students who wish or need to earn such credit, but they also are open to those who prefer to take part as auditors and do not ask for credit.

Where PBS stations regularly schedule some sort of catchall, locally produced programs, these do offer an opportunity for the publicist. The formats usually are flexible and vary a lot, but they sometimes do handle the sort of material the person doing p.r. for a program or other activity can latch onto. These might include panel discussions on a controversial or especially interesting topic related to the theme of the program which is just over the rise, or even a call-in program on that topic. Watch the PBS target station and see where the openings exist.

Public educational radio offers a riper opportunity for the publicist than does TV. Stations which are related to an educational institution frequently have a format which allows them to tape concerts, speeches, and other programs for later broadcast.

Many have shortspots—5 minutes to a half hour—with titles like "The University Report." These focus on one aspect of an institution's activity, with a guest member of the faculty doing the voice.

Publicists within major educational institutions have several gambits for getting programming on the air in stations other than the ones serving the campus locality. There are direct-dial news spots tapes, a different item each day, which a newscaster can dial on his or her station phone; the message goes straight onto the air from the on-campus phone where it originates.

On specified and usually seasonal occasions, commercial radio and TV stations can send tapes to a campus and receive them back with a program for the stations' use—a Christmas concert by student groups, for example, or the annual message of the institution's spokesperson on the state of its activity.

These outreach efforts are appropriate to and are being heavily used by educational institutions. However, the approaches can be transferred with little or no alterations to use by nonprofit and public-service organizations and agencies.

Public-Service Announcements and News/Press Release Mechanics

A publicist's first concern is to give newsrooms (both print and broadcast) the material for release about the project in a form which can be used with little or no editing or rewriting (see pages 61–64).

A simple way to accomplish this goal is to follow patterns which generally are used in the media.

After a little practice, you will find that preparing information according to these patterns will become a comfortable habit.

In brief, a public-service announcement (PSA) is the type of notice given to forthcoming events during "Community Calendar" spots or spots called by similar titles.

Although several lengths of PSAs are accepted by TV and radio stations (see pages 58–60), the shorter sizes are best, because they have greater chances of being used. (More separate "goodwill" PSAs can be fitted into a given number of minutes.)

Anatomy of a Public-Service Announcement

1. Figure about 20 words for a 10-second announcement, 60 words for a 30-second, 120 words for a 60-second. Longer is not always better. A tight, well-aimed 10-second announcement can have a greater impact than a poorly done 60-second version.
2. A good rule of thumb for a PSA is five typewritten lines long, and don't cheat on the margins. That's 15 to 20 seconds, depending on how fast or how slowly the announcer reads.
3. Always *time* your PSA by reading it (and then having someone else read it), and *count the words*. List the time and the number of words on the left-hand side of your PSA handout. Like so:

> PUBLIC-SERVICE ANNOUNCEMENT
> Time: 20 seconds
> Words: 42

Another reason for reading (and then having someone else read) your PSA is to make sure that you are avoiding any difficult words or hard-to-pronounce combinations of words—i.e., inadvertent tongue twisters. Also triple-check your who, what, when, where, why, and how ingredients, and make doubly sure that you have listed a contact address and/or telephone number.

4. It is a good idea to put the text of the PSA on the right-hand side of your

handout, about halfway down. (This is a stylistic pattern at some stations, and many broadcasters think it makes a PSA easier to read.) Head it "FOR IMMEDIATE RELEASE," and give an expiration date—a date after which it should not go out on the air because of some reason, which you need not specify, by the way. An example would be that after that date, registration would have been closed, or the prize would have been awarded.

5. Write it in caps.
6. Triple-space it.
7. In a small- to medium-sized setting, forget the above—put it on a postcard.

Most of the warnings re accuracy and conciseness (how can you be anything *but* concise in 20 seconds?) listed under the guidelines for press releases (pages 61–64) also apply here. Review them each time before you write a PSA.

```
IUPUI DIVISION OF CONTINUING STUDIES, 1201 E. 38th
ST., INDIANAPOLIS, IN 46205, 264-4501

                                    July 20
Contact: Nancy Garber,
         Media Coordinator        FOR IMMEDIATE RELEASE
         Home: 255-0724
         Office: 264-4702         Expires: September 15


PUBLIC SERVICE ANNOUNCEMENT
TIME:   20 seconds
WORDS: 50


FROM ASSERTIVENESS TO ZOOLOGY-AD WRITING

TO YOGA, GUITAR, BIORHYTHMS, CAREER PLANNING, ART,

MUSIC AND VOCATIONAL COURSES-A HUNDRED AND FIFTY

CLASSES FOR ADULTS THIS FALL.  JOIN ELEVEN THOUSAND OF

YOUR FRIENDS IN NONCREDIT CLASSES AT IUPUI.  CALL FOR

A FREE SCHEDULE.  264-4501.
```

IUPUI DIVISION OF CONTINUING STUDIES, 1201 E. 38th
ST., INDIANAPOLIS, IN 46205, 264-4501

July 20

Contact: Nancy Garber,
         Media Coordinator   <u>FOR IMMEDIATE RELEASE</u>
         Home: 255-0724
         Office: 264-4702   Expires: September 15

<u>PUBLIC SERVICE ANNOUNCEMENT</u>

TIME: 15 seconds

WORDS: 43

FROM ASSERTIVENESS TO ZOOLOGY—AD WRITING TO YOGA. ART,

CAREER PLANNING, VOCATIONAL COURSES—A HUNDRED AND

FIFTY CLASSES FOR ADULTS THIS FALL. CALL NOW FOR A

FREE SCHEDULE. ADULT NONCREDIT CLASSES. CONTINUING

EDUCATION AT IUPUI. 264-4501.

IUPUI DIVISION OF CONTINUING STUDIES, 1201 E. 38th
ST., INDIANAPOLIS, IN 46205, 264-4501

July 20

Contact: Nancy Garber,
         Media Coordinator   <u>FOR IMMEDIATE RELEASE</u>
         Home: 255-0724
         Office: 264-4702   Expires: September 15

<u>PUBLIC SERVICE ANNOUNCEMENT</u>

TIME: 10 seconds

WORDS: 33

FROM ASSERTIVENESS TO ZOOLOGY—AD WRITING TO YOGA—A

HUNDRED AND FIFTY CLASSES FOR ADULTS THIS FALL. CALL

FOR A FREE SCHEDULE. CONTINUING EDUCATION AT IUPUI.

264-4501.

Mailed: Jan. 20
Release: Immediate

FROM: UNIVERSITY OF ILLINOIS
CONTINUING EDUCATION AND PUBLIC SERVICE

PUBLIC SERVICE ANNOUNCEMENT

Ralph Nader, consumer advocate, will speak on "Public Rights and Public Policy" at 7:30 P.M., March 21 at the Holiday Inn, Harvey. The public is invited. For registration information, call Paul Caponera, Thornton Community College, (312) 555-7622.

—hsf—

Dennis Jahn
Public Service Announcements
WGN-AM
2501 Bradley Place   Mailed: Jan. 20
Chicago, IL 60618   Release: Immediate

FROM: University of Illinois
      Continuing Education and Public Service
      Press Information, Helen Farlow (217) 333-0517

PUBLIC SERVICE ANNOUNCEMENT

Ralph Nader, consumer advocate, will speak on "Public Rights and Public Policy" at 7:30 P.M., March 21 at the Holiday Inn, Harvey, during a forum on access to environmental information. The public is invited. For registration information, call Paul Caponera, Thornton Community College, (312) 555-7622.

—hsf—

MECHANICS OF A PRESS RELEASE

Newswriting instructors often describe the standard news story—for this is formula writing in its strictest form—as an inverted triangle.

What they mean is that you put all necessary facts, the

Who
What
Why
Where
When
How

in the *lead*, which is at the very beginning—the first paragraph (or, at most, the first and second paragraphs).

They are right.

It is what's up front that counts.

The reason for the inverted triangle model is that you begin with essentials. You then trail off into minor details so that the article can, if necessary, be cut when it gets to the news desk, to fill a smaller space without losing punch or power.

I prefer to call the news story format—for exactly the same reasons—a kite. If you build a pretty fair kite and give it a long, trailing tail (of minor importance), the tail can be lopped off almost anywhere along its length, and the kite will still fly.

Press releases are no different. Not at all. If they are properly and professionally written, you can cut off their tails, and they still will fly.

When you sit down to write a news release, you must follow basic guidelines— guidelines which in most cases boil down to old-fashioned common sense.

They are the kinds of things about which people say, "Everybody ought to know enough to do that!" Sure they should. But you would be surprised to know how few really do.

Press-Release Guidelines

1. Be accurate. Gather the information carefully. Don't take anyone's word for anything. Check and recheck (at more than one source, if possible). Be thorough, and include all necessary materials, but follow the kite example. Put the nonessentials way down in the tail.
2. Stick to the facts—don't editorialize.
3. Put your grabber in the first paragraph. First, remember that you've got to catch the interest of a busy, overworked, and ofttimes jaded news desk person who

Anatomy of the News Release

1. <u>Doublespace</u> on 8½ x 11 typing paper.

2. <u>Type it</u> or get someone to type it. Handwriting is not acceptable.

3. <u>Use only one side</u> of the paper. This is manda-tory.

4. <u>Allow 1" margins</u> on all sides.

5. <u>Do not break</u> a sentence or a paragraph at the bottom of the page.

6. <u>Number your pages</u> and give them a slug so they can be identified. For example, Page 1—Coal Con-ference. At the bottom of the page, then, in par-entheses, put (More—Coal Conference). Your sec-ond page, then, could start, COAL CONFERENCE—Page 2. Parentheses are used at the bottoms of pages but not necessarily at the tops. However, no harm will be done if you find this little rule hard to remember and use parentheses at the tops as well as the bottoms; harm <u>might</u> be done if you reversed the thing and used no parentheses at all.

7. When you get to the end of your article, use some kind of a <u>symbol to indicate that you've finished.</u> It can be the symbol "—30—"; or simply a hash mark "#"; or, if a number of people from your institution are sending out releases, you may want to use your initials, "—hsf—." Anything to indicate, "that's all, folks."

8. It's a good idea to put something with the re-
    lease that tells <u>where you can be reached</u> if the
    editor/reporter/newscaster has questions. One
    way to do it is this: After your hashmark or
    other closing symbol, and <u>again in paren-
    theses,</u> put something like this: (PRESS INFORMA-
    TION: Josie Marcus, Gideon Junior College, Sham-
    baugh, Iowa, 01234, Phone 555-1981, Ext. 123).

9. A point on punctuation. Always use your punctua-
    tion marks <u>inside</u> the quotes.

10. Latch onto a current <u>AP (Associated Press)
    Stylebook</u> if you can. Printshop style is neither
    academic nor literary. The cost is small. How-
    ever, an old one (discard) from a newspaper or
    broadcast friend will do almost as well.

11. At the top of the page, be certain to include (a)
    the date the release is sent; (b) the name of the
    contact person (yourself); (c) the name of the
    agency sending the release; and (d) the release
    date—usually immediate.

 Avoid adjectives and adverbs wherever pos-
sible. Your nouns and verbs should be
your color-action words. Avoid using substitutes for the verb "said." It slows
down the action of your sentence if you
use "remarked," "uttered," "pronounced,"
etc., unless such descriptive insistence
on the substitute is actually necessary to
the point the words are making.

will be the release's first obstacle as it progresses to print or broadcast—or into the wastebasket.

4. Don't get into the trivia department. Make sure that when a release goes out over your initials it says something that is important, interesting, and timely. Trivia is great, if you are giving a columnist a cutesy item or are suggesting a fluffy little feature story. But not in basic press releases.

5. Crisp, clean, short sentences and paragraphs delight an editor's soul. Leave out long, awkward phrases. Don't use jargon or technical language which a typical reader might find confusing. It is only when dealing with some of the hard, exact sciences (and how often will your average program promoter deal with those?) that rather precise and not easily translatable nomenclature is necessary—and even then, you'd have to translate.

6. Your news release should look good, too. Neatness counts.

7. Don't submit a headline. They write their own.

8. Date all copy—prevents arguments.

WATCH YOUR LANGUAGE: MISCELLANEOUS BAD WORDS, SEXIST WORDS, COPYRIGHTED WORDS

LOOK OUT FOR THE BAD WORDS

There are several kinds of language that a publicist (a person whose written word may be translated into the public prints and into the spoken broadcast) must be aware of.

These are:

1. Materials which could be suspect in your use of them under the stringencies of the revised *copyright law*. An explanation is below.

2. Inferences or statements which could bring about a suit for *libel*. This also is treated below. There is a very good additional treatment of libel in *The Associated Press Stylebook* (see "Bibliography" and pages 64–68).

3. "Dirty words." You probably are not publicizing many programs in the underground or *porno* press, so do not use even borderline "dirty words." If you are quite young, some words which are not in polite social usage among older or more conservative people may seem to you to be commonplace language. They are not. If you would not say these words in the presence of your most sheltered, unsophisticated, and conventional older friends or relatives, do not use them in anything which might get out to the general public. No matter what you want to say, there are polite, "square" ways to say it that will offend no one. The newspapers and magazines and broadcasters probably wouldn't use dirty words, even if you included them in a news release, but (particularly with camera- or scanner-ready copy) something might slip through. Don't chance it.

You'd be committing professional suicide. Also watch brochures, flyers, posters, etc., to make certain that nothing like this slips by.

Watch out, in this area and in the area of libel, for *double meanings.* A word that carries a double meaning, even such a historically innocuous phrase as "great and good friend," can be tricky.

Be very fussy about words and statements which could reflect *bad taste* or a violation of even purely *local mores and taboos.*

A publicist should not use street talk.

A publicist should not use epithets and putdowns.

A publicist should not use blurred words, words which have lost their original meaning and (sometimes) have taken on shadings which hold unsavory (to some readers or listeners) implications and suggestions.

A publicist should not use outhouse language or "humor."

Watch out, too, for jargon intelligible only to another of the same career or cultural orientation.

In these days (see below) you can get into trouble if your words reflect sexism.

 **These are among the reasons why all copy should be read, not only by the originator but also by one or, preferably, two other people—people who, it is hoped, don't share the writer's background, biases, or office.**

The proof is in the proofing.

SEXISM

Women are very touchy about the sexism which still is rife in many publications as well as the broadcast media, and they have a right to be.

Most touchy of all are women who are newsmakers by virtue of professional competency or civic leadership. These usually are the women who will be among platform people in programs you may be called upon to publicize.

Women of this caliber, and their colleagues and associates of both sexes, will not tolerate the use of such words in regard to them as "chick," "doll," "broad," "baby," "dear," and the dozens of others you can think of in 30 seconds.

Such women prefer to have the news of their activities reported on news pages and on newscasts and not in special sections or programs (by whatever name) devoted largely to material which editors seem to think appeals mainly to women.

As a publicist, you should take particular precautions not to offend either the subject of your news release or the readers.

In the International Women's Year (1975), the President's National Commission for the observance of that year brought out a report on media guidelines with regard to women and a leaflet summarizing the report. The leaflet states:

> *The media have an enormous impact on the formation and reinforcement of behavior and attitudes. When women are constantly portrayed in stereotyped ways, these images affect their aspirations. Increasingly, women have been more concerned about the limited portrayal of them by the media . . . [and] a predominance of discrimination against women throughout the media industry . . . ranging from under-representation in policymaking and news positions to ridicule of women's activities in daily coverage.*
>
> *Women are rarely presented accurately in radio, television, newspapers, magazines, film, entertainment programming, and advertisements.*
>
> *Despite progress in some areas, news relating to women is still very seriously underreported.*

The leaflet sets forth ten media guidelines, many of which deal with news and feature presentations of women's activities and of women in other spheres of work and prominence. The following are helpful to the publicist:

> *The present definition of news should be expanded to include more coverage of women's activities, locally, nationally, and internationally. In addition, general news stories should be reported to show their effect on women. For example, the impact of foreign aid on women in recipient countries is often overlooked, as is the effect of public transportation on women's mobility, safety, and ability to take jobs.*
>
> *The media should make special, sustained efforts to seek out news of women. Women now figure in less than 10 per cent of the stories currently defined as news.*
>
> *Placement of news should be decided by subject matter, not by sex. The practice of segregating material thought to be of interest only to women into certain sections of a newspaper or broadcast implies that news of women is not real news. However, it is important to recognize and offset an alarming trend wherein such news, when no longer segregated, is not covered at all. Wherever news of women is placed, it should be treated with the same dignity, scope, and accuracy as is news of men. Women's activities should not be located in the last 30–60 seconds of a broadcast or used as fillers in certain sections or back pages of a newspaper or magazine.*
>
> *Women's bodies should not be used in an exploitive way to add irrelevant sexual interest in any medium. This includes news and feature coverage by both the press and television, movies and movie promotion, "skin" magazines and*

advertising messages of all sorts. The public violation of a woman's physical privacy tends to violate the individual integrity of all women.

The presentation of personal details when irrelevant to a story—sex, sexual preference, age, marital status, physical appearance, dress, religious or political orientation—should be eliminated for both women and men.*

It is to be hoped that one day all titles will be unnecessary. But in the meantime, a person's right to determine her (or his) own title should be respected without slurs or innuendoes. If men are called Doctor or Reverend, the same titles should be used for women. And a woman should be able to choose Ms., Miss, or Mrs.

Gender designations are a rapidly changing area of the language, and a decision to use or not to use a specific word should be subject to periodic review. Terms incorporating gender reference should be avoided. Use firefighter instead of fireman, business executive instead of businessman, letter carrier instead of mailman. In addition, women, from at least the age of 16, should be called women, and not girls. . . .

Copyright Laws and Ethics

Don't Be a Thief

Anytime a writer, instructor, or speaker uses copyrighted material without permission of the author or whoever else holds the copyright—e.g., publisher, agent, heir—he or she is a *thief.*

He or she is stealing the author's talent and livelihood just as much as if the stolen material were cash out of a person's wallet. It is theft by underhanded means of the author's very job.

If you would not steal goods off a merchant's shelf, do not steal an author's merchandise—which is his or her copyrighted material.

---

*Note: The matter of personal details not related to the news story itself is of particular abhorrence to some of us who have been professional women for many years. If you would not mention certain details in announcing the program appearance of a man in a job like mine, don't do it for me or any of the others.
Would you say, for example:

> Robert E. Harrison, head of Information Services at Upper Oregon University, will present a special workshop, "Publicizing and Promoting Programs," during the forthcoming conference on continuing education administration on his campus.
> Harrison, 55, the blond, 6-foot grandfather of three, will speak at 3 P.M. on November 21 in Memorial Hall. Flashing a dimpled smile and swinging an elegant expanse of leg, Harrison said that he will key his talk and the accompanying materials to the assistance of newcomers in the field of educational public relations.

Get it?

There are exceptions to this prohibition, and the revision of the nation's copyright laws which took effect on January 1, 1978, attempts to spell these out in some detail.

However, the law in many ways is ambiguous and in need of interpretations by the courts—interpretations which will go on for some time until the issues are clarified.

Please note that among the major changes under the current statutes as opposed to the older versions are (1) to lengthen the time that a copyright is in effect, and (2) to extend the various prohibitions very specifically to include the pirating or otherwise lifting of such materials by means of photocopying machines.

Basically, the copyright laws still comprise legal recognition of the ownership of a particular creative work on the part of an author, artist, or composer.

How Do I Get Permission to Use Copyrighted Materials?

You may obtain permission to use material which is under a copyright by getting in touch with the person or agency which holds that copyright. In some cases this is the person who wrote or otherwise created the material. In other instances, it is the publisher or producing agency. You can learn the identity of the holder of the copyright by looking on the copyright page in the front matter of the book, or the masthead of the publication for the address of the publisher. Or write to the author or person who originated the material. To locate the person, find the city; look in the phone book or city directory for the address.

Be certain to get all the permissions *in writing.* You may have to pay a small fee.

Anthologists and others who use long quotes, or complete chapters or articles of another person's work usually get permission to use such materials through their publishers. Most major publishers have "permissions departments" which clear such matters, through systems of payments, credits, or exchanges.

Again, get it in writing.

DIRECT MAIL

Direct mail is the most popular device used in publicizing and promoting programs. It is the only tool for promotion which most program development people have had any experience with.

In addition:

It is easy.

It is fast.

When it is well designed, it can be attractive. Kept plain and simple, it still can have impact.

You don't have to think about it very much. Development of a brochure or other direct-mail piece can become almost an automatic reflex for the program developer.

Yet, direct mail as a publicizing and promotion tool is only as good as:

Its visual effect.
The people-pulling power of its pitch (i.e., how well it is written).
The mailing lists which are used.

Direct-mail pieces—flyers, even three-folds to six-folds, brochures, or catalogs—have to have immediate eye appeal and copy which will trigger an unhesitating response and which represents a product that meets a need or a desire.

People receive so many, many flyers at their homes or workplaces that they are apt to become thoroughly immunized to this kind of approach. Think about the situation for a second.

Direct-mail pieces come from all kinds of sponsors, from banks to amusement parks and from liquor dealers to churches.

EFFECTIVE DIRECT MAIL

How can you make yours stand out?

First, your mailing piece should be an eye-catcher, both in design and in whatever words you place on its cover.

Second, it should be written in a clear and catchy style. Unless it is addressed to a segment of the public which is highly specialized in a technical field where the terminology is extremely basic to communication among colleagues, it should be bare of jargon.

Third, it should be specific as to what your program will include and as to how the program can benefit the participant or that person's organization or agency.

Fourth, it should be as *inclusive* as possible, given all time factors. The fact that you don't have *all* the names of the panelists or instructors confirmed should not preclude your stating in your brochure the names and identities of those who definitely will be platform people. (Check your copy to be sure *all* necessary facts are included—Who? What? Where? When? Why? and How?)

Fifth, it should play up any pluses you can offer: big-name speaker? attractive location? expertise not available elsewhere? Review the "P's" on pages 20–21, and use those which are applicable as points to cover in the mailing piece.

Sixth, returning a blank for registration and/or more information should be made as painless as possible for the prospective participant. The blank should be easy to separate from the rest of the copy. In some cases, you may want to go as far as to have postage imprinted or to include a stamped and addressed envelope. Beware, however, of wrecking a program's budget on the shoals of postage.

Seventh, it should be completely honest as regards the activity, its platform people, the facilities, the possible rewards, and the costs for those who will enroll or attend. There should be no hidden baddies among the stated goodies. The participants should be told what they will get—and *exactly* what they will get! And then don't disappoint them; give them a little more than you promised.

Eighth, to cut down on your mailing piece's immediate disposition—unread—in the trash barrel, mail it to the person's place of business, and not to the home address. Less "junk mail" comes to offices, which increases the chance of your mailing piece being read.

Ninth, think a whole lot about mailing lists.

1. Find a good direct-mail business list brokerage firm, and cleave to it. How do you find one? Ask people in your line of activity who themselves have good track records. They can make recommendations. Or you always can consult the *Standard Rate and Data Service* lists of mailing lists for an appropriate source. (The *Standard Rate and Data Service* references can be found in any large public library.)

In selecting a mailing list from a mail-order broker, look for purchasing or demographic characteristics suggesting an interest in a particular subject. (A person subscribing to a cookbook-of-the-month club might like to take a course in Indonesian cooking.)

A good broker will be a good right hand. The person you deal with at the brokerage firm will recommend the right lists to you for your program offering.

One thing to watch carefully is the age and veracity of a purchased mailing list. Ask the broker: "How long ago was this list laundered?" The word "laundering," in this context, refers to a list's being tested out through a trial mailing (first-class mail, always) and then meticulously corrected on the basis of returns (no such address, moved, gone out of business, etc.) and changes of address.

But to reemphasize, an established, respectable, dependable mail broker can be of infinite help and can be so exact in fulfilling your requirements that a newcomer to the experience will be amazed.

A competent mail broker can identify a target mailing down to one city block within a ZIP-Code area. This sort of firm can do some pretty exotic pinpointing of potential audiences or target groups—all the pediatricians in a specified region who are 49 years old and blue-eyed, and who have wives named Mary.

Well, not quite.

That is an extreme and facetious example. But brokers are almost that specific!

The wise p.r. person with a project large enough to warrant such an approach demonstrates that wisdom by taking advantage of a mail house's potential for specificity. The money, in most cases, will be well spent.

2. An organization in the field you are attempting to serve may be willing to share mailing lists, or your program's cosponsors can give you their lists.

3. For general public interest or for class enrollments, build a list of current and previous participants, request names of interested friends from current students or clients, put an aide to work compiling lists of neighbors of current and former students or participants through use of the city directory.

4. Some other sources that can point you to good lists or help you develop your own are:
   a. The U.S. Department of Commerce (census reports on population, retail establishments, wholesale establishments, industry).
   b. The Bureau of Labor Statistics (type of business, employment, average earnings).
   c. The county and city data book (population, taxes, firms, business establishments).
   d. Local and state chambers of commerce (names of members, types of industries). Some chambers of commerce have developed splendid packets analyzing and making accessible in a single place all the demographic and other data obtainable for their area from the sources above and immediately below.
   e. Trade associations.
   f. Unions.
   g. City and trade directories.
   h. State commerce departments.
   i. Sales management magazines' surveys of buyer power (spending power, population, income, sales by major category by county and major metro area).
   j. Sources of information which you, as a publicist, should have in your office anyway *(Ayers Directory, Editor and Publisher Yearbook, Broadcasting Annual).* These can tell you a lot about population, and *Ayers* also lists industry and similar information for every community it mentions.

How do you get the information and lists suggested in "a" through "i"? Write or call the offices and agencies which the list suggests.

DESIGN

Your mailing piece will be designed in one of three ways:

1. *It will follow a set pattern.* This means that it will carry the same logo (identifying symbol, catchword, or initial—usually a design), typefaces, or color as every

such mailing piece from your office or agency. The purpose is one of instant identification with your operation by the recipient.

The "look-alike" idea can be varied. For example, the design (logo, typefaces) can remain identical for a number of mailing pieces, but the color can be changed to make certain that the recipient doesn't think he or she is getting a duplicate of something which arrived earlier.

 **If you are going to use the "look-alike" pattern over and over and over, loosen your purse strings and get a one-time job done by a good graphics designer. It will pay off in effectiveness, and you'll be a whole lot happier (as will your associates) about the fifth time you have to look at the same design. This "look-alike" design can be carried over to posters, letterhead, printed programs, etc.**

2. *It will be especially designed for the activity being promoted.* A telephone information service might, of course, have its announcement brightened by a picture of a phone; a garden club conference would have something floral; a refresher course for driver training teachers—what else? A car? Or maybe a stoplight. You have to be pretty careful about the design of an activity-connected brochure. It can look busy, cutesy, or blatantly obvious if it is not carefully designed and laid out.

3. *It can be completely plain,* with the only "design" being the contrast provided by the use of varying typefaces and perhaps the contrast afforded by ink of one color and paper of another.

If you don't have the assistance of someone professionally qualified in the graphic arts and you want to try to come up with some ideas of your own, your printer can provide you with a sheet or booklet showing all the type sizes and typefaces available in his or her shop, and also with a color wheel, which will help you choose colors of paper and ink.

But don't let yourself get carried away with all those colors and typefaces. Don't use too many of either; the plainer the better. Too much of either will result in an unattractive mailing piece—and it will run the cost up sky-high.

The principal point to remember is to put your most important fact—probably the program's title—in the biggest type.

NOMENCLATURE: A BROCHURE BY ANY OTHER NAME. . . .

What do you call your mailing piece? Purists would have it that booklets, broadsides, bulletins, and leaflets are different sorts of instruments. However, you will find that, whatever the format, if you call your mailing piece a "brochure," most people will know what you mean. It is an umbrella term for "mailing piece."

 **Don't forget (or discount) the lowly postcard. People will read a postcard who will throw away an envelope or three-fold (obvious promotion pieces). Postcards are dandy for appetite whetting in a prolonged promotion campaign, and also as second reminders.**

Brochure Formats

1. The easiest kind of brochure to design and to use is a three-fold which can be used as a self-mailer. That is, it is folded in three from top to bottom and stapled shut. Then the address or address label is placed on the outside. You stamp it and drop it in the mailbox sans envelope.

2. The next easiest is a leaflet—a single sheet bearing print on one or both sides, used as an envelope stuffer. This is a good format if you are including your announcement/invitation with a sponsor's or a friendly business' mailing—for example, statements from a major bank or bills from the major department store or an organization's newsletters for its members.

3. The more elaborate program may call for a printshop job on heavy paper, which also will be mailed in an envelope.

4. A really prestigious effort may be publicized and promoted by an engraved invitation in a hand-addressed envelope (perhaps with an engraved reply card included). Only a high-budget activity could justify spending this kind of money.

Do-It-Yourself Art and Type: Camera-Ready Copy

A saving ploy is the preparation of "camera-ready" copy.

"Camera-ready" art is usually one piece of artboard with all the elements of the layout (headlines, copy, art) arranged and pasted in the exact position in which they will appear on the printed piece. Size of paper or artwork is not too important. The piece can be enlarged or reduced by the printer or photo lab as necessary. If you plan to enlarge or reduce the page, talk to your printer about type sizes. In any case, 8 × 10 inch sheets are easier to handle and work with in the preliminary stages.

In addition, all elements (artwork and lettering) on the page must be in the proportion of the finished page. If the page is to be reduced to one-fourth, the artwork and type should both be four times as large. Elaboration on this point can be provided by your printer.

In preparing "camera-ready" copy, consider using transfer type (Press Type or

Ink-smudged hands with calloused, nimble fingers, they gave the world the gift of
ABCDEFGHIJKLMNOPQRSTUVWXY abcdefghijklmnopqrstuvwxy \$123456789
12 point (Large) Clarendon Semi Bold   Caps, lower case, figures

Ink-smudged hands with calloused, nimble fingers, they gave the wo
ABCDEFGHIJKLMNOPQRSTU   abcdefghijklmnopqrstu \$12345678
14 point Clarendon Semi Bold   Caps, lower case, figures

Ink-smudged hands with calloused, nimble fingers, they g
ABCDEFGHIJKLMNOPQR abcdefghijklmnopqr \$1234567
18 point Clarendon Semi Bold   Caps, lower case, figures

Ink-smudged hands with calloused, nimble fin
ABCDEFGHIJKLMN abcdefghijklmn \$123456
24 point Clarendon Semi Bold   Caps, lower case, figures

Ink-smudged hands with calloused, n
ABCDEFGHIJK abcdefghijk \$12345
30 point Clarendon Semi Bold   Caps, lower case, figures

Ink-smudged hands with callou
ABCDEFGHIJ abcdefghij \$1234
36 point Clarendon Semi Bold   Caps, lower case, figures

Ink-smudged hands with
ABCDEFG abcdefg \$123
42 point Clarendon Semi Bold   Caps, lower case, figures

Ink-smudged hand
ABCDE abcde \$12
60 point Clarendon Semi Bold   Caps, lower case, figures

Letraset), which comes in a wide range of styles and sizes and is available at art supply stores. Body copy can be typewritten; a typewriter which accommodates different elements with different typefaces works well.

Add interest to your homemade copy by using capitals, italics, differences. But remember the warning about overdoing it; keep it fairly simple.

DEEPDENE BOLD
ABCDEFGHIJKLMNOPQRSTUVWXYZ&
abcdefghijklmnopqrstuvwxyz $1234567890

DEEPDENE BOLD ITALIC
ABCDEFGHIJKLMNOPQRSTUVWXYZ&
abcdefghijklmnopqrstuvwxyz $1234567890

DELPHIN NO. 1
ABCDEFGHIJKLMNOPQRSTUVWXYZ&
abcdefghijklmnopqrstuvwxyz $1234567890¢

DELPHIN NO. 1 ITALIC
ABCDEFGHIJKLMNOPQRSTUVWXYZ&
abcdefghijklmnopqrstuvwxyz $1234567890¢

DELPHIN NO. 2
ABCDEFGHIJKLMNOPQRSTUVWXYZ&
abcdefghijklmnopqrstuvwxyz $1234567890¢

DELPHIN NO. 2 ITALIC
ABCDEFGHIJKLMNOPQRSTUVWXYZ&
abcdefghijklmnopqrstuvwxyz $1234567890¢

DE ROOS ROMAN
ABCDEFGHIJKLMNOPQRSTUVWXYZ&
abcdefghijklmnopqrstuvwxyz $1234567890c

DE ROOS ITALIC
ABCDEFGHIJKLMNOPQRSTUVWXYZ&
abcdefghijklmnopqrstuvwxyz $1234567890

DE ROOS SEMIBOLD
ABCDEFGHIJKLMNOPQRSTUVWXYZ&
abcdefghijklmnopqrstuvwxyz $1234567890c

DEVINNE
ABCDEFGHIJKLMNOPQRSTUVWXYZ&
abcdefghijklmnopqrstuvwxyz 1234567890

DEVINNE ORNAMENTED
ABCDEFGHIJKLMNOPQRSTUVWXYZ&
abcdefghijklmnopqrstuvwxyz $1234567890

DEVINNE ORNAMENTAL ITALIC
ABCDEFGHIJKLMNOPQRSTUVWXYZ&
abcdefghijklmnopqrstuvwxyz $1234567890c

DEVINNE EXTRA BOLD
ABCDEFGHIJKLMNOPQRSTUVWXYZ&
abcdefghijklmnopqrstuvwxyz $1234567890

DIDI
ABCDEFGHIJKLMNOPQRSTUVWXYZ&
abcdefghijklmnopqrstuvwxyz 1234567890

DIMENSIA
ABCDEFGHIJKLMNOPQRSTUVWXYZ&
abcdefghijklmnopqrstuvwxyz$1234567890

DOMINANCE BOLD
ABCDEFGHIJKLMNOPQRSTUVWXYZ
abcdefghijklmnopqrstuvwxyz 1234567890

DOMINANCE AD HEAVY/Darling Ad Heavy
ABCDEFGHIJKLMNOPQRSTUVWXYZ&
abcdefghijklmnopqrstuvwxyz $1234567890

DOMINANCE DIFFIDENT/Darling Open
ABCDEFGHIJKLMNOPQRSTUVWXYZ&
abcdefghijklmnopqrstuvwxyz $1234567890

DOMINANCE OVERBEARING/Darling Bossy
ABCDEFGHIJKLMNOPQRSTUVWXYZ&
abcdefghijklmnopqrstuvwxyz $1234567890

DOMINANTE
ABCDEFGHIJKLMNOPQRSTUVWXYZ&
abcdefghijklmnopqrstuvwxyz $1234567890c

DOMINANTE ITALIC
ABCDEFGHIJKLMNOPQRSTUVWXYZ&
abcdefghijklmnopqrstuvwxyz $1234567890c

DOMINANTE BOLD
ABCDEFGHIJKLMNOPQRSTUVWXYZ&
abcdefghijklmnopqrstuvwxyz $1234567890c

DOMINANTE BLACK
ABCDEFGHIJKLMNOPQRSTUVWXYZ&
abcdefghijklmnopqrstuvwxyz $1234567890

DOMNING ANTIQUA
ABCDEFGHIJKLMNOPQRSTUVWXYZ&
abcdefghijklmnopqrstuvwxyz $1234567890¢

DUKE/Duomo
ABCDEFGHIJKLMNOPQRSTUVWXYZ&
abcdefghijklmnopqrstuvwxyz $1234567890

DUTCH OLD STYLE CONDENSED
ABCDEFGHIJKLMNOPQRSTUVWXYZ&
abcdefghijklmnopqrstuvwxyz $1234567890

EGIZIO MEDIUM
ABCDEFGHIJKLMNOPQRSTUVWXYZ&
abcdefghijklmnopqrstuvwxyz $1234567890¢

EGIZIO MEDIUM ITALIC
ABCDEFGHIJKLMNOPQRSTUVWXYZ&
abcdefghijklmnopqrstuvwxyz $1234567890¢

EGIZIO MEDIUM CONDENSED
ABCDEFGHIJKLMNOPQRSTUVWXYZ&
abcdefghijklmnopqrstuvwxyz $1234567890

EGIZIO BOLD
ABCDEFGHIJKLMNOPQRSTUVWXYZ&
abcdefghijklmnopqrstuvwxyz $1234567890¢

Copy can be typed on 8½ × 11 inch white bond paper. Use a relatively new black ribbon in the typewriter. Don't erase mistakes—use liquid correction fluid. Proof your copy and make the necessary corrections. (It is usually best to have at least two persons read proof.) Avoid wrinkling when pasting up. Use paste sparingly (rubber cement is best), and use rulers and T squares to keep your copy straight.

Brochure Timeframe

Allow plenty of time for the production of your brochure or flyer. What do we mean—"plenty of time"? It can take 8 to 10 weeks to get a flyer from square A (its writing and design) to the hands of your potential students or program participants.

This Timeframe is based not on the date of your program or your registration but *on the day you have set to mail out the brochure.*

1. Three months in advance of the *mailing* date:

    Arrange for the collection or procurement of mailing lists.

    Hire a writer and a graphic artist if you aren't going to keep this as an in-house do-it-yourself product.

    Get rough copy ready, if you are going to write the brochure and design it yourself.

    Line up a printer, and specify your deadlines so he or she can order paper and ink (if necessary) and get you on the sometimes hectic schedule.

    Decide on the style of your mailing piece, and prepare a rough layout.

2. Two months in advance of your mailing date, go see your printer—with, let us hope, your copy in hand.

    How do you choose a printer? The choice of a printer will be made for you if you are fortunate enough to have a printshop in your own agency. Otherwise, it depends a lot on how magnificent a mailing piece you have planned and how many copies you need. A lowly speed printshop can be less expensive than a conventional printer if you only have a few hundred copies to print. Letterpress and offset procedures are usually priced per thousand.

    In any case, bring your rough copy and design to the printer, and follow his or her advice and instructions for producing a workable original.

    Give your printer a deadline for proof copy, which is the set type of your material as it will be printed in the end product. This deadline should be no later than 1 month ahead of the mailing date. Also give the printer a deadline for picking up the final product—"*x* number of brochures." That deadline should be no later than 2 weeks ahead of mailing.

3. One month ahead of the mailing date, go to your printer and pick up your proof copy. Proof it to death (read it carefully at least twice), and have others proof it. Once more to your checkwords—Who? What? Where? When? Why? and How?

Are they all covered? It is so easy to leave out a vital fact; you tend to overlook such facts just because you are so familiar with the activity. Familiarity, in this context, may not breed contempt, but it certainly can breed forgetfulness. A carefully planned brochure can show up in a prospective participant's hands without the place of the activity; without the time of the activity; without particulars regarding registration or other fees.

Do you know the easiest thing to do wrong on a brochure (or in a news release, for that matter)? You have a day of the week and a day of the month which *do not* agree. You have Wednesday, the 27th, on your brochure (in your article). Wednesday actually is the 28th. Which is right? Nobody looked at a calendar while proofing.

Another common mistake is in the spelling of names. Are you certain that it is *Frederick Reed*, not *Reade*, *Read*, or *Reid*? Both first and last names are tricky. As an example, some people spell "Frederick" without the "k" or the second "e."

If you are not absolutely sure, check!

 **This is your last time to make changes in the brochure or other mailing piece, so *be sure it is right*. Be sure the color, size, the *whole bit are the way you want them*.**

4. Two weeks ahead of the mailing date, pick up your brochures. Get them ready to mail by ZIP Code or whatever little tricks (see page 110) you are using to cut postage costs.
5. *Mailing date* (usually 5 to 6 weeks in advance of the program).

COPY PREPARATION

Copy preparation is the last line of defense against error, against misunderstanding by the printer, editor, or newscaster and the readers, and against sloppy material.

Copy preparation is a stool with three legs. They are copy correction, copy marking (commonly called "proofing"), and copy fitting.

Material to be printed in any form—as a brochure, a newspaper or magazine article in the form of a news release, a book, or an advertisement—should be double-spaced on one side of the paper only.

The contributor or publicist only rarely would be in a situation to proof anything which will appear in a newspaper. It's now unlikely that anyone else will proof it, either. The old-time proofreader is another endangered species. However, the contributor usually gets an opportunity to proof copy for a brochure, an advertisement, a book, and even sometimes a magazine article. When you do get a proof, it will be in the form of a long, continuous sheet called a "galley."

Proofreading

A project involving a major book or advertisement (or sometimes even a proceedings) enables you to get another crack at last-ditch corrections. You will be able to read a page proof, which is just what it says it is: page after page of material as it will appear in the book or the completed ad.

Either form of proofing involves:

a. The use of standard proofreading marks. (Page 79 lists them and shows how they are used.)
b. Marginal corrections you make using the standard marks.

Take full and careful advantage of your opportunity to correct proofs. Printers do not charge extra for correcting errors made in their shops, but they do levy an extra charge for the time an employee spends correcting errors in your original copy that were not spotted earlier. They also charge extra for the time they spend resetting lines for an editor (in p.r. work, *you*) who makes last-minute changes. The longer you delay in checking for errors and revising copy, the more it will cost.

How to Prepare Copy for the Typesetter

Typewrite on 8½ × 11 inch bond.

Allow a 1½- to 2-inch margin at the left for typesetting instructions.

Leave a ¾-inch margin at the top of each page.

Double-space lines and keep them as nearly equal in length as possible.

Read and reread copy carefully before submitting—changes after type is set are costly.

Number each page to avoid mix-up.

If many corrections are made in a paragraph, rewrite it and paste it into position.

Indicate headings in capitals or use three lines below; for small capitals use two lines; for italics use one line; for boldface, underscore with a wavy line or write "bf."

Paste small scraps of copy on 8½ × 11 inch paper, for easy handling.

Indicate paragraph indentation or flush left if you have a choice.

If you have a preference for a certain typeface, make a note to that effect, and write it on the copy, or put it in the cover letter or memo of instruction.

proofreader's marks

Mark	Instruction		Mark	Symbol	Meaning
	Delete		⊙	.	Period
	Delete and close up			,	Comma
□	Quad (one em) space			'	Apostrophe
⊔	Move down			" "	Quotation marks
⊓	Move up			;	Semicolon
⊏	Move to left			:	Colon
⊐	Move to right		?/	?	Question mark
eq #	Equalize spacing between words		!/	!	Exclamation mark
X	Broken letter		=/	-	Hyphen
¶	Begin a new paragraph			–	En dash
no ¶	No new paragraph			—	Em dash
stet	Let type stand as set			——	Two-em dash
?	Verify or supply information		(/)/ ( )		Parentheses
tr	Transpose letters or marked words		[/]/ [ ]		Brackets
sp	Spell out (abbrev) or 7				
∪	Push space down				
=	Straighten type				
‖	Align type				
run in	Run in material on same line				
bu	Change (x/y) to built-up fraction				
sh	Change x/y to shilling fraction				
	Set s as subscript				
	Set s as exponent				
lc	lowercase Word				
cap	Capital letter				
sc	SMALL CAPITAL LETTER				
bf	**Boldface** type				
ital	*Italic* type				
rom	Roman (type)				
wf	Wrong font				
#	Insert space				
◡	Close up				
9	Turn letter				

Send along magazines, professional journals, or samples of ideas you might have which will assist the artist in his or her design.

Type a period only at the end of a sentence. *Do not* type a period at the end of a title, headline, etc.

Make three copies of the material—one for the designer, one for the typesetter, and the third copy for your file.

Newspapers across the country are switching from hot type (molten metal) to cold type (a chemical process). When a target newspaper goes to a photo-letterpress type of computer-related production, there are strategies the publicist can use to give his or her releases an edge over the traditionally typewritten copy sent in by a competitor.

In other words, if a paper using computerized production gets two news releases of about equal news value (or lack of it), the release which has been prepared to be compatible with its computer-related typesetting system will be used, and the other may not be. The former will save the paper's staff time and money, since it requires no additional work in the newsroom and particularly on the news desk.

In this competitive world of publicity and promotion, this is important to you.

So OK. What do you do to gain that competitive edge?

It will not be entirely easy, principally because the printing industry (and particularly the newspaper production segment of that industry) is in a wild state of flux. Mechanization and computerization products and equipment are coming out in bewildering numbers from multiple sources. The situation is confusing and annoying.

The first thing you do is to ascertain from a staff member of your target newspaper (or by looking it up yourself in *Ayers Directory* or *Editor and Publisher Yearbook*) whether or not the plant uses a system called optical character recognition (OCR).

Such a system involves machines called *readers* or *scanners.* An optical scanner can convert typewritten copy to tape or memory, which is then used to drive a computerized photocomposition machine.

You don't have to remember all that jargon. It simply means that an IBM Selectric typewriter element can be purchased whose letters or code can be "read" by the scanner.

 **Be sure to ask your newspaper source *which* font or element is compatible with the particular paper's scanner.**

The copy is simply fed into the machine—the reader or scanner. The machine converts the copy at the speed of hundreds of words per minute, and the converted copy is then ready for photocomposition. If there are errors, changes can be made by using a pen whose colored ink is not "recognized" by the computer.

It may have been a while since you visited a newspaper's editorial office or newsroom. You may get quite a shock when you make that first visit to outline your project and leave background material with an editor or reporter.

Instead of seeing the typewriters you are used to, you'll see reporters and editors typing on keyboards before what look like little TV screens. These are video display terminals (VDTs).

These, again, will feed material directly into a computer. The computer can store material for later use, or it can punch a tape that runs a computerized phototypesetter.

The fact that VDTs are used instead of typewriters by both the Associated Press and United Press International has brought about a chain reaction: VDTs have been widely adopted by newspapers which do business with these wire services.

Is it going to take a lot of extra time to retype your releases once for OCR systems and another time for the nonmechanized papers?

Not at all. The fact is that the nonmechanized plants can use the scannable copy just as well as any other kind of typewritten copy, while a computerized paper gets a bonus.

Type it once, with the appropriate Selectric element and a carbon ribbon, and send it out in that typeface to all your media targets.

PHOTOGRAPHY

Promotion-publicity campaigns usually involve the use of photography, somewhere along the line.

WHEN WILL PHOTOGRAPHY BE USED?

You will use photography for:

Advance publicity in newspapers.

1. A picture of your planning committee, if it is not too large, or of your cochairpersons, codirectors, co-coordinators, or whatever, if the committee is sizable.

    When is a committee "too large"? Most newspapers do not like to use pictures with more than three or four people in them. A photograph with more than three people in it will look like a crowd scene or take up too much white space. Or if they reduce it down to a couple of columns, the faces will be so tiny as to be unrecognizable.

2. Pictures (the head-and-shoulders, studio-processed kind) of your platform people—speakers, panelists, performers. These can be offered to newspapers, magazines, journals, and TV news departments and inserted in your activity's brochures, posters, programs, and proceedings.

3. Maybe a photolayout. An extremely friendly news or feature editor might go so far as to give you a panel of pictures, showing various committees at work, or even a full page, such as the front page of a Sunday-edition feature section. To get such advance coverage, even from a small, community-oriented local paper, you have to have a strong and important group of sponsors and usually a "cause," i.e., a charity or fund-raising ball or other project held for a worthy purpose. In middle-sized cities, the papers are disposed to give such a panel or page to the United Fund Drive, the symphony fund-raising event, and the like. A large bank or other company may sponsor advertising for your project as part of its *own* public-service program.

Advance publicity in other print media, such as magazines geared toward the kind of activity you are conducting. Head-and-shoulders and informal shots are good here.

 **Remember that magazine deadlines are 3, 6, or even 9 months ahead of publication.**

Advance publicity on your TV station(s). A picture can take the form of a background slide for use with a public-service announcement. (See pages 50 and 54).

Publicity at the time of your event or activity.

Perhaps, given a generous budget, candids for the files, scrapbook, records, and ego gratification of your committee and your platform people. (Your chairperson would love a picture of himself or herself with the senator. Can't you just hear the chairperson, moving nimbly into position, saying, "Oh, you don't want a picture of *me*, do you?")

The photographer definitely should be on hand for any and all press conferences, and on tap for the reporter who needs a picture to go with a feature or interview but is from out-of-town or who otherwise lacks an on-the-spot photographer.

USE A PRO

The kind of financial support a steering committee is prone to provide for publicizing is limited. You have to live within it, and so you will have to trim the edges somewhere. However, in these two places you must not trim your budget: postage and photography. Photography which is not done right should be eliminated entirely.

What do we mean—"done right"?

We mean *use a professional photographer.*

Never, *never* an amateur, no matter how experienced, well trained, well equipped, and even gifted. Don't let them foist one off on you with an assurance like "George [or Georgia] has won seven awards at photographic competitions." Tell them to go away and let you handle a professional challenge in a professional manner. Nine-tenths of all photographs which hit an editor's desk are returned or discarded because a very capable person—for an amateur!—took them.

A professional photographer, as opposed to the amateur who is considered a semipro, has channels not open to George, Georgia, and their counterparts.

The professional photographer:

Keeps abreast of the latest developments in film, chemicals, and equipment. He or she not only relies on experience and the professional journals but also has a network set up for exchanging ideas and new techniques with others in the profession. In addition, seminars and short courses are open to him or her which are not open to Georgia/George and the others.

Knows how to pose and light a subject—and do it properly—*to produce the best results for the different media*! The pro knows that a given situation which could be handled in one way for a newspaper shot should be handled another way for a magazine, still another way for a business brochure, and so on.

Knows how to shoot *fast.* He or she is aware that the subjects are busy, that they don't have much time for photography. Fast shooting provides a spontaneity that a good amateur loses. The pro can be in and out of a place while the amateur still is fussing with the equipment.

Has developed the art of being unobtrusive, again adding to the liveliness and authenticity of the end product.

Knows local editors and what they like in the way of photos. The pro is thus able to gear the technique for the editor he or she most wishes to reach.

Is aware of the pitfalls into which the unwary photographer can fall. Photography is an art governed by intangibles—engendered by cameras, lights, film, chemistry.

It is, at base, not a difference in equipment which differentiates the amateur photographer from the professional. It is a difference in conditioning and dedication. An amateur who flubs a job can—after embarrassment and chagrin have passed—shrug and say, "Oh, drat." Your professional has to come back with a *usable picture*, or the rent won't get paid and the children will not eat.

Where do you get a professional photographer?

The fortunate few have a pro—a full-time professional photographer—in the photo lab or publicity department of their own shops.

 **Never hire a photographer (or approve the use of an amateur) on the basis of a picture or an album of pictures. Anybody, over the period of a year, can take enough pictures and then try to look pretty good by selecting samples carefully. Insist on looking at sample *proof sheets from rolls of film*. In other words, insist on seeing the sheet of proofs from a roll. (The proofs should be numbered in sequence on that sheet.)**

You will look for a pro in one of these:

1. Established studios. (Be sure they give you the top photographer, not a learner.)
2. Moonlighters. (Photographers from your local papers on their days off.)
3. Hotels and conference centers. (They often have photographers. There will be a fee, but use them.)

In hiring a professional photographer, all other elements which go to determine your choice are subordinate to this: the photographer's reputation. Check the photographer's reputation among peers, among persons (preferably in your field of endeavor or of your personal acquaintance) who have used the photographer's service, and among those whom the photographer designates as references.

Be thorough. If, indeed, photographs are an ingredient of your publicity mix, the choice of the right photographer can be crucial.

COST

Photographic service prices vary from location to location and even vary widely within a location. A "name" photographer can charge astronomical prices. A photographer from a local newspaper can bring in a good job very reasonably. Get prices from two or three—after you have seen their proof sheets.

One photographer may charge for time, materials, and prints. Another may charge for time, materials, and prints plus 10 percent for overhead and for the additional time wasted in conversation and on nitty-gritty questions, ideas, and negotiations by you and your committee. A third—or even either of the above—probably will give you a complete job estimate. You may be able to say to this photographer, "Here are the things I need. Do as good a job for me as you can, but keep the entire thing under $200."

 **If you want a lot of good candids, tell your photographer, "Shoot it like a wedding." If the photographer does not know, completely and instantly, exactly what you mean, fire that person—he or she is not really a pro.**

A rule of thumb is that a professional photographer will spend 2 hours in the darkroom for every 1 hour of taking pictures. In the darkroom, the photographer may be performing the most important part of the process for which you are paying him or her. You may not see the photographer at work in the darkroom, but you must pay for the darkroom time.

Rates will vary according to geographic location, competition, how you will use the photos, the time of day, and even the season of the year.

STATE OF THE ART

In the last 20 years, photography has undergone so many changes that even a pro finds it difficult to keep up. Like the White Queen in *Through the Looking Glass*, he or she has to run twice as fast just to keep up. There is as much difference between photographic technology then and the technology now as there is between "Howdy Doody" and "60 Minutes" on television. So something you (and good old George or Georgia) think you know for sure probably is no longer a fact.

Twenty years ago, news photographers were using Speedgraphic and similar cameras and flashbulbs on a normal, daily basis. Little if any professional work was done using 35-mm cameras.

Fifteen years ago, professionals started using Rolleis and other cameras of like size (variously called "120 size" or "2¼ × 2¼ or "two and one quarter") on a day-to-day basis. Also, roll film for news photographs came into general use. Electronic flash (strobes) began to be used. And with smaller, more compact equipment, not to mention greater depth of field with the shorter, faster lenses and faster film speeds available, the news photographer's versatility was increased immensely.

Today that time of change is regarded as a virtual revolution in technology. Almost all news photography is done with 35-mm cameras. We are seeing fully automatic cameras and strobes; interchangeable and zoom lenses; faster and faster films, and the chemistry that enhances processing and makes film speeds even faster. Special kinds of film—infrared, water penetration, aerial, high-speed recording—are available for use on special assignments and with special techniques.

Today the photographer you will hire to publicize your program will go on a day's assignments and carry with him or her several camera bodies, a raft of lenses complete with filters and accessories, an assortment of film, strobes, umbrella lighting equipment, a tripod, cable releases, and many other pieces of equipment in the same space in which a photographer used to place one Speedgraphic (or a similar camera, by whatever firm or name), two flashguns, and forty film holders.

The ludicrous part is that the equipment has changed entirely, but the weight has remained the same. The good photographer is still half pack mule.

 **Remember, good photographers are as independent as blazes—like any other professionals whose callings are based on a blend of creativity and technology.**

MECHANICS: POSITIVES VERSUS NEGATIVES, SIZING, PRINT QUALITY

OK. Now you know the basic rules of photography in a publicity-promotion effort.

1. Hire a pro.
2. If you can't hire a pro, eliminate the photographic element in your effort.

But there are times, as we all must realize, when a pro is out of the question and when the steering committee insists on some pictures. So you go to good old George or Georgia, who may or may not be up to date on any newer wrinkles or approaches in publicity pictures. Here are a few things which, if you know about them, may help you direct George or Georgia in a more effective manner than if you were ignorant of them.

1. Do the print media with which you are working want negatives or positives?

Column-sized positive halftone prints are *most* acceptable in mechanized newsrooms. You know what a negative looks like—a shiny black plastic photographic "plate." A positive, on the other hand, is an actual photograph made from a negative—an ordinary picture.

A screened print halftone, *not* a "glossy" as you may know this type of print from former days, is one step ahead toward a finished product. It already has, through screening, been reduced to a dot pattern, so it already looks like the pictures you see in newspapers.

2.   How should pictures for use by the media be sized?

You will be playing it safe if you have them made to column size, which, of course, may vary from newspaper to newspaper and certainly from newspaper to magazine to journal. In any case, let your pro (and I do hope you have one in the wings, even if George/Georgia does the actual shooting) do the cropping, that is, cutting down on the extraneous borders to bring the focal point of the picture up front.

Sized to column width? What does that mean? You have a ruler, haven't you? Take it out and measure a picture in the publication you are hoping will use your photo. Have the width of the finished picture you present be exactly the same as the width of the picture you are measuring, whether it covers one column, two columns, or three columns.

If you are still in doubt, uncertain about sizing pictures to column width, play it safe by sending or taking 8 × 10s. Almost any darkroom or photo lab is equipped to handle them.

 **Plan to be happy if you get a one-column picture printed and well satisfied if you get a two-column picture. You'll be smart and lucky if you can wangle a three-column; such allocation of white space is rare in routine p.r.**

3.   What about engravings?

By and large, most newspapers today have ceased using old-fashioned metal engravings for pictures, although some magazines and journals still do. Newspapers today are apt to have a Fairchild engraver (or a similar device from another company, although a Fairchild is the commonest) in the shop—a machine which produces a plastic "engraving." In the old days, a Fairchild could only produce a plastic engraving the size of the picture which was placed on its cylinder. Time marched on, and the Fairchild people and their fellow manufacturers improved their products.

Fairchilds today have enlarging and reducing capabilities, so if your town's newspaper uses Fairchild or similar engravers, don't worry too much about the size of the photo you submit.

Always include, with your positive halftone print, a regular uncropped print of your picture. This cossets the occasional editor who fancies herself or himself an artiste, and who likes to do her or his own cropping.

With the increasing mechanization of newsrooms and composing rooms—using offset and cold type—we are seeing photomechanical processes used more and more.

Additional newspapers each month, and some magazines, are accepting (and welcoming) positive halftone prints made to column size which they can paste up directly onto a page of copy. This means that the pages and the photographs they include can go directly to the graphic arts cameras; no darkroom work is necessary. To repeat, the publicity chairperson will improve the chance of getting mileage from a mechanized newspaper by sending it positive halftone prints.

Nevertheless, a few old-timers in the p.r. area still think it is a good idea to send negatives to the publications they service. This can be tricky. A lot of newspapers, in particular, don't want to use them—too much trouble. So, if you are tempted to take this path, query in advance.

There is another block to sending negatives, even when a publication likes to get them. This is the current practice of photographers of not releasing their negatives. A photographer who does release negatives is losing his or her chance of selling prints to people who are in the pictures or who are interested in the project. Many times a good photographer, recognizing the possibility of additional sales, will work for you at a rate that is cheaper than the usual scale, just to enjoy this possibility of added income.

4.   What about print quality?

Two of the most overused terms heard about photography from the lips of nonprofessionals (and some editors) are "glossies" and "contrast." Don't concern yourself (or let others concern you) with glossies, which are prints with a smooth, shiny surface, although there is nothing wrong with them. Many top professional photographers prefer paper that is *not* glossy—untextured paper, which basically is the same as glossy, but without the gloss—because it is easier to spot, retouch, and airbrush, and because it causes few reflection problems for the graphic arts camera people and engravers in reproduction.*

"Contrast" is a much abused term. The contrast for the photographic print which you would frame or hang on the wall in your house is not necessarily of the same quality as the one which will reproduce the best in a paper or magazine.

A good engraver can always add more contrast for proper reproductive quality, but he or she cannot cut contrast. Therefore, a good photo for reproduction which you send out should be slightly flat. "Flat"? Slightly dull or uncontrasty.

If you run into a newsroom desk editor who is not aware of this (and you will!), you will have to either try to educate him or her or supply him or her with a too-contrasty print which will suffer in the final reproduction (lots of luck!).

5. What about photographs for television?

Refer to the section on television graphics (pages 53–54) for essential information on the very great differences between TV art (including photographs) and that which is to be used in the print media. Different proportions, different paper, that entire important set of dissimilarities.

A final word about professional photographers:

One eminent editor has come up with this slightly jaundiced advice: "After you have found the best photographer for your needs, *marry* him or her! The photographer is as important as your best fishing partner or favorite colleague—maybe more so, because your career does not depend on the fishing buddy or bosom friend."

PEOPLE-REACHER TOOLS

Word of mouth may be the most potent device which can be used in attracting audiences and enrollments.

Social scientists have found that when they really need to reach, inform, and influence members of a minority or ethnic group, they must first find and convince the "Delores" or "Albert" in the neighborhood—the person to whom others turn for support and advice, the opinion leader.

The "laying on of hands," i.e., the warm, person-to-person contact as between

---

*Purist-professionals tell me that photofinishing is something which amateurs do in their basement darkrooms, alias laundries, and the sort of thing you get when you leave your film at the corner drugstore. Although metal plates are not involved, the professionals who process film with an eye to ultimate excellence still call the process "engraving" and themselves "engravers."

friends, neighbors, relatives, and associates, is the informal term for this. If Joe takes the course, Sally or Jim may follow. If Mary goes to a program, John or Marietta probably will accompany her.

"I'm going; why don't you go with me?" is the most powerful people puller for all kinds of programs and activities.

There are organized ways in which the person-to-person contact network can be expanded, and these can be set up by a publicist's task force:

1. You can *set up a Speakers Bureau* and offer to make appearances at clubs and other meetings to tell about your program or activity. You might make a brief announcement and provide handout material (a brochure or facts sheet). Or you might make a full-fledged presentation—useful in publicizing year-round activities—with slides or a motion picture to accompany the spoken script.

 **Most organizations plan their next year's program in the spring. Those planning fall programs and activities should get to the program planners early if these are to be admitted to the schedule.**

An elaborate Speakers Bureau in a city will need a coordinator and will itself need to be publicized. A small Speakers Bureau in a smaller community can have a less formal operation, and its availability to those planning programs can be made known by telephone or a mailed flyer.

2. You can *organize a telephone chain*, a device that is especially good when you are trying to attract members of your organization or constituency to an event or activity. It employs the "personal invitation" idea, which sometimes works even when the person extending the invitation is a stranger.

    A "telephone tree" as a formalized structure can be used in announcing special programs or (as with the one used as an illustration) the cancellation of an event which is one of a series (in this case, an extramural class). The illustration happens to be for academic use, but many clubs and institutions have similar ones.

 **Get your most reliable member or student to accept the post of "first person to be called."**

Another type of telephone chain is one-purpose-only. Each member of your group of committees—*all* committees, not just the steering committee or

CALLING TREE

During this course, bad weather may cause the cancellation of a meeting. The Extramural Classes Office (333-3061) can notify one of the members of this class of the cancellation. He or she can call two more, and so on, in order that everyone is notified and does not make an unnecessary trip to class.

To make this possible, this blank calling tree is supplied in quantity. The following procedure is suggested.

1. At the first class meeting, the class members agree who should be the first person called by the university. Enter the name and phone number (home and work) at position #1.

2. Next choose persons for positions #2 and #3.

3. Complete the entire tree in this way.

4. Each person keeps a copy so as to know whom to call. (Don't break the chain of calling. If you can't get your person, call the next one.)

5. The instructor should bring a completed copy back to the Extramural Classes Office, 101 Illini Hall, the following day.

6. If there are late registrants, it would be helpful if the person at position #1 would see that they are placed at the end so they will receive notification.

INSTRUCTOR: Please turn this in promptly. It may be necessary to use it the second week.

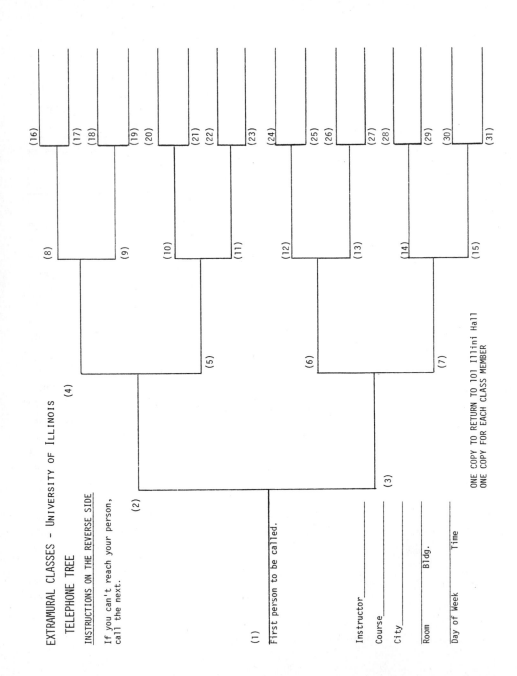

EXTRAMURAL CLASSES – UNIVERSITY OF ILLINOIS

TELEPHONE TREE

INSTRUCTIONS ON THE REVERSE SIDE

If you can't reach your person,
call the next.

(1)

First person to be called.

Instructor _____

Course _____

City _____

Room _____ Bldg. _____

Day of Week _____ Time _____

ONE COPY TO RETURN TO 101 Illini Hall
ONE COPY FOR EACH CLASS MEMBER

publicity task force—agrees to telephone *x* number of people from a list or from among his or her acquaintances.

3. A *talkabout* (coined word, and we admit it) is similar to a telephone chain. When you organize a talkabout, you mobilize every committee member and, in some cases, every member of your entire organization. Each person is asked to agree to "talk about" your program and activity to a half-dozen or ten more individuals per day until whatever participatory goal you have set is reached.

 **Arm talkabout workers and volunteers with brochures or facts sheets.**

4. *Promotion packets* are similar to press kits (pages 186–199) but are less elaborate and are used as an auxiliary to facts sheets. They are packets which you would use as handout materials for people who can help or hinder your activity or program—the principal of a school whom you may be prompting to send a classful of students and pay their fee out of activities funds, for example. They give an administrator (whether an educator, a business or industrial executive, an organizational president, or a member of the clergy) something to go on in deciding whether or not to support your program and also something to justify the effort or expenditure.

5. *Billboards and marquees* are not the most dignified devices for publicity and promotion, but they do get attention. A billboard message, unless it is donated by a friendly advertising agency or an advertiser who uses billboards, can be very expensive. If your program warrants such a promotional ploy, go ahead and ask. All they can say is "No."

An outside sign with movable letters, such as a sign outside a motel or a realtor's office or a shopping mall, has changeable type so that the message, unlike a billboard, can be changed every day if the mood strikes the owner-operator.

Space on such a signboard is limited, so you must condense your message into as few words and letters as possible. The owner or manager of the property where it is located can tell you exactly how many letters and spaces you have to work with.

Try to get your message over with some punch. "FALL SEMESTER REGISTRATION—NOW—TRINITY COLLEGE" does not have much punch, although it does get the message over.

THIS WAY TO THE ROOM AT THE TOP
FALL REGISTRATION—NOW!
TRINITY COLLEGE

takes more space but does a bit better in creating action-response.

A billboard message's impact should be immediate and dramatic. Here is one place where a staff artist or a hired graphics expert with outdoor advertising experience and know-how is a "must." However, if an agency or advertiser has been persuaded to donate the space, maybe that donor will go the whole way and give you some help with composition and copy.

6. *Piggybacking,* that is, the inclusion of your invitation or brochure with someone else's mailing, is dealt with on page 110. Persons with a commendable program, activity, or cause sometimes can get a major bank, department store, or other sponsor to let them piggyback. Another form of piggybacking is when a sponsor's paid advertisements include a notice about your program.

   Piggybacking is achieved through the altruism of the prospective sponsor and the sponsor's goodwill toward your particular activity or cause. Frequently, there is a close relationship between the sponsor and the person seeking permission to piggyback.

   An interesting instance was the inclusion in a recent Neiman-Marcus catalog of the announcement of the sale of the Dallas Junior League's cookbook. Makes you wonder which Neiman or Marcus daughter or granddaughter is in the league.

7. *Oddments*, far-out kinds of promotion tactics, work well in one location, poorly in another. It's a take-a-chance choice when you use one of these approaches. Sample: a balloon ascension.

8. Exhibits, displays, and demonstrations are used by a number of urban-located colleges, universities, and organizations. "We put up a display wherever people congregate and have a staff member there at the busiest times," reports a major university.

   What kinds of places? Airports, shopping malls, conventions, fairs. . . . The list went on.

   Such promotion areas should always be well stocked with informational material and with cards to send in for more information. They are best used for the year-round promotion effort (see pages 220–229) but also can sometimes be helpful in publicizing a single program or series of activities.

9. *Bumper stickers, bus cards, and public-address systems* are among the less dignified devices for promotion, but some publicists dote on them. Continuing education promotion staff members at the Indiana University—Purdue University campus in Indianapolis tried *bus cards* and learned that their principal constituency was drawn from neighborhoods whose residents do not customarily ride buses. The cards were found to have little people-pulling power. A colleague at the University of Michigan heard of this finding and reported that her own experience in using bus cards was just the opposite. She made the experiment when the area was on a heavy energy kick and people who drove autos in Ann Arbor—as opposed to those who rode bicycles or took the bus—were considered un-American and viewed as social pariahs. So there are, indeed, intangibles involved.

Bumper stickers and auto window stickers, in my view, have a kind of snickery, "hee-hee" connotation in most people's minds. My advice is: Don't use them unless your activity has a definite entertainment or sports slant. They would seldom be appropriate for promoting a public discussion series, a lecture series, or even a class, unless they are carefully designed with the use of good art. However designed, they usually are all right if what you are publicizing is a student circus or an organization's bazaar.

The same holds true for *public-address systems*. Again, don't use them unless there is an entertainment-sports flavor to your program, or unless you want to call people's attention to your booth, display, or demonstration in a hotel, arena, or other public place.

DEVELOPING THE SPECIAL-INTEREST MEDIA MAILING LIST

When building mailing lists of publications and (rarer) broadcast outlets which address the clientele you are trying to attract to your program, it is necessary to make full use of the "Basic Bookshelf," outlined on pages 96–100.

In particular, you will want to cross-check among the various directories on the "Basic Bookshelf" to make certain that your list covers the available publications in the most effective way. Several reference works list publications by category—e.g., agriculture, banking and finance, engineering. Local directories and area guides can be used as well.

The important factor is to decide how many publications in which categories you will include.

A first step toward this decision can be taken on the basis of the scope of the activity you are publicizing *and* the amount of money for postage. Is it a program to which you are attempting to draw a national audience or participation? Is it regional—i.e., New England, Midwest, West Coast, Southeast, etc.? Is it subregional, drawing from your state and perhaps abutting cities in other states? Or is it local?

It is silly to waste paper, envelopes, stamps, mailing labels, and time (spent in building lists) on a national mailing for a program intended for residents of your state—e.g., "Native Wildlife of Idaho," "School Tax Laws of Ohio," "Missouri and the Energy Crisis." Obvious? Not to everyone; such "obviously" misdirected efforts have happened.

It is equally silly to limit to one state or area, not using the national publications, a program for which a national audience is appropriate and being sought.

It should be very obvious that you do not use the *same* mailing list (except perhaps for the selected newspapers to which you mail copy about most of your programs, regardless of topic) to publicize a program for school music instructors that you use for mechanical engineers or legal secretaries.

Do not neglect special outreach instruments found in the media—the foreign language press can be very useful if you are presenting programs of possible use to its readers.

Examples: courses in English as a second language, programs of a "know your community" or "know your neighborhood" type; courses in basic (English language) literacy; courses leading to a certificate or diploma (equivalency credit); courses or other programs preparing people for admission to United States citizenship.

Do not under any circumstances ignore or use only marginally the many publications grouped under the general rubric "black press." These often have large circulations and are read by members of a public glad to be aware of and take part in all sorts of educational and adult-oriented self-enrichment activities.

Programs keyed to young adults also may reach an audience through the underground press.

Chambers of commerce and public libraries often have giveaway lists of organizations, publications, and service groups. Publicity for a local program can be profitably placed in the newsletters of the organizations and service groups, and publications you might not otherwise be aware of can be located from such lists.

THE PUBLICIST'S BASIC BOOKSHELF

Anyone who does publicity on a fairly regular basis—as many as three or four times a year—needs a set of basic reference books in the immediate office. In the long run, it will save your operation a lot of time and money if these references are at hand, and not tucked away in some library across town or even down the block. The person who has a publicity assignment only once a year or so may be wiser, however, to trek over to the library to consult these.

In your office or out, the following sources will help you identify local, national, and general-interest or special-interest media which can help you get the word out about your programs.

Take special note, as you consult them, of the publication dates and days.

Several of these types of publications are organs of firms which also provide an array of other services which p.r. people find useful—clipping services, mailing services, etc.

Sad to say, quite a few otherwise efficient publicists are not making full use of these valuable servants, or else they are unaware of or have not thoroughly explored their contents.

I have an idea that in quite a few colleges and offices, graduate students and comparable serfs are painstakingly compiling the sorts of lists of information almost pathetically easy to find in these established and dependable references.

The Basic Bookshelf for Publicizing Programs

Bacon's Publicity Checker This valuable background source is published annually. It is one of the references which list publications by category and also alphabetically. *Bacon's* is unusual in that several times a year customers are sent gummed correction slips which they can use to keep the book up to date—slips which record such changes as "out of business" and "new address." The companion volume in this set lists the nation's daily and weekly newspapers.

Ayers Directory of Publications *Ayers* is a rich reference with many types of information in it. It offers background demographic information of a basic nature, as well as lists of newspapers and magazines by category, alphabetically, and by state and community. It is particularly helpful to a publicist who is trying to blanket a community or an area in a promotion blitz, since it lists *every* publication in a community, from newspapers to college publications to specialized journals-magazines.

The Editor and Publisher Year Book and *the Broadcasting Year Book* These are the annual editions of the magazines by the same titles. They are gold mines of information. No publicist's desk should be without them. Again, certain basic demographic information is included, as well as information on rates and agencies, associations, names of contact persons in the media, etc. A publicist who is attempting to keep media mailing lists current also should subscribe to the magazines.

Your state press association's directory and your state broadcasters association's directory You really need these. They are not expensive, and they are extremely valuable to those working in their own backyards.

Regional media directories Not every area of the country has a regional directory, but where regional directories are available, they are sensationally helpful. *Midwest Media*, which covers the greater Chicago area with outstanding thoroughness, also covers the rest of Illinois. It gives you not only talk show hosts but also their contacts; it not only lists columnists but also gives you their subject areas. The New York area version is called *New York Publicity Guide* and covers outlets within a 50-mile radius of Columbus Circle.

Telephone directories (Yellow Pages) These include your own community's directory, the directory of the largest city you operate in or around, and the state capital's phone book if it is not the same as that of your community or your metropolitan target community. In addition to these three, if you are operating or planning to operate a program in any other community, get that city's telephone directory at the start.

The Associated Press Stylebook Get it and follow the style right out the window.

Let's face it. These reference books are expensive. However, the splendid timesaving and fingertip information they contain makes them very much worth the money.

Once you work with them, you'll be hooked. There is no way that I can rank these references as to their value or degree of indispensability. You need the package.

What's more, with the publications and broadcast world and the publications and broadcast people in a constant state of flux, you have to buy these references once a year.

But perhaps the best advice this book can give you, other than that on accuracy, is to get the costs of these reference works into your annual budget and keep them there.

 **Why the suggestion that you have "yellow page" phone books on your "basic bookshelf"? Why your largest city target, why the state capital? Easy. Most of your larger area publications will be in one of the two. Most of your larger organizations will have state headquarters in one of the two.**

The "Basic Bookshelf" stipulates that you should have the directory of your *state press association* and the directory of your *state broadcasters association*. Lists of the newspaper and state broadcasters associations in existence are at the end of this section, pages 126–129 and 131–133.

A "Syndicates Directory," cross-indexed as to subjects and writers, each year is included in a July issue of the *Editor and Publisher* weekly magazine, and it can be purchased separately at a low price. A list of the larger news services (which include major syndicated services) also is at the end of this section, pages 129–130.

SPECIAL STEPS IN DEVELOPING MEDIA LISTS

1. Look at your program from three points of view:
   a. What kinds of clients are you trying to attract?
   b. What kinds of newsletters, house organs, daily or weekly papers, journals, and magazines will these people be likely to read?
   c. What kinds of television-radio programs are they apt to turn on? Where are the outlets located which carry such programs? Can you latch onto their use through talk shows, PSAs, public-service programming?
2. Determine how many categories of publications and broadcasts your program's components suggest. How can your program be analyzed for possible appeal to various publics and to the media they read and tune in?

MEDIA MAILING LISTS:
WHERE TO FIND WHAT
Print

	Bacon's	Ayer's	Editor and Publisher Year Book	Regional Media Guide	State Press Association Directory	AP Stylebook	Yellow Pages	
Listings of daily papers and editor, address, circulation			X	X	X			
Listings of weekly papers, publication dates, editors, addresses, circulations			X	X	X			
Department heads, special-interest writer-editors, columnists, daily papers			X		X			
Special pages, seasonal sections; topic and when published			X					
Sunday magazines used by dailies			X					
Magazine and journal listings, by topic, circulation, acceptance of materials	X	X						
Black press, ethnic press, underground press	X	X						
Syndicates and their "stables"	X		X					
Basic market information		X	X			The AP *Stylebook* should be your constant reference. Newspaper-broadcast styles are not like the educational style or literary style. Consult the AP *Stylebook* at all junctures. It also provides fine chapters on libel and the right to privacy.		Your state press association's directory lists "specialty newspapers" and papers by county (with maps). *Bacon's* lists most dailies and *financial* editors.
Basic demographic data		X	X		X			
Vendors and services—graphic artists, printers, rental equipment, etc.							X	
Locations, bureau chiefs, press association bureaus								
Rosters—national press corps, UN, congressional, etc.		X						
Rosters—regional, state press corps, legislative, etc.				X				
Clipping services	X		X					
Mailing services	X		X					
Sets of media addresses on envelopes or labels, by area, type, topic, selectively	X		X					
Advertising rates					X			
Advertising placement (group, package)					X			

WHERE TO FIND WHAT

Broadcast

	Broadcasting Year Book	State Broadcasters Association Directory	Regional Media Guide	Yellow Pages	Stylebook				
Listing of TV and radio stations by call letters, addresses	X	X	X	X					
News and program directors	X	X	X						
Newscasters accredited to legislature, Congress	X		X						
Basic demographic and market information	X								
Black, foreign-language, ethnic stations	X	X	X						
Special programming emphasis (at least 20 hours a week)			X						
Vendors (services, supplies, other things purchased or rented)	X			X					
Radio stations' formats	X	X	X						
Advertising rates in general (seasonally vary)	X								
Advertising placement (group, package, time slots)		X							
In your area, department heads, talk show stars and formats, contacts			X						

Note: The basic demographic and market information, added to the *Broadcasting Year Book* information and charts (which can be obtained from *Ayer's* and *Editor and Publisher Year Book*), as well as the mailing services (except addresses and labels) available in *Bacon's* is equally applicable to broadcast media where publicity and promotion are concerned.

Note: Instead of seeking out vendors, you usually can do better on slides and other materials to use with PSAs or advertising spots if you pay the cost of having them staff-produced at a local station.

3. Decide *how much time* and *how much money* you have to spend on (a) preparing special mailing lists and special materials and (b) mailing the materials or otherwise getting them to the media.

FIRST EXAMPLE: A minimally technical program on alternative sources of energy for housing would be of interest to magazines, journals, columnists, and commentators addressing themselves to the interests of architects, contractors, engineers, realtors, environmentalists, city planners, housing developers, city managers, representatives of groups like the League of Women Voters and the Municipal League, manufacturers, and those of a scientific bent.

SECOND EXAMPLE: A conference called "Beyond Divorce" was originally developed for social workers but was found to be of interest not only to publications and commentators (and their constituencies) in the field of social work but also to publications intended for clinicians in psychology, and to physicians, mental health workers, attorneys, and counselors in a variety of specialties.

THIRD EXAMPLE: You are doing publicity for a 2-day program called "Challenges in the Teaching Process." This one is a little harder than the other two. At first glance, your target audience (and the publications with which to reach that audience) seems pretty well limited to academicians in the colleges of education.

From the early, rough, advance program copy, you try to pick out several "presenters" who might make news.

You start your special media mailing list, then, with appropriate columnists and journals.

You next look at journals dealing with connected research specialties. Medically connected learning disabilities? Speech and hearing? Child psychology?

Another possibility would be the newsletters of parents organizations and the magazines in this area.

For an exercise, try to think of some other kinds of magazines, journals, and air columnists who might be interested in that topic.

4. At this point, and always thinking within your budget, go to *Bacon's*, to *Ayers*, go to the other publications on your "basic bookshelf," and find the correct category in the index. Go to work.

 **If you have to limit your mailing, look first at the degree of applicability which each particular publication or broadcast medium has to whatever the topic of your program or activity. Among the more applicable publications and broadcast opportunities, which have the largest circulations or the widest listening-watching audiences?**

COSTING IT OUT

GENERAL CONSIDERATIONS

An old-fashioned rule of thumb is that the publicity-promotion funds for a given activity should amount to 10 percent of the total budget for that activity.

This does not hold true. It is not even a good place to start in building a publicity-promotion budget.

Take, as examples, two kinds of conferences.

1. The first is addressed to a specific target audience—perhaps religious workers—but does not have a base group immediately on tap. That program will require a heavy promotion-publicity effort if it is to pass the break-even point.
2. The second has a built-in constituency. Let us say that it is directed toward power plant engineers. The coordinator, with a simple mailing of a brochure and a registration blank to the state's institutional power plant engineers—who enroll each year in an on-campus refresher program designed to address their interests and needs as part of their on-the-job training—can pass the break-even point of the total budget. Any additional registration income from engineers outside that core of state employees is gravy.

In both, the secret of p.r. success is that in building the program's total budget, you make an honest estimate of the effort it will take to bring in the number of people your conference directors will need if they are to break even and/or generate income.

Unlike the *total* conference budget, with fixed costs for renting a hall and providing the needed services (visual equipment, sound equipment, catering, stipends, etc.), the publicity-promotion budget is flexible. It also should vary according to the need to attract participants to the course, program, or other activity being publicized.

This is a reason why it is often a stepchild—skimped until a last-ditch effort is necessary to get the program over the top.

The following Checklist covers both "absorbed costs" and "vendors' charges." "Absorbed costs" are those carried by the sponsor or facilitating agency and not charged to the particular activity—the office rent and the costs of janitorial help, the services of a professional, salaried staff, etc.—the usual items that the publicist must cover when he or she is forecasting the p.r. campaign's probable expense and/or checking on the actual expenditures after the completion of the activity.

"Vendors' charges" are the costs of all the goods and services you have to buy.

In every instance, careful coding can and does pay off. Careful coding will prove the accuracy of your cost estimates and will serve as the basis for an assessment of what you really spent—and how. This not only will be helpful in your reports to the conference staff and the steering committee but also will help you plan future p.r. campaigns with an eye to the effectiveness of the contents of your tool kit.

Predicting the dollars involved in a publicity campaign is not an easy task. There are many variables and intangibles involved which may be mixed and matched, or mismatched, in an astronomical number of combinations.

COSTING IT OUT
CHECKLIST

Name of activity: _____   Dates covered by column:

Date(s): _____

Item	Absorbed costs	Vendors' charges	Estimated total	Actual total
POSTAGE				
Direct mail (brochure)				
Press releases				
PSAs				
Press kits Facts sheets Misc. media information				
Photos				
Posters, flyers				
Letters Invitations				
House organ Newsletter Bulletin Announcements				
Other (specify)				
DIRECT MAIL (BROCHURE)—PREPARATION				
Writing				
Graphics Layout Design Illustration				
Printing Copying Folding Binding Other (specify) Distribution (other than postage)				

Item	Absorbed costs	Vendors' charges	Estimated total	Actual total
MAILING LISTS				

Media
  General
  Immediate
  Targeted
  Special-interest				

Prospective participants				
PRESS RELEASES, PSAs, PRESS KITS, FACTS SHEETS—PREPARATION				
Writing				

Graphics
  Layout
  Design
  Information				

Printing
  Copying
  Folding
  Stuffing
  Other (specify)
  Distribution
  (other than
  postage)				

PAID ADVERTISEMENTS				
Radio spots TV spots Special broadcasts				

Newspapers
Special press (specify)
Professional magazines,
  journals
Special-interest magazines,
  journals
Other (describe)				

(Note: In the cost files or on the backs of cost estimate sheets be very descriptive as to place of ad, its distribution, time and date, and coded response.)				

Item	Absorbed costs	Vendors' charges	Estimated total	Actual total
VISUALS (Other than still photos) Posters Flyers for posting Slides Tape Film Displays Exhibits Logos Signs Other (specify)				
RENTALS (specify)				

SUPPLIES AND
FACILITIES
 	
Phones and
phone charges
(break down)
 	
Paper
  Duplicating
  Letterhead
  Brochure
  Posterboard
  Other (specify)				

TRAVEL, TRANSPORTATION, DELIVERIES (specify)				
COURTESIES, AMENITIES (media) Press badges Press meals Press supplies Use of phones Press parties Entertainment				
SALARIES AND WAGES (be *very* specific)				
MISCELLANEOUS CRISES AND CONTINGENCIES				

Often, in good faith but nevertheless mistakenly, a steering committee, finance committee, or conference coordinator will try to get a quick answer on what the publicity campaign will involve in the way of money.

Certainly, he or she is in a hurry.

Certainly, time is slipping away.

Certainly, a report (to whomever the chairperson is reporting to in these particular circumstances) is long overdue. But. . . .

Don't be rushed.

Take your time.

Go over the items in the chart thoroughly.

Get bids.

Check references.

Study rate cards.

Look for freebies wherever you can.

Refuse to settle for what seem to be obvious economies, for that reason only, because (1) the cheap version may not do the job you are assigned to do and (2) it may prove more expensive in the long run.

Do all the above. Then, and only then, provide the budget people with an estimated publicity-promotion expense rundown.

This is one of the points at which the steering committee can begin showing symptoms of the supermarket syndrome—feeling impelled to stuff its p.r. shopping basket with all manner of goodies—one of each.

The only hope for a miraculous cure lies in your application of the absolute truth. Be very candid with the committee members. Show them, *on paper*, exactly what kind of money they are talking about.

Suggest trade-offs and substitutes—e.g., if they will be happy with a brochure in which contrast is achieved by using only one color of ink on paper of a different color, they may be able to afford the development and provision of press kits as well.

In costing out the p.r. for your program, it will pay you to shop around and use whatever is at hand.

1. Use in-house staff people, whose salaries are already paid by your institution or organization, as much as possible, and augment their work with that of volunteers (carefully monitored) when necessary.

2. Get at least three bids or estimates *in writing* on any sizable job you are farming out, on materials rented or purchased, and on any other services commissioned from outside.

3. Be absolutely *firm* about schedules. Late deliveries and the resulting scurryings and substitutes can be costly. Get all deadlines *in writing*, too.

4. Be very *flexible* about relatively unimportant details. If your printer overbought

on a nice buff stock and will make your brochures up in that (instead of the blue you planned on)—at half the paper cost—snatch up the offer.

5. Look for quality. Settling for a shoddy job is false economy. Check samples—lots of samples—of the vendor's work. Before accepting any bids or estimates, check references.

6. Be selective. Some of the p.r. output or arrangements which may seem of prime importance to your steering committee undoubtedly are frills. Think each item through carefully before you make a commitment or include the item in your budget.

In this case, do you really *need* the services of a clipping bureau, or can careful coding serve adequately as a tracking instrument?

Is a three-color print job on this brochure really necessary?

Can a three-fold self-mailer suffice, instead of a stapled booklet-type brochure which necessitates the use of an envelope, has to be stuffed, and perhaps takes more postage?

Is the program heavy with news appeal? If so, can paid advertisements be eliminated?

On the other hand, is its pulling power so limited to a specific group that huge mailings to individuals outside that inner circle are not necessary and will not be productive? The Checklist on pages 103–105 furnishes the clues for economies which can be applied to this program or that (although, of course, each one you may think of will not be appropriate in every case).

MAILING COSTS

The only fixed price structure in a publicity-promotion campaign is the cost of postage. Anything else can be negotiated.

That is a flat and arbitrary statement, and of course even it has exceptions, since the major factor affecting postage costs will be your (and your steering committee's) decisions on how inclusive your mailing lists will be and how many mailings will go out.

Consult the postage chart on pages 108–109; then consider these questions:

Brochure—How many copies of your mailing piece—your brochure in whatever form—will be mailed out?

How heavy is the mailing (i.e., how much postage will it take per item)? Will your return card be prestamped? In other words, will you pay the cost of having the card mailed back to your shop?

What class of mail will you use for your mailing? (See the caution on deterioration of mailing lists given on page 110.)

U. S. MAIL CLASSIFICATIONS

Service	Weight	Cost	Remarks
FIRST CLASS			
Letters	1st oz.	.15	Must have over 500
	each add'l. oz.	.13	pieces to qualify for
	over 12 oz.	use priority mail	presorted rate
Postcards	.10		
BUSINESS REPLY			
Letters	1 oz.	.25 + first-class postage	
	each piece	.12 + first-class postage	Must pay $30 annual fee
	each piece	.035 + first-class postage	Must pay $75 annual fee; maintain advance deposit at post office
TRANSIENT SECOND CLASS	first 2 oz.	.10	Newspapers and periodicals
	each add'l. oz.	.06	sent as separate issues by the public or a publisher
THIRD CLASS			
Single-piece Rate	2 oz.	.20	
	4 oz.	.40	
	6 oz.	.53	
	8 oz.	.66	
	10 oz.	.79	
	12 oz.	.92	
	14 oz.	1.05	Over 14 oz., use fourth-class rate if lower
Bulk Rate			Minimum of 200 pieces, must
Regular	per piece	.084	be presorted
	by pound	.36	books and catalogues
		.41	circulars
			Maximum weight per piece: 3.278 oz.
Nonprofit	per piece	.027	books and catalogs
	by pound	.14	circulars
		.17	Maximum weight per piece: 2.541 oz.

What will your mailing *area* be? A single neighborhood? An entire city (persons selected by special interest or occupation)? A state? The nation?

News and feature releases, PSAs—Almost universally, these will and must go out as first-class mail.

Will you cover an area near where the activity will be held?

The state?

Service	Weight	Cost	Remarks
FOURTH CLASS			
Special (book)	1st lb.	.48	
	2-7 lbs.	.18	
	each add'l. lb.	.11	
Library	1st lb.	.14	
	2-7 lbs.	.05	
	each add'l. lb.	.04	
Parcel post			See parcel post chart
PRIORITY MAIL			See priority mail chart
SPECIAL DELIVERY	up to 2 lbs.	$2.00	
	2-10 lbs.	$2.25	
	more than 10 lbs.	$2.85	First class, priority
SPECIAL HANDLING	up to 10 lbs.	.70	
	over 10 lbs.	$1.25	
REGISTERED			
Value in dollars	$ 100	$3.00	
	200	3.30	
	400	3.70	
	600	4.10	
	800	4.50	
	1000	4.90	
INSURED			
Limit in dollars	$ 15	.50	
	50	.85	
	100	1.10	
	150	1.40	
	200	1.75	
	300	2.25	
	400	2.75	
CERTIFIED		.80	First class, priority Mail must not have any intrinsic value
COD			
Limit in dollars	$ 10	$1.10	
	25	1.35	
	50	1.65	
	100	1.95	
	200	2.30	
ADDRESS CORRECTION		.25	

The nation?

Will you mail it to the general news media?

To a columnist, a special section (sports, for example), or a friend on the news desk (all of them)?

To the special-interest media, according to the program's subject-matter emphasis?

 **Don't forget to save first-class postage, if you have one or more programs/activities in the works, by piggybacking several releases in a single envelope.**

Remember that you can get six sheets of the most commonly used duplicating (20-pound) or copying machine paper into an envelope carrying a single first-class stamp.

Other mailings—Are you sending out photographs? Press kits? Facts sheets? Information packets? Letters of invitation? Letters to speakers and others regarding vitae and press conferences?

And what about mailing posters?

Notices for house organs and for club, church, union, professional, and other magazines and newsletters?

Tactics—In using bulk mailings, carefully weigh the arrival factor. Is the time element more important than the money saved? Considering the costs of design, writing, printing, and paper, sometimes it is a whole lot more prudent to use first-class postage than to take a chance on bulk mail arriving in time for the intended respondents to profit by it—i.e., attend your program or enroll in your class.

News Release, Public Service Announcement Distribution Checklist

Many publicists (myself included) find it useful to work with printed Checklists, especially for news releases.

This kind of distribution Checklist serves a number of purposes:

It helps in planning the promotion package;

It helps in your record-keeping;

It helps keep your coworkers (committees, task force, etc.) tranquil and confident;

It is a valuable checkpoint in costing out a news release.

The sample on page 111 is one developed for my own shop. It is a multicopy form—an original and three copies—obtained by ordering the blanks printed on NCR (carrying its own carbon) precollated sets. Such "carbon sets" or "carbon packs" as they are sometimes called, can be obtained with a total of two, three, four, five, or six parts. They come in 8½ × 11 sheets, but can be cut to any size. My original is white, and each of the other copies is a different color. I can, if I wish, keep one copy in my file for one activity, one in an easy reference file mirroring duplicating

The University of Illinois
Information Services
114 Illini Hall 333-0517

DISTRIBUTION CHECKLIST

Continuing Education and Public Service
and
Statewide Programs and Services

Specifics

Account Number _____

Name of Project _____

Location _____

Date _____

Chairperson/Coordinator _____

Distribution	Number of copies
Locals _____	
Basics _____	
All Illinois Dailies _____	
All Illinois TV _____	
All Illinois Radio _____	
Special List (specify):	
_____	
Police Training List _____	
Firemanship Training List _____	
Home Towns as Listed _____	
Other (specify) _____	
File Copies _____	
Copies to _____	
Campus Routing _____	
Cost	
Number Run Off _____	
Brochure enclosed _____	
Cost of Duplicating _____	
Cost of Mailing _____	
Other Cost (specify) _____	
Total Cost _____	

111

and distribution, and give one, when appropriate, to the coordinator. Sets are available from any good paper house.

Mailing Piece Sizes (Postal Considerations)

It's great to be inventive, but eschew the temptation to "create" when you get materials ready to mail.

On April 15, 1978, the U.S. Postal Service started charging more for mail that does not meet dimensional and weight standards.

Extra postage is now required on first-class mail weighing 1 ounce or less, and third-class mail weighing 2 ounces or less, that is not proportioned according to the new size standards.

Envelopes cannot be higher than 6⅛ inches or wider than 11½ inches. Envelopes and postcards smaller than 3½ × 5 inches are not mailable at all.

According to postal officials, the rates for odd-sized first-class mail can increase as much as 50 percent in the immediately foreseeable future, and there are plans for across-the-board rate increases (as always).

THE LITTLE COSTS ADD UP—DUPLICATION AND SLIDES

It is not the slick job by an outside printer or the professionally produced promotion film show that most publicists of programs have to cost out.

The services which they use dozens or even hundreds of times a year as compared with the few times they may go to an outside printer are, simply, duplicating services and slide preparation services.

Duplicating Costs

Often it is not necessary to take brochure or poster copy to an outside printshop. It almost *never* is necessary to take copy for press releases and other support materials to an outside printshop.

Duplicating rooms abound in agencies, organizations, colleges, and universities. As long as they do a good job on 20-pound paper at a good price, they are a preferable choice for the publicist.

In your own shop, one connected with your institution, 100 copies of a one-page release or other statement can cost as little as $1.70. This price is rock-bottom, but certainly you should be able to buy this amount of printing for under $5.

In this in-house duplicating room, they charge an additional 50 cents or so per hundred sheets for machine folding.

All price ranges suggested are as of this book's publication date.

 **Always have news releases and facts sheets which will go to a news desk folded so that the lead shows when the envelope is opened. Saves an editor a lot of time if he or she knows immediately what is at hand.**

Most institution-connected duplicating rooms will charge about one-third to one-half more than the low-priced but very efficient shop whose director I am quoting.

However, if you go to an independent printer, you will be talking about a price three or even four times as much.

If you are servicing three or four major dailies, at most, in a metropolitan area, there is some advantage in doing the final clean copy of your release on a composer—a typewriter-style typesetting machine—with the font actually used by the newspapers, so that the copy will be camera-ready. In this situation, use photo paper (positive mechanical transfer—PMT); it can be pasted up in a computerized newspaper or magazine typesetting operation "as is."

 **Do not ever fold camera-ready PMT copy.**

It is unlikely that you as a p.r. person, or professional or volunteer program coordinator, will have a composer in your immediate department. The use of this machine is available through printshops or graphic shops at the present time. If you do, you are fortunate. However, it is useful to know what to ask for, and what kind of paper to specify, and what you should look for in future equipment plans. Those who are thinking about adding to their print capability should look seriously at the composers on the market. With any volume of use, composers can pay their entire costs in 1 year. They also can be rented.

One factor in considering composers is that you save a great deal on paper costs, and there is little or no waste. They do a good job on brochure copy. It can be very simple to use composers. They do not require high degrees of skills on the parts of the operators. Another factor in their favor is that they do not require justifying. Also, they turn out beautiful copy.

 **On very small jobs, another way to save on costs is to take your nice, clean release to a fast-copy shop. You can find one in almost any business district, certainly in any business district adjoining a campus. This kind of shop charges from 2 cents up to 10 cents per sheet. Copying machines in public places (hotels, airports) require 25 cents or more per copy.**

Cost of Slides

A television presentation, whether it is a simple PSA or a paid announcement, picks up a lot of impact and class when it takes the form of a slide, with voice-over.

A finished slide which is used in a slide show or for a "how I spent my vacation" evening with friends can be made by almost anyone in the business of photofinishing.

However, a finished and bound slide which is for TV use should be professionally made—preferably in the TV studio's art department. They do it every day. They know what is effective and what is not. And the cost is minor.

At this writing, the first finished slide costs you $5 or so. After that, slides are $4 each. Artwork costs are based on the staff artist's time. Usually, anywhere from $8 to $15 is about standard for a fairly simple slide—one for which you have brought in ideas and suggested copy. When the artist is called upon for original work, the charge is higher, of course, because he or she uses more time.

Don't be surprised if the artist asks you to cut down on words. Artists on TV staffs know what they are doing. Listen.

PAID ADVERTISING

An extensive operation involving the purchase of paid advertisements in newspapers, magazines, journals, TV, and radio requires the services of a professional in both buying and the preparation of copy. Go to an ad agency.

A single-shot ad campaign usually can be handled by the publicist or program coordinator, with the help of an advertising salesperson at the paper, other publication, or TV or radio station.

It is only logical for a person, even one with no p.r. experience, to expect that an ad in a news outlet in a small community will be light-years cheaper than an ad in the metropolitan areas. He or she will be absolutely correct.

Yet there are a few avenues in either place which the person buying an ad to publicize a program can take to reduce the cost of the campaign.

First, look around your institution and see if you can tie in with some other agency or unit within that institution which already is placing ads in the outlet you are planning to use.

Ads in Magazines and Newspapers

An ad in a regional edition of *TV Guide* which you buy to advertise a television correspondence course can be considerably cheaper than otherwise, if your institution-connected public broadcasting station already has a contract with the *Guide.* They can cost you in at the contract rate.

An ad in a chain of suburban weeklies which you take out in order to promote a new series of evening humanities courses in that area may be considerably cheaper if your institution's athletic department or concert series already is placing ads in that chain.

Anytime you take out an ad on your own—without the help of a pro—ask for the nonprofit rate (sometimes there is one, sometimes not). Likewise, if you are connected with an educational institution, ask for the institutional rate.

There are special newspaper editions which often offer advertising bargains. A program which falls into the category which a special edition addresses can reach a target audience with an ad. Costs in a special edition also are lower than usual rates. Such editions are "back-to-school" or "farm" or "fashions" (usually just before Easter) or "sports" or the like.

It also helps to get on the pages where the audience you are addressing makes up the readership. A conference for bankers, for example, might be advertised on the financial pages.

Getting on the page you prefer is "iffy." Large contracts may specify such and such a page or section. The one-timers usually have to take whatever spot they can get.

The cost of newspaper advertisements varies with the circulation. Your state press association directory is usually also a rate book, and a good source of comparative figures—both as to circulation and as to cost.

The press association also functions as a placer of ads in package deals and as a go-between in getting you a good rate when such deals are structured.

A three-quarter-page ad placed by an educational institution in a large-circulation Chicago daily costed out at a whopping $1,700.

At this writing, a comparatively small daily with a circulation of about 44,000 was charging $180 for a quarter-page ad, and a metropolitan daily, $597 for a quarter-page ad.

In placing ads, as in placing news releases, do not forget the people-pulling power of suburban weeklies. The big chains which ring some of America's larger cities can claim both high circulation and high readership. As far as advertising goes, they often reach the target audience that program planners are seeking, and also they can offer the advertiser attractive package deals.

Larger chains sell ads by circulation zone so that the advertiser can pinpoint a specific target audience by area.

Take these factors into consideration when you are placing all your ads, in whatever media:

1. What audience does this outlet reach? Is it the same one you are trying to reach?
2. What is the outlet's circulation or listener rating? More circulation, more impact on greater audience.
3. How much does the ad you want to buy cost? Think of the cost, again, in terms of (a) type of audience and (b) size of audience.
4. Does the ad promise to pay off? Will your dollars spent generate enough registrations or enrollments to recoup the cost?

It doesn't hurt to take a little flier now and then, just to test the water and see what the pull of a particular publication or station may be. Don't invest a lot in this kind of "research," however.

There is very little reason why a person engaged in publicizing and promoting continuing education programs would want or need to use general-readership magazines for this purpose.

There are, as always, exceptions. One is that of a program which has a television component. The television viewers of the area would need to be informed in a striking way.

Another is that of certain travel-abroad programs directed toward participants who are well-to-do and who also have a high cultural quotient. Several universities which offer these sophisticated tours advertise them through the magazines that have an equally sophisticated readership—*Smithsonian, Harper's,* and the like—with good results.

Journals and special-interest magazines, however, are another matter.

 **Most of the publications which fall into these categories have deadlines which fall from 3 to 6 months ahead of the publication dates. Check the specific journal, or look up the special-interest magazines in *Bacon's* (see the "Bibliography"). For best results, get your copy in early.**

Again, study the journals and magazines which you think may be appropriate for your use in publicizing a particular program. Look at their circulations (see *Bacon's* or *Ayers*), and compare each circulation with the cost of an ad.

It will be wise to write to them for their current rates; these fluctuate.

TV and Radio Ads

Television and radio are more specific. Within limits, you can buy whatever time spot you choose. A spot with a high-rated viewing or listening will cost you more than a spot that attracts less viewing or listening.

At this writing, a 30-second spot on a metropolitan TV station will cost from $24 to $1,300, depending on the time of day and the pull of the TV program on at that time, while a 60-second spot on that same station, under the same circumstances, will cost from $50 to $2,600. The very low rates apply to "dead" times, such as 2–3 P.M.

Turning to radio, a top-listenership metropolitan station (200,000 people tune in every 15 minutes) charges $56 to $172 for a 30-second spot and $70 to $214 for a 60-second spot.

A medium-sized radio station with a good listenership charges $8.55 to $13.02 for a single spot, 30 seconds, and $9.60 to $121.50 for a single spot, 60 seconds. As most medium-sized and small to tiny stations do, it offers package deals with packages of slots, ranging from $102.75 for 30 seconds (15 spots per week, assorted times) to $121.50 for 60 seconds, same package.

Broadcast stations, both TV and radio, have rate books or cards, as do newspapers and often magazines. They'll be glad to give them to you.

However, the rates are not constant. They usually are good only for a few months at a time. In the medium-sized to smaller stations, rates are changed several times a year, following ratings examinations. Larger stations may change them even more often, since ratings are under continuous examination by the stations' or networks' marketing and research departments. Newspapers are a little slower to change, but make certain of costs before you place an ad.

COLUMBIA BROADCASTING SYSTEM

WDWS

Established 1937

OWNED BY

THE CHAMPAIGN NEWS-GAZETTE, INC.

South Neil Street Road - Champaign, Illinois 61820

LARRY STEWART, Station Manager
CONSTANCE VOGT, Assistant Manager

Area Code 217
Telephone 351-5300

Rate Card
No. 19

Effective January 1, 1978

General Information

1. WDWS-AM—Operating Power 1000 watts (day), 250 watts (night)
   1400 kh.
   WDWS-FM 50 k.w. 97.5 mh.
   Operates on Central Standard Time
   Operating Schedule:
   > Weekday 5:00 a. m. to 12:15 a. m.
   > Sunday 7:00 a. m. to 12:15 a. m.

2. LENGTH OF COMMERCIAL COPY: In accordance with NAB standards and Code.

3. NEWS SERVICE: A.P.

4. MUSIC CLEARANCE: BMI, ASCAP, SESAC

5. NO BROADCASTS IN FOREIGN LANGUAGES.

6. COMMISSION AND CASH DISCOUNTS:
   a. No cash discounts — bills due and payable when rendered.

Local Broadcast Advertising
TIME RATES
Effective January 1, 1978

CLASS AAA—5 a. m.-1 p. m. Monday through Saturday
CLASS AA —1 p. m.-7 p. m. Monday through Saturday
CLASS A —ALL OTHER TIMES

	Minutes			30 Seconds		
	AAA	**AA**	**A**	**AAA**	**AA**	**A**
1x	15.20	12.35	9.60	13.05	11.15	8.65
52x	12.05	10.30	7.90	10.65	9.15	7.15
156x	11.10	9.55	7.40	9.95	8.50	6.55
260x	10.60	9.05	6.90	9.15	7.75	5.95
520x	9.80	8.30	6.35	8.30	7.15	5.55
1000x	8.90	7.60	5.80	7.60	6.45	4.90

PACKAGE RATES WDWS AM and FM
TOTAL AUDIENCE PLAN

	60 Seconds		30 Seconds	
15 per week	10 AM (9.65)		10 AM (8.15)	
	5 FM (5.00)	121.50	5 FM (4.25)	102.75
25 per week	15 AM (9.00)		15 AM (7.55)	
	10 FM (4.75)	182.50	10 FM (4.00)	153.25
35 per week	20 AM (8.75)		20 AM (7.30)	
	15 FM (4.50)	242.50	15 FM (3.75)	202.25

All Local Rates are Net to Agencies

IDS — MINIMUM 20 per week $6.00 per spot

PROGRAM RATES

	15 Minutes	5 Minutes
1x	38.10	18.20
52x	33.05	15.35
156x	28.30	13.80
260x	25.30	11.75

DISCOUNTS allowed retroactively on the number of broadcasts given within a year. Announcements and programs cannot be combined to earn larger discounts.

The above rates are for convenient reference. They are not to be considered as an offer of facilities and are subject to change without notice.

Contract And Other Requirements

Contracts subject to conditions of Standard NAB and AAAA contracts.

Representatives
McGAVREN-GUILD

WDWS-AM simulcasts with WDWS-FM Monday through Sunday from sign-on to 12:00 noon FM Stereo is separate from 12:00 noon to sign-off.

Stereo FM Rates
RATE CARD 2
Effective January 1, 1978

Operating Power 50,000 KW

	60 Seconds	30 Seconds
1x	6.25	5.25
30x	6.00	5.00
90x	5.75	4.75
180x	5.50	4.50
360x	5.75	4.25

Area Code 217 351-5300
Operating Schedule: Noon to **Midnight**

AFFILIATED WITH

The News-Gazette
"Your Newspaper Since 1852"

Program Promotion in this daily newspaper readily available. Daily circulation in excess of 40,000.

 **Shop around. Newspaper and TV-radio advertising rates are competitive.**

Newspaper Inserts as Catalogs

You may want to gear your paid newspaper advertising around seasonal or topical newspaper inserts, and even use inserts instead of continuing education course catalogs. In fact, colleges and other nonprofit service organizations or agencies with multiple course offerings and programs in specific areas frequently opt for newspaper inserts instead of catalogs. They are printed immediately prior to registration or enrollment periods and may be as small as a half-page ad listing courses, or as large as a two-page spread which lists not only courses but also outreach programs.

The use of an entire pullout section is advocated by some colleges and agencies (e.g., the United Fund in some areas). The University of Arizona has made good use of this promotion tool in publicizing its entire summer outreach program.

Allowing for Inflation

An inflationary cushion must be added in costing out any activity which will take place more than a few weeks away.

For ordinary programs or other activities, 8 to 10 percent a year is about right. If you are going sophisticated and there are electronic or other potentially expensive ingredients, 19 to 20 percent is not too high an annual inflationary increase projection.

The lack of foresight in taking inflation into account has had a killing effect on many outreach activities.

Way back in February or March, a group begins planning for a program which will take place in October and costs it out at a certain dollar figure. By August to October, when the heavy expenditures are being leveled against that dollar figure, the dollars have shrunk, the money is not there, and vital portions of the program have to be eliminated.

THE MAGIC MIX OF PUBLICITY INGREDIENTS

FINDING A FORMAT

You now are ready to decide on the exact format of your publicity push. Think along these lines:

1. The "three-notice" rule.
2. The subject matter of your program: hard to sell? easy to sell?
3. The size of your program.
4. People pullers which are based on factors other than the program topic.
5. The size of your task force.
6. The assets and tools available in your Inventories.
7. The amount of money you have to spend.

The magic mix may be a matter of worry. It need not be.

But there are items to take into consideration, a principal one being the "three-notice" rule:

It takes three contacts with a person in your appropriate target group to make up his or her mind about enrolling in or registering for your course or program.

These do not have to be formal contacts—e.g., the receipt of a brochure or the reading of a newspaper article. They can be a variety pack.

Let's say that the person you are trying to reach is a schoolteacher. He or she might get one notice in the form of a brochure. He or she might hear about the course or program at a teachers meeting. He or she might read about it in some periodical, or see a poster, or hear a radio announcement. The teacher might, in fact, be exposed to the idea of coming to your program or taking your course in any one of the dozens of ways which have been discussed in the portions of the book just read.

Why does it take three contacts? "Three" seems to be a behavior-triggering number.

The first contact results in "Oh, that's nice" (or "that's a good idea," or "that would be fun," or "that might be valuable," or "that's in a good place," or "so-and-so may go").

The second is a little nudge. "Maybe I'd better do something about enrolling [or making a reservation]."

The third prompts an instant, almost panic reaction—the kind of do-it-*now* feeling that leads to an immediate response.

Now there are more exceptions to this rule than to most. Many people—even the appropriate clients—will rule out a given program immediately on grounds of disinterest, busy schedule, lack of money, etc.

But it is a fact that for the average program (whatever its format) there are three humps in the time schedule of enrollments or registrations.

Of the people who will accept the various invitations and enticements to participate, a sizable percentage will be the early enrollers—those who take up pen and enroll almost immediately upon receiving the first notice.

Then there will be some who get around to it during the weeks before the event—as they come across the brochure or clipping, or as they sit down to write monthly checks or otherwise clear the tops of their desks.

But of the three groups we are talking about—people who will come but make decisions and take action on differing schedules—by far the largest will be the third-notice entrants. So your magic mix—the particular formula which you will follow in this publicity push—must take into consideration the three-notice rule.

Research, both formal and experiential, shows that people (usually motivated by a hope of upgrading themselves occupationally) will drive 50 miles, but not much more than that, one evening or weekend day a week to attend a class or program. A single activity with a strong appeal to a special-interest group or with star-quality speakers or entertainment value will draw from a considerably wider area, 100–200 miles.

SAMPLE MIXES

A. A small, locally based activity with a topic of interest and concern to the community or area and with some grass-roots support should pull a suitable audience through the following mix:
   1. Three news releases.
       a. A bare-bones release, as early as possible.
       b. A full release, giving details and particulars (with photographs).
       c. A wrap-up release with last-minute additions and changes, to spark action.
   2. A public-service announcement on local radio-TV.
   3. Insertion of notices in various kinds of calendars.
   4. Distribution of posters.
   5. A set plan for the laying on of hands—personal approaches through a talkabout or a calling tree.
   6. An invitation to the press to cover your activity, and early provision of a facts sheet.

B. A medium-sized program which is supposed to attract regional or statewide attention, with a topic of interest and concern to particular constituencies, should rely on all the items in mix A, plus:
   7. Attempts for advance feature coverage in the area—newspapers, radio-TV.
   8. Special attention to Nowlen's list of "P's" and to the people-puller attractions and ploys (pages 20–21).

9. Personal visits to newsrooms *throughout* the drawing area.

10. Four press releases, instead of three, with "d" being an article heavily loaded with audience appeal through emphasis on the attractive or compelling features—star speakers or the like.

11. A press conference, depending on the caliber of the speakers and the hotness of the topic.

C. If you have a real biggie which may attract national notice if not national audience participation, go with all the items in mix A and mix B, plus:

12. A press room, press kits, lots of photographs.

13. A staff and amenities such as are specified under "D Day Operations" (pages 168–180).

14. A pro. When you get a really big event to publicize, one which will generate revenue as well as interest, you and the steering committee may want to give serious consideration to augmenting your efforts by getting backup for this or that specific task from a pro who is a specialist in that particular area of expertise.

In all of these, keep the dollar signs and schedules dancing before your eyes. Promising more than you can produce or embarking on too many support activities which you cannot finance with the budget allowed can be fatal to the effort.

```
FROM:  Helen Farlow
 FOR:  Program Development Staff


      A PUBLICITY TIMEFRAME FOR ACTIVITIES WHICH
      NEED PROMOTION TO "BRING IN THE BODIES"

At Least Six Months Ahead

 1.  Prepare special-interest mailing list
 2.  Initial announcement

At Least Three Months Ahead

 3.  The next article-release giving program particu-
     lars
 4.  Public-service announcements
 5.  IF and ONLY IF your activity merits it, arrange-
     ments for advance features (printed media) and
     broadcast spots
 6.  Be SURE that you--or whoever is fronting for the
     activity--have cleared your calendar to the ex-
     tent that you will be free to keep the commitments
     implied
 7.  Get your activity on all appropriate calendars
```

<u>Six Weeks Ahead</u>

8. If you REALLY have to bring in the bodies, start
    your countdown:
    a. Release on complete program (pictures where
       available)
    b. Release giving added features and details
    c. Wrap-up release
9. IF AND ONLY IF your activity <u>merits</u> it, set up
    your press conference(s)
10. Observing the cautions of #5 and #8 above, assem-
    ble your press kits

<u>Immediately Ahead</u>

11. Reminders to media; check all details of press
    conferences, special coverage and/or interviews,
    air time, etc. Make arrangements to have your
    speakers/front people/guest experts at appointed
    places at appointed times
12. Relax and gird for the crises ahead

Note: Scale your effort to the scope and stature of
   the activity being planned. Do not attempt to pull
   out all the stops for each and every program; those
   of moderate scope and importance will not need--or
   deserve, or attain, even if you try--all of the media
   attention implied above. Indeed, it may contribute
   to diminishing returns if you attempt to do the whole
   bit every time; you soon will wear out the welcome
   for you AND your institution or department.

Note: This Timeframe does not include the functions
   ordinarily assumed by conference coordinators, such
   as obtaining organizational membership mailing lists
   and mailing out brochures. Neither is it in the least
   <u>inclusive</u>--there are many other p.r. tools and ploys
   used as the situation indicates, rather than regularly; such are not mentioned above.

NEWSPAPER ASSOCIATIONS

Daily Associations

Allied Daily Newspapers
18601 Pacific Highway South,
Room 181
Seattle, WA 98188
Mgr., Paul R. Conrad
206-248-0770

Massachusetts Newspaper Publishers
Association
56 Wyman Street
West Medford, MA 02155
Mgr., Joseph L. Doherty
617-395-2773

New York State Publishers Association
Newhouse Communications Center
215 University Place, Room 305
Syracuse, NY 13210
Mgr., W. Melvin Street
315-475-0012

Publishers Bureau of New Jersey, Inc.
2040 Millburn Avenue
Maplewood, NJ 07040
Mgr., David J. Winkworth
201-762-8080

Texas Daily Newspaper Association
3701 Kirby Building
Houston, TX 77098
Mgr., John H. Murphy
713-529-3531

Regional and National Associations

American Newspaper Publishers
Association
Box 17407, Dulles International
Airport
Washington, D.C. 20041
Mgr., Jerry W. Friedheim
703-620-9500

Canadian Community Newspapers
Association
12 Shuter Street, Suite 201
Toronto, Ontario M5B 1A2, Canada
Mgr., Dorry Gould
416-366-4277

Canadian Daily Newspaper Publishers
Association
321 Bloor Street East, Suite 214
Toronto, Ontario M4W 1E7, Canada
416-923-3567

Inland Daily Press Association
100 West Monroe Street
Chicago, IL 60603
Mgr., William G. Boykin
312-782-0513

National Newspaper Association
491 National Press Building
Washington, D.C. 20045
Mgr., William G. Mullen
202-783-1651

National Newspaper Publishers
Association
400 1627 K Street
Washington, D.C. 20006

Southern Newspaper Publishers
Association
P.O. Box 28875
6065 Barfield Road, Suite 222
Atlanta, GA 30328
Mgr., Reed Sarratt
404-394-5550
(does not distribute a directory)

Suburban Newspapers of America
111 East Wacker Drive
Chicago, IL 60601
312-644-6610

State Associations

Alabama Press Association
100 Professional Plaza
921 Third Avenue East
Tuscaloosa, AL 35401
Mgr., Stephen E. Bradley
205-345-5611

Arizona Newspapers Association
Financial Center, Suite 417
3443 North Central Avenue
Phoenix, AZ 85012
Mgr., Katherine S. Smith
602-264-4631

Arkansas Press Association
212 Wallace Building
Little Rock, AR 72201
Mgr., Louise Bowker
501-374-1500

California Newspaper Publishers
Association
1127 11th Street, Room 1040
Sacramento, CA 95814
Mgr., Ben D. Martin
916-443-5991

Colorado Press Association
The Press Building
1336 Glenarm Place
Denver, CO 80204
Mgr., William F. Lindsey
303-255-1707

Connecticut Editorial Association
The Lakeville Journal
c/o *The West Hartford News*
20 Isham Road
West Hartford, CT 06107
Mgr., Robert Estabrook
203-435-2541

Florida Press Association
306 South Duval, Room 204
Tallahassee, FL 32301
Mgr., Reg. E. Ivory
904-222-5790

Georgia Press Association
1075 Spring Street, N.W.
Atlanta, GA 30309
Mgr., Julia Dyar
404-872-2467

Hawaii Newspaper Publishers
Association
c/o *Hawaii Catholic Herald*
Honolulu, HI 96813
Mgr., Monsignor Francis A. Marzen
808-536-5494

Hoosier State Press Association
1542 Consolidated Building
115 North Pennsylvania Street
Indianapolis, IN 46204
Mgr., Richard W. Cardwell
317-637-3966

Idaho Newspaper Association
P.O. Box 1067
604 Idaho Building
Boise, ID 83701
Mgr., William Moon
208-343-1671

Illinois Press Association
1035 Outer Park Drive
Springfield, IL 62704
Mgr., David R. West
217-753-8100

Iowa Press Association
511 Shops Building
Des Moines, IA 50309
Mgr., Don J. Reid
515-244-2145

Kansas Press Association
P.O. Box 1773
701 Jackson
Topeka, KS 66601
Mgr., Donald M. Fitzgerald
913-233-7421

Kentucky Press Association
63 Fountain Place
Frankfort, KY 40601
Mgr., Jesse R. Shaffer
502-223-8821

Louisiana Press Association
680 North Fifth Street
Baton Rouge, LA 70802
Mgr., Max N. Franz
504-344-9309

Maine Press Association
101 Lord Hall
University of Maine
Orono, ME 04473
Mgr., Howard A. Keyo
207-581-7588

Maryland-Delaware-D.C. Press
Association
801 St. Paul Street
Baltimore, MD 21202
301-837-6070

Massachusetts Press Association
Malcolm T. Barach
Department of Journalism
Suffolk University
41 Temple Street
Boston, MA 02114

Michigan Press Association
P.O. Box 71
257 Michigan Avenue
East Lansing, MI 48823
Mgr., Warren Hoyt
517-332-4610

Minnesota Newspaper Association
84 South 6th Street, Suite 400
Minneapolis, MN 55402
Mgr., Robert M. Shaw
612-335-8844

Mississippi Press Association
P.O. Box 1789
Jackson, MS 39205
Mgr., Evelyn Traylor
601-354-1524

Missouri Press Association
8th and Locust
Columbia, MO 65201
Mgr., William A. Bray
314-449-4167

Montana Press Association
P.O. Box 1186
315 Allen
Helena, MT 59601
Mgr., Sam Gilluly
406-443-2850

Nebraska Press Association
Suite 723, Sharp Building
Lincoln, NE 68508
Mgr., Philip A. Berkebile
402-432-2851

Nevada State Press Association
P.O. Box 722
Carson City, NV 89701

New Jersey Press Association
206 W. State Street
Trenton, NJ 08608

New Mexico Press Association
P.O. Box 1058
704 Gunnison Avenue
Grants, NM 87020
Mgr., Ward E. Ballmer
505-287-2867

New York Press Association
Newhouse Communications Center
215 University Place
Syracuse, NY 13210
Mgr., Frank H. Haugh
315-478-3195

North Carolina Press Association
907 Runnymede
Raleigh, NC 27607

North Dakota Newspaper Association
Box 8137, University Station
Grand Forks, ND 58202
Mgr., Eugene G. Carr
701-777-2574

Ohio Newspaper Association
145 E. Rich Street
Columbus, OH 43215
Mgr., William J. Oertel
614-224-1648

Oklahoma Press Association
3601 North Lincoln
Oklahoma City, OK 73105
Mgr., Ben Blackstock
405-524-4421

Oregon Newspaper Publishers
Association
2130 S.W. Fifth, Suite 2
Portland, OR 97201
Mgr., Roger Williams
503-227-2526

Pennsylvania Newspaper Publishers
Association
PNPA Press Center
2717 North Front Street
Harrisburg, PA 17110
Mgr., G. Richard Dew
717-234-4067

South Carolina Press Association
P.O. Box 11429
Columbia, SC 29211
Mgr., Dr. Reid H. Montgomery
803-777-5169

South Dakota Press Association
Box 1147
Brookings, SD 57006
Mgr., William J. McDermott
605-688-5623

Tennessee Press Association
P.O. Box 8123
Knoxville, TN 37916
Mgr., Glenn E. McNeil
615-974-5481

Texas Press Association
718 West 5th Street
Austin, TX 78701
Mgr., Lyndell Williams
512-477-6755

Utah Press Association
467 East 3d South
Salt Lake City, UT 84111
Mgr., Thomas Garry Payne
801-328-8678

Virginia Press Association
410 Virginia Building
One North Fifth Street
Richmond, VA 23219
Mgr., Edwin O. Meyer
804-648-8948

Washington Newspapers Publishers
Association
3838 Stone Way North
Seattle, WA 98103
Mgr., Jerry Zubrod
206-634-3838

West Virginia Press Association
409 Hoyer Building
Charleston, WV 25301
Mgr., Charles R. Cline
304-342-1011

Wisconsin Newspaper Association
Washington Square
33 North Dickinson Street
Madison, WI 53703
Mgr., Romain C. Brandt
608-257-3941

Wyoming Press Association
503 South 24th
Laramie, WY 82070
Mgr., Nancy R. Shelton
307-745-8144

NEWS SERVICES

AP   Associated Press
AP Newsfeatures
50 Rockefeller Plaza
New York, NY 10020
212-262-4000

CanP   Canadian Press and
Broadcast News
36 King Street East
Toronto, Ontario M5C
2L9, Canada
416-364-0321

CN   Capitol News Service
301 Capitol Mall, Suite
300
Sacramento, CA 95814
916-445-6336

CNS   Copley News Service
P.O. Box 190
San Diego, CA 92112
714-299-3131

CPS   College Press
Service/Center for the
Rights of Campus
Journalists
1764 Gilpin Street
Denver, CO 80218
303-388-1608

CQ   *Congressional Quarterly
Service*
1414 22d Street, N.W.
Washington, D.C. 20036
202-393-7130

CSM   *Christian Science Monitor*
News and Photo Service
Box 4994
Des Moines, IA 50306
515-284-8250
Telex: 478-472

CT-NYN   *Chicago Tribune*–New
York News Syndicate
220 East 42d Street
New York, NY 10017
212-949-3400

DJ   Dow Jones News Service
22 Cortland Street
New York, NY 10017
212-285-5182

ERR   Editorial Research Reports
1414 22d Street, N.W.
Washington, D.C. 20037
202-393-7130

FNS	Field News Service 401 North Wabash Chicago, IL 60611 312-321-2801	NYT	*New York Times* News Service 229 West 43d Street New York, NY 10036 212-556-7087
GNS	Gannett News Service 1281 National Press Building Washington, D.C. 20045 202-393-3460	RN	Reuters News Agency 1700 Broadway New York, NY 10019 212-582-4030
HHS	Hearst Headline Service/Special News Service 959 Eighth Avenue New York, NY 10019	SHNA	Scripps-Howard Newspaper Alliance 200 Park Avenue New York, NY 10017 212-867-5000
KNT	KNT News Wire 1195 National Press Building Washington, D.C. 20045	UPI	United Press International World Headquarters 200 East 42d Street New York, NY 10017 212-682-0400
LAT-WP	*Los Angeles Times/Washington Post* News Service Times Mirror Square Los Angeles, CA 90053 213-625-2345	WN	World News Syndicate 6223 Selma Avenue P.O. Box 449 Hollywood, CA 90028 213-467-7024
NANA	North American Newspaper Alliance 200 Park Avenue New York, NY 10017 212-557-2333	WNS	Women's News Service 200 Park Avenue New York, NY 10017 212-557-2333
NEA	Newspaper Enterprise Association Editorial HQ—200 Park Avenue New York, NY 10017 212-661-6600 Business Office—1200 West Third Street Cleveland, OH 44113 202-621-7300	WWD	*Women's Wear Daily* Fairchild Syndication Service 7 East 12th Street New York, NY 10003 212-741-4315
NNS	Newhouse News Service 1750 Pennsylvania Avenue, N.W., Suite 1320 Washington, D.C. 20006 202-298-7080		

STATE BROADCASTERS ASSOCIATIONS

Alabama Broadcasters Association
Box 6246
University, AL 35486
205-758-6240

Alaska Broadcasters Association
3910 Seward Highway
Anchorage, AK 99503
907-279-9437

Arizona Broadcasters Association
Box 654
Scottsdale, AZ 85252
602-266-1726

Arkansas Broadcasters Association
2311 Biscayne Drive, Suite 100
Cantrell Place
Little Rock, AR 72207
501-375-2545

California Broadcasters Association
1107 Ninth Street, Suite 907
Sacramento, CA 95814
916-444-2237

Colorado Broadcasters Association
7138 West Frost Drive
Littleton, CO 80123
303-979-8787

Connecticut Broadcasters Association
15 Highland Park Road
North Haven, CT 06473
203-771-6433

Florida Association of Broadcasters
3131 N.W. 13th Street, Suite 37
Gainesville, FL 32601
904-372-0708

Georgia Association of Broadcasters
6065 Roswell Road, Suite 604
Atlanta, GA 30328
404-252-0964

Hawaiian Association of Broadcasters
1534 Kapiolani Boulevard
Honolulu, HI 96814
808-537-3991

Idaho State Broadcasters Association
Box 884
Boise, ID 83701
208-375-7277

Illinois Broadcasters Association
726 South College
Springfield, IL 62704
217-753-5720

Indiana Broadcasters Association
1111 East 54th Street
Indianapolis, IN 46220
317-636-0724

Iowa Broadcasters Association
1230 Marston Avenue
Aimes, IA 50010
515-294-4340

Kansas Association of Broadcasters
1052 N. Waco
Wichita, KS 67203
316-265-8901

Kentucky Broadcasters Association
Box 680
Lebanon, KY 40033
502-692-3126

Louisiana Association of Broadcasters
Box 16078, Louisiana State University
Baton Rouge, LA 70893
504-388-4472

Maine Association of Broadcasters
Box 307
Augusta, ME 04330
207-623-3878

Maryland–District of
Columbia–Delaware Broadcasters
Association
Route 1, Box 125
St. Michaels, MD 21663
301-745-5155

Massachusetts Broadcasters
Association
20 Franklin Street
Worcester, MA 01600

Michigan Association of Broadcasters
Box 16015
Lansing, MI 48901
517-371-1729

Mississippi Broadcasters Association
Box 758
West Point, MS 39773
601-494-7334

Missouri Broadcasters Association
1800 S.W. Boulevard
Jefferson City, MO 65101
314-636-6692

Montana Broadcasters Association
213 Fifth Avenue
Box 503
Helena, MT 59601
406-442-3961

Nebraska Broadcasters Association
Box 31802
Omaha, NE 68131
402-551-4360

Nevada Broadcasters Association
Box 2427
Reno, NV 89505

New Hampshire Association of
Broadcasters
Rochester Hill Road
Rochester, NH 03867
606-332-0930

New Jersey Broadcasters Association
Radio Center, Rutgers University
New Brunswick, NJ 08903
201-247-3337

New Mexico Broadcasters Association
709 Fruit Avenue
Albuquerque, NM 87102
505-242-2211

New York State Broadcasters
Association, Inc.
9 Herbert Drive
Latham, NY 12110
518-783-5821

North Carolina Association of
Broadcasters
Suite 300, BB & T Building
Raleigh, NC 27602
919-821-7300

North Dakota Broadcasters
Association
Box 5347, University Station
Fargo, ND 58102
701-237-8321

Ohio Association of Broadcasters
100 East Broad Street, Suite 1207
Columbus, OH 43215
614-228-4052

Oklahoma Broadcasters Association
Box 457
Shawnee, OK 74801
405-273-9084

Oregon Association of Broadcasters
530 Center Street, NE
Salem, OR 97301

Pennsylvania Association of
Broadcasters
407 North Front Street
Harrisburg, PA 17101
717-233-3511

Rhode Island Broadcasters Association
c/o Richard Rakovan
WPRO East Providence, RI 02915
401-433-4200

Rocky Mountain Broadcasters
Association
Box 220
Pocatello, ID 83201
208-233-5020

South Carolina Broadcasters
Association
University of South Carolina, College
of Journalism
Columbia, SC 29208
803-777-6783

South Dakota Broadcasters
Association
4609 West 12th Street
Sioux Falls, SD 57106
605-336-7110

Tennessee Association of Broadcasters
Box 2688
Nashville, TN 37219
615-254-5761

Texas Association of Broadcasters
P.O. Box 14787
Austin, TX 78761
512-476-3061

Utah Broadcasters Association
Box 401
Provo, UT 84601
801-225-6942

Vermont Association of Broadcasters
Box 608
Burlington, VT 05401
802-862-5761

Washington State Association of
Broadcasters
Suite 1015, 1411 Fourth Avenue
Building
Seattle, WA 98101
206-622-2991

West Virginia Broadcasters
Association
1910 Parkview Street
Huntington, WV 25701
304-522-2905

Wisconsin Broadcasters Association
702 N. Midvale Boulevard
Madison, WI 53705
608-238-7171

Wyoming Association of Broadcasters
Box 1873
Cheyenne, WY 82001
307-634-5871

PHASE II

CARRYING THROUGH: THE SIX-WEEK COUNTDOWN

CHECKING PROGRESS

Stop.

Stop right here.

It is time to look around, to see where you are in publicizing your program, and to plan the final steps of your campaign.

You have accomplished all the tasks you were assigned during the gearing-up period.

Or *have* you?

And look, too, at a second list of reminders on pages 137–138. Your Timeframe is on pages 124–125. Look *it* over again. Make a copy of it, so you can check each item off without marking up the book to the possible detriment of its use another time.

Are you absolutely sure of every detail?

Did you entrust anything to

An assistant or student?

Your best friend?

Your secretary?

Any other member of your staff or organization?

An associate or a task force member?

Someone from another department?

A volunteer?

A vendor (i.e., a printer, a graphic artist, etc.)?

Anyone other than yourself?

Check it out.

If the task that you assigned the person in question (or which that person volunteered to do) is not entirely completed to the exact point which the Timeframe and the Checklist specify, take it away, albeit against his or her arguments and dictates, and *do it yourself.*

Take it away even if the person involved is your boss on the organizational charts. No one is your boss when it comes to publicizing that program. It is your responsibility, and you will be accountable for all slipups.

Look.

The program is only 6 weeks away.

Right?

You can't let rank or clout or anything else (including the fact that you are operating on a personal schedule which already is about to give way at the seams) get in your path.

This one precaution on your part may not win you any popularity contests, but it may be one of the five or so most important things we tell you about in this book on publicizing and promoting.

When you find a weak spot, take that part of the assignment over and do it yourself.

It would be nice if you had the time and patience to help the person who flubbed up learn how to do the job and how to keep to a Timeframe. But you don't, not now. Maybe someday—but not now. Not with a program only 6 weeks off.

Again, about that matter of checking on details as you enter the countdown period.

Be certain that you—you, yourself, and not a surrogate—actually check in person every deadline that you and a vendor or a service arm of your agency have agreed upon. Get out your original bid. Beware of such wriggly and undependable phrases on agreements and orders as "about February 1," or "as soon as possible." They should read "at 11 A.M. on February 1." You'll be in the clear here if you followed the directive (page 106) to get it in writing.

The phase of your activity we are calling "Carrying Through" should be an orderly 6-week period if everything is in order and you have practiced early-bird tactics.

Your calendar now is marked up, almost day by day, as to what must be accomplished during that work span.

You know that on Tuesday, the 21st, you must get proof sheets back to the photographer.

You know that on Friday, the 24th, you must finish up the news release for the following week and get it to the duplicating room.

It's all there.

It's all in writing on your schedule.

Or it had better be.

And so, with all advance preparations made and materials prepared, and with a schedule as elaborate and as rigid as one for a presidential tour, you again are at a stage of "ready, set, *go.*"

Where should you be by now? Here is a list of reminders to supplement the Timeframe on pages 124–125. These are on the nitty-gritty level. They all should be behind you.

By this date:

1. Any special TV shows, features for the press, etc., have been scheduled or programmed and prepared for release during the countdown.

2. Media mailing lists (including special-interest lists) have been prepared and *sets* of envelopes have been made up so that they are ready to be stuffed and mailed. If time has permitted, a volunteer or other helper has sorted them by ZIP Code.

3. Lists of prospective clients who may enroll or attend have been prepared and those envelopes or brochure labels are ready.

4. The Speakers Bureau (if you plan to use one) will have been activated, and its representatives' schedules are pretty well jelled.

5. Brochures are ready.

6. Posters are ready.

7. Signs are ready or have been ordered.

8. Press tickets have been ordered or are ready.

9. The press badges have been ordered or are ready (see page 168).

10. At least the bare-bones release (see pages 124–125) has been written—plus as many more as you have fodder to prepare.

11. The public-service announcements have been written. In metropolitan areas they are mailed 2 to 4 weeks ahead of the start of the countdown. This kind of early foot (fast start) is not required in smaller communities; in fact, if you get PSAs to smaller stations too early, they may not be aired at the most effective times.

12. The slide(s) to accompany your PSA is all ready for use.

13. You have written to the platform people (speakers and panelists) for photos and speech copies.

 Photos should be printed as they come in, and the prints should be assembled into sets. A good task for a volunteer. When a print comes back, ready for mailing to an outlet, have someone write the person's name on the back, way at the bottom so it won't show through on the final printed copy. *Never* write across any person's face; even writing on the back of a photo sometimes shows through.

14. Background information on the event and all its cosponsors should be ready in your shop. This information should be put in the press kits (which should be ready and waiting) as it comes in. Slight rearrangements of materials can be made later on.

15. Advertisements—if you use them—have been written and assembled, and the ad orders placed.

16. Initial press contacts have been made. (They were made long ago—by mail, by phone, by personal visits to the newsrooms.)

17. Schedules have been drawn up and other items in your magic mix—the detailed formula for the countdown period—have been formulated and circulated.

There are two elements of the 6-week countdown period to keep uppermost in your mind at all times and to impress upon your associates:

First, there is the need to adhere strictly to the various schedules. Check constantly, and tighten up the act when necessary.

Second, there is the need to work effectively and harmoniously with others:

The p.r. task force

The coordinators, chairpersons, and steering committee

The internal and external publics

Your staff and other near associates

Volunteers

The media

WORKING WITH THE TASK FORCE

Most p.r. people, paid or amateur, are great to know. Somehow imaginative, humorous, and interesting folk gravitate to p.r. committee assignments or jobs.

Frequently, they also are:

Insecure

Ambitious

Flighty

Unrealistic

Nervous about position and prerogatives

As the publicity coordinator, information officer, or committee chairperson, you will have as one of your major duties—and headaches—the task of soothing their jangled nerves. Sad to say, their jangled nerves do not unjangle easily and once unjangled are apt to get jangled again at the slightest pretense.

Whether you are publicizing a single program or working on multiple activities, the publicity crew probably will be one of these combinations:

1. You and your own staff
2. You and your staff—with the activity's director or the steering committee chairperson nodding in at frequent and usually inconvenient intervals
3. You and your staff with a publicity committee or p.r. people from other sponsoring agencies
4. You and your staff with professionals (but nonpublicity types) from other agencies
5. You and your staff with outside volunteers
6. You alone (without a paid staff) and any of the people listed immediately above

How do you keep this complex operation going? How do you work with the task force, whatever its makeup?

The key is to treat your coworkers tenderly and be sincere about it. This is one of the places where good manners breed goodwill. Goodwill, in turn, generates comfortable working relationships.

While being gentle and mannerly, and while showing respect for their interests and talents, you also must keep control of the task force's operation. It must not be allowed to develop the confusion which is inevitable when committee members take off on their own.

Here are some strategies to consider as ways of helping your coworkers from the outside feel secure and become operationally effective.

TASK FORCE ASSIGNMENTS

1. Have regularly scheduled task force meetings so that all the members are involved and are kept up to date on the progress of the p.r. campaign.
2. Arm them with agendas, Checklists, Timeframes, and all possible information which can help them be well informed and on schedule with their assignments.
3. When you divide up the chores, have a plan of organization and operation already in hand, and be certain the others request—or are assigned—pleasant

and also necessary tasks which will be to their liking and will cast them in roles which carry some clout.

4. Offer to take over the unpleasant nitty-gritty tasks yourself. Freed of the drudgery which is the most necessary component of a publicity campaign, they will surprise you with the quality and quantity of their effort. (Once in a while, by sheer luck, you will find in your task force a nitty-gritty lover—someone who has a passion for detail. When you find such a person, turn all your nitty-gritty tasks over to him or her, and everyone will be happy.)

5. In this example, we are assuming that you are from the "Big U," or the state league, or the regional office, or some other unit which is larger than the rest. Come on quietly. Forget the gangbuster bit. You are not there—nor is your agency—to take over.

   This is a cooperative venture, remember?

   Again, even if you or your agency controls the budget and format and the whole package, remember to treat others sincerely, at all times as equal partners.

   Remember, *and require staff members to remember,* that even if others come from smaller operations and are totally inexperienced or less experienced than you, they are valuable assets to the effort.

   You can be of value to them, also. Working with you should be a learning experience for them. But you don't have to underscore the fact.

6. Promise them, and their agencies, full billing on all materials released or otherwise used to promote the project. And make certain they get it.

TASK FORCE MEETING SITES

Spend some thought on the *site* of the sessions with the task force. Plan the task force meetings carefully. You will need to schedule three, possibly four. You are going to have to choose one of three approaches:

1. Hold your meetings in the same place each time. This can save time and prevent confusion, since people will not have to remind themselves of different locations for the various meetings.

2. Have each meeting at the headquarters of a different sponsor. This may cause confusion within the group ("Hey, John, do you remember where we're supposed to meet Monday?"), but it will make the task force members look good to their own associates. Many times, when meetings follow this format, you'll find the committee people calling in their bosses to meet the group. On such a bright occasion, the institution or agency may even treat you to lunch! Happens all the time.

3. Have your meetings at a single, neutral location, not connected in any way with any of the project's sponsors. This may be:

a. A conference hall or a convention hall or another kind of public building.
b. An airport meeting room. If your people are coming from various other cities, a meeting room can be reserved at the airport in the city where you are having your session—that is, of course, if you or one of the others belongs to the private "club" of the airline which makes the meeting space available. Almost all the major airlines have such a club, and it is worth the annual dues for one to be able to enjoy this kind of convenience.
c. A hotel meeting room. Also near the airport or near the confluence of interstates, should most of your people be driving in, it is possible to rent a hotel meeting room. If your meeting will last overnight—i.e., if you might meet on Monday evening and until early afternoon Tuesday—a hotel meeting room may be made available to your group without charge if enough of its members are lodged at the hotel.
d. A restaurant or club. Going back to the supposition that most of you are from the same area, a private room in a restaurant or club is a happy solution to "where shall we meet?" In fact, when your task force is made up of busy people on tight schedules, the opportunity to combine a meal and a meeting can be most acceptable.

Wherever your group meets, check the meeting place out—if it's in another city, have a trusted acquaintance check it out—before your first session in it.

It should look and be comfortable.

It should be well ventilated and well lighted—a pleasant and efficient amount of light; light without glare.

There should be ample table space, for people will want to take notes.

A blackboard (don't forget the chalk!) and a paper flip-board are musts for all your task force meetings, especially the first one.

There must be a supply of paper tablets and some pens and pencils. If smoking is to be permitted, plenty of large ashtrays.

There should be ice water and plenty of glasses or paper cups.

When a meeting is scheduled to last more than 1 hour, coffee and soft drinks should be available, as well as some little extras like sweet rolls or cookies. These can be on hand when the committee members enter, or they can be brought in by a waiter after the first hour of the meeting has elapsed.

It helps to know where the nearest copying machines are located, and the locations, also, of the nearest telephones and rest rooms.

 **Parking facilities should be convenient.**

PLANNING TASK FORCE MEETINGS

Six months ahead, or as soon as the project takes shape, you will call the first task force meeting—for organization, the assignment of responsibilities, and "getting to know you."

Two weeks prior to the first task force meeting, you will send each of the members:

1. An agenda. (See the sample on page 145)
2. Any background materials which you can supply, and which explain the project. You *mail* out these materials as a matter of routine—even if you see the other people every working day of your life.

Come to the first meeting prepared with an additional supply of the materials you mailed out originally. About half the p.r. task force members will have forgotten or lost the materials that were mailed to them.

Changes may have been made in the agenda. Additional materials about the project may be available. Have new agendas/materials ready to distribute.

Attendance Record

Open the meeting, and send around an attendance record. This is another must even if half the members belong to the same bridge club, bowling team, or "Friday Forum" discussion group.

Be certain that the signup sheet (attendance record) gets back to you and *that you keep it.* Records have a way of taking on lives of their own and going into hiding.

Copies of the attendance record can be sent later to other task force members—for their information, reports, and files.

A publicist who does a lot of p.r. jobs probably will want to have this form printed up in quantity. It will be easily identifiable on your desk and retrievable in your files if it is on paper that is some color other than white. People who seldom are on such assignments can get the form photocopied in the quantities needed on colored paper.

A person who does p.r. only once or twice a year can add a little dash by having, instead of a blank line for the name of the project, an imprinted title—for example, "Conference on Collective Bargaining by Public Employees," or "Noncredit Course Sequence in the Humanities."

But why have such a fancy attendance record? You all already know each other. Right? And wouldn't a piece of scratch paper or a sheet from a lined yellow pad serve the purpose? Not as well.

Here is why:

P.R. TASK FORCE ATTENDANCE RECORD

PROJECT ——————————— DATE ———————

YOUR NAME	YOUR AGENCY AND TITLE	ADDRESS AND PHONE NUMBER(S)

Notes and Special Instructions:

1. A formal attendance record makes your life easier, because you don't have to look up a bunch of phone numbers and addresses every time you want to communicate with your group.
2. It helps you keep track of the progress of your project by giving you instant recall on who attended each meeting. This is important. If Joe Dunn didn't show up and he was to have been briefed on an assignment or have reported on one, a follow-up on your part is imperative.
3. It helps in reports to your supervisors, whether they are department heads or deans or presidents, or simply the chairpersons of a lay steering committee.
4. Since you will have enough copies made of the sheet used at your meeting to send one to each member of your task force (see above), it encourages a sense of group identification. This team spirit contributes to the high morale needed for a good publicity push.
5. It looks professional. This, again, can be a plus for your p.r. task force. It makes members feel, correctly, that they are a part of an important, well-run operation.

As the attendance record (page 143) is going around, pass out duplicated or updated agendas (see the sample on page 145).

Now begin an explanation of the project. Your people may have had some of this information in the material mailed to them in advance, but it bears repeating. You can do this yourself, or you can have a spokesperson present from the steering committee (the project director would be nice) and let that person do the exposition.

A publicist on a very large project or a cluster of activities which makes up a project may find it useful to have several specialists in attendance at the meeting.

One from program development
One on the budget
One or more from the subject-matter field

First Meeting Agenda

At this earliest meeting of the p.r. task force, goals should be very carefully outlined. The p.r. people should be told:

What the project is
Why it is appropriate to carry out
Something about its format, including dates, hours, and site, if these details have been arranged at this early date
What kinds of people we hope to get to take part—as the audience, on the one hand, and as speakers-panelists-instructors-resource people, on the other

AGENDA, FIRST PUBLICITY COMMITTEE MEETING
10 A.M. September 10,
Conference Room (Room 134), Calumet Bldg.
1416 Maple Street, Freeport

for

THE CAMEL'S BACK

A Conference on Community Values and Tax Referenda

(to be held in February)

1. Introduction of committee members

2. Discussion of the program (title, date, site,
    cosponsors, possible cost to participants,
    target enrollment)

3. The publicity-promotion possibilities and lim-
    itations:

        a. Recommendations to the program committee
        b. Alternative components of the promotion
           campaign
        c. Resources on hand
        d. Budget

4. Assignment to subcommittees or volunteers for
    the first round of tasks:

        a. Media mailing lists
        b. Preparation of initial materials
        c. Early-bird press contacts
        d. Speakers bureau

5. Distribution and discussion of a Timeframe

6. Next meeting date

The cost factors, including a rough idea of what kind of money will be available for publicity

All of this should be very short, in capsule form. After all, you've got 6 months in which to talk about it—haven't you?

Allow a half hour for questions and discussion, but don't let the conversation drag on. Cut it off with "one more question?" After that question, proceed to the next item without delay.

At this point, you can begin talking about the p.r. job which will be demanded of you and the task force if the project is to be completed satisfactorily.

Allocation of Duties

You now go on to assign duties in one of several ways:

1. You can have chosen the p.r. subcommittees in advance, perhaps in consultation with the steering committee chairperson or others who have some knowledge of the character and interests of the various task force members. In this case, be sure that every primary sponsor has at least one of its representatives as a task force subchairperson.
2. You can go to the meeting having appointed the chairpersons, always with their consent, but not other specific members of their committees.
3. You can start from scratch with your task force assignment sheet (not to be confused with your attendance record). An example is on page 148. This sheet was designed for use with a locally based program of modest size. An assignment sheet for a larger, more sophisticated activity would have to be of a more detailed and sophisticated nature. After the signup sheet is returned, you can appoint a chairperson from each group, *or* you can let each committee elect its own chairperson.
4. There is another method of organizing committee work for the promotion-publicity effort involved in a simple local activity addressed to a community's general public. In this form of organization, you divide your people into general committees rather than among specialized functions.

    These groups are:

    Publicity-promotion
    Recruitment (or attendance, if you prefer the term)

    The publicity-promotion committee would work for press contact assistance, would develop the media mailing lists, and would take charge of graphics and printing.

    The recruitment committee members would be first-line workers on attracting participants—the people reachers.

The members of the recruitment committee should receive instructions as to analyzing the community for maximum impact as the publicity and promotion materials go out. Its specific tasks would include:

a. Assembling up-to-date lists of organizations and the addresses of the members of those organizations—people who should receive a mailing, a telephone call, or both.

b. Calling on all the resources of the community, attempting to get endorsement and mailing lists from businesses and from the Chamber of Commerce, the Convention Bureau, the Federated Women's Clubs, the Ministerial Association, and similar organizations.

c. Answering these kinds of questions and acting on the answers: Will the program have a special appeal for the professional men and women listed in the Yellow Pages of the telephone directory? Would senior citizens, city employees, recreational specialists, social service employees, law enforcement officers, farmers, and legislators be interested?

Which is the best way to organize the task force? Each has advantages, each has disadvantages. Most pros take the number 2 approach (p. 146) for task force organization.

Other Task Force Meetings

You call three additional meetings of the publicity task force.

1. Two months after the first organizational meeting, a check session is required. Put these things on the agenda:

a. Signup and introductions. (You will have this every time; attendance will vary from meeting to meeting as people have conflicts and send substitutes or as others join or drop out of the group.)

b. Reports on and discussion of all publicity-promotion activities to date in relation to the Timeframe.

The media mailing lists
Preparation of materials
Press contacts
Speakers Bureau
Budget
Problems, concerns, and bright ideas

c. Progress of the program. By now, the major program slots should have been filled in by the program committee, and the publicity task force should analyze the rosters of speakers, instructors, or panelists as to their drawing power.

(For a simple local program or class
addressed to the general public)

Publicity—Promotion Task Force Assignment Sheet
Subcommittee Preferences

Press contact assistance
(local)
1.
2.
3.
4.
5.

Media mailing lists
assistance (local, special—
interest, 50—mi. radius)

1.
2.
3.
4.
5.

Graphics and printing
assistance (bids, schedule,
arrangements)

1.
2.
3.
4.
5.

Typing, stuffing, mailing
assistance

1.
2.
3.
4.
5.

Press contact assistance
(50—mi. radius)

1.
2.
3.
4.
5.

Speakers Bureau*

1.
2.
3.
4.
5.

Distribution of promotional
materials

1.
2.
3.
4.
5.

Press kit assistance*
1.
2.
3.
4.
5.

*The press kit and the Speakers Bureau will be needed only
in a larger program, one where your target audience is up—
wards of 150—200 people.

2.   The third meeting is crucial. It will be 6 weeks, give or take a day or two, after your second publicity committee session, and 6 weeks before your D day. It will mark the start of the promotion blitz, the 6-week countdown.

　　　The format will follow that of the first two meetings, except that the group will get down to specifics, with the various subcommittees filling in the rest of the overall committee on such things as plans for press conferences and the press room.

　　　Duties and responsibilities for D day will be allocated, either through assignment or through volunteering. For an indication of the various duties which are appropriate, see the section on D day. However, these will include the press room aide(s), floaters at registration, the press conference aide(s), and the gopher(s) or subordinates.

　　　In some cases, people may want to "volunteer" a fellow staff member for typing, gophering, and other duties, themselves remaining free for the more socially involved tasks such as serving as floaters—in the press conference slots—and in facilitating coverage for the visiting press.

3.   A wrap-up meeting about a week before the program may be necessary. However, it may be more efficient to put it off until the night before or the morning of the activity itself—late enough so all functions except those for D day should have been performed, but early enough so that you can set up an emergency operation if something has fallen between the chairs.

WORKING WITH THE STEERING COMMITTEE

Good relationships with the steering committee of your program are critically important. The steering committee, if you remember, is made up of the key planners and coordinators of the entire program or other activity. They are representatives of the sponsors; they are special-interest or departmental experts; they are the organizers of the overall activity and those who will carry it through to completion. They are the brass.

　　　Good rapport and good working team attitudes can, of course, help the p.r. campaign; a lack of them can diminish it. So it is a matter of both courtesy and good operation that this central group be made aware of your plans and progress all along the way.

　　　In an early phase of the project, as soon as it begins to take shape, give the steering committee an outline of what your campaign will consist of. Include estimates as to the cost of each component of that campaign.

　　　Then, on a regular basis, bring it up to date. If the program is 6 months or so in the planning, one report a month will suffice during the initial weeks, the gearing-up phase, and carrying through. As D day approaches, it may be necessary for you to consult with at least the chair or cochair daily.

　　　Put all reports to and for the task force in writing; date them; circulate them to all who conceivably could need to know anything about the particular matters you are reporting on, and keep *at least two copies for your own files.*

As chief publicist, you meet regularly with the steering committee (program committee, codirectors of the project, conference staff, whatever they call themselves as a group). If you do not meet regularly with the steering committee, you have flubbed that part of the responsibility we advised you to assume on pages 16–17.

Or half-flubbed it. You certainly have failed in the part of the job in which you were advised to deal yourself in early. But all is not lost—or need not be. The program still is 6 weeks off. Be very firm about the fact that you *now must*—repeat *must*—be advised of and present at all future meetings of the committee and its subcommittees—right up into D day.

Working with the program's planning and administrative body takes tactics tailored to their knowledge of your role or lack of it.

You will find that, except in cases so rare as to be unheard of, the steering committee members are pretty dim about exactly how effective p.r. is achieved. And that makes them unsure of themselves and of you. To put their minds at rest, keep them well apprised of what is going on as you go about promoting the activity they have been working on for so long.

Each time you meet with the steering committee, give them something to look at and read. This makes the average person comfortable. Something, they tell themselves, is being done; something is being accomplished. Good. We're getting on.

What will you give them? Your p.r. schedule of releases, broadcast dates, press conferences, all those things, if you have not done this already during the gearing-up period.

Second time, perhaps a sample facts sheet, together with written information on any change in or additions to the schedule. *Written,* I said. Committee members tend to forget the spoken word as soon as they leave for the coffee break.

And on subsequent dates, why not a copy of the layout for the brochure? Or copies of a favorable answer to your request to the program's star speaker that he or she arrive early enough for a press conference?

Samples of the public-service announcements which (you have been told) will be on local radio this week. Committee members will ask you why you did not include this bit of information or that, or the other. You will have a chance to explain to them the mysteries of PSAs and why they have to run just a certain number of lines. They will be impressed, informed, and satisfied.

Be very certain that your steering committee members themselves block out segments of their own personal time for possible interviews, statements, and photographs. This becomes a special concern if the topic being addressed has even a smidgen of controversy.

The steering committee members want publicity. They want the program to attract a large attendance or enrollments.

But when the press calls to schedule interviews with steering committee members, don't allow them to plead a conflict or be "just too busy." Insist on their leaving or making time for the press.

And, as in working with any others in the course of publicizing a program, deal with the steering committee with good humor and good manners.

Your associates and *their* associates, particularly when the sponsors include agencies not associated with your own institution, business, or organization, may from time to time request a memorandum to present to a parent committee or funding source.

This memorandum should be as detailed as you can make it. In drawing it up, you should:

First, indicate the important time factor.

Second, bear down on the support factor of temporary help—or permanent, if the venture is an ongoing activity.

Third, be realistic about costs without going into dime-by-dime pricing out.

Fourth, be careful to remain realistic and not arouse false hopes on the part of the inexperienced people on the committee.

Example: The memorandum on page 152–157 is an actual supporting memorandum for a proposed pilot project in which storefront adult counseling centers were to have been placed in two communities—a large, metropolitan area and a smaller, middle-sized city. Only a couple of minor editorial changes to generalize the memorandum for wider use as a pattern have been made.

The program did not jell until spring, making the lead time for such an elaborate effort slim to the point of nonexistence. The project self-aborted.

WORKING WITH VOLUNTEERS

Volunteers can be an asset to any publicity task force if their talents are used wisely and selectively.

It sometimes is hard for one of the paid staff members—the hired hands on the year-round payroll—to take into consideration that the volunteers we work with are *not* being paid for the hard work they put into the project. The volunteers become indignant or disinterested because:

The regular staff is impatient with them and is not giving them open credit for their efforts.

People treat them gruffly and/or try to saddle them with trivial tasks which hold no challenge.

P.R. Timeframe for Steering Committee Information

TO: Project Director

FROM: Helen Farlow

RE: Public information activities in connection
        with the ADULT COUNSELING PROJECT. Target date
        for the opening of the pilot centers is Sept. 1.

A. PRELIMINARY (PRECOUNTDOWN) PUBLICITY
    1. At least two general releases should go in late
May or early June. The first should describe the project in attractive, general terms. The second should
give details on the pilots.
    2. At that time (June) preliminary approaches
should be made by the information services staff to
the news media in the two locations, re feature
stories, talk show appearances, etc. This is the time
for the spadework.
    3. Also at that time (or in early July; at any
rate, six to eight weeks before the countdown), the
public service announcements should go out in both
areas (see below, C-2).
    4. Late May and early June also is the period when
preparation of all special mailing lists for the project should be completed.
    5. All contacts should be made with organizations,
industries, and others whom we hope will use information about the project in their magazines or newsletters, and/or (in the smaller city) book a short appearance by one of our spokespersons at their meeting or
staff conference.

B. THE BUILDUP
    1. The objective is to get the project director and
possibly others on television (a) in the smaller city
and (b) in the metropolitan area, in talk show appearances. For this purpose, the p.r. person will have to
spend several days in the larger city on at least two
occasions, plus a third stay of up to a week (this last
time with the director) during which the previously
scheduled appointments will be honored.
    2. The same kind of work must be done, simulta-
neously, in regard to the radio talk shows and "call
in" shows.

3. The newspapers, magazines, news bureaus of national publications, the whole works. Same kind of thing, simultaneously.

C. THE COUNTDOWN

1. Six releases, at weekly intervals, each giving NEW information, but also briefly recapping the vital facts, starting the week of July 21.

2. Public-service announcements (see D for mailing lists) on TV and radio.

3. In the larger city, p.r. saturation, using all available tools and approaches in the neighborhoods of (a) the facility to be used and (b) the neighborhoods of the cosponsors.

4. The radio-TV appearances should take place during this period.

5. Posters, flyers, brochures should go out--but everywhere--and supplies of the first two should be replenished on a regular schedule.

6. "Speakers Bureau" (E-5) should be activated. Note that these contacts must be made in late spring, as many organizations are comparatively inactive during the summer months and their newsletters often are suspended during that period.

D. THE MAILING LISTS

Not all of the releases will go to every media outlet on all of the mailing lists; the cost would be prohibitive. However, we should try to cover as wide a spectrum as possible. We will piggyback with other compatible mailings wherever possible, in order to save postage.

1. The combined pilots ("pilots" are trial runs or exemplary patterns of operation)
   a. All dailies in the state
   b. The press associations, city news bureau, p.r. wire, etc.
   c. The national bureaus in the larger city (Monitor, *Time* magazine, etc.)
   d. Statewide magazines
2. The smaller city pilot
   a. Heavy coverage to the locals--the daily papers; the television stations (all three commercial networks and the educational network); radio (the commercial stations giving heavy news coverage, plus one educational station and a campus-based "student" station); sporadically, some underground press.

Note: At some time, we will have to make a decision on
        the radius to be covered: will it be the commu-
        nity only? the county? the communities included
        in the junior college district? a 30- 50- or
        75-mile radius?

        b. All kinds of local publications—club, church,
            civic (chambers of commerce, etc.), profes-
            sional, educational, women's movement, etc.;
            the possibilities are infinite. This takes a
            lot of work; not hard, just time-consuming,
            and is one of the places we can use temporary
            help.

    3. The metropolitan area pilot. This is a biggie.
There will be many decisions to be made re the breadth
of coverage, and this will have aspects other than the
obvious one dealing with geography.

        a. All on the combined pilot list (D-1, above)
        b. Neighborhood coverage (both as to sponsors
            and as to facility site).
        c. Citywide coverage, including features in
            newspapers (the metropolitan dailies, the big
            chains, and again the neighborhood; TV and
            radio talk shows; "house organs" (business
            and industry); the labor press; the under-
            ground press; the ethnic press; the black
            press; the religious press, etc.
        d. We must not ignore the foreign language radio
            station(s) and special programs; those beamed
            at the inner city; and the educational sta-
            tion(s). Again, early decisions are needed on
            area of coverage. The city? the county? the
            metropolitan area (which includes several
            counties)? One thing that only your friendly
            neighborhood demographer knows for sure—
            with a few publicists thrown in—is that not
            all the suburbs are glossy and affluent. Many
            of them are, in fact, suburban slums, and
            others have great pockets of underprivileged.
            These are some of the people we most want to
            reach.

E. AUXILIARY EFFORTS
    We will need:
    1. Large quantities of
        a. Brochures—fairly complete and explanatory
        b. Flyers—one sheet come-ons; throwaways

  c. Posters--to be put where people pass or congregate: banks, supermarkets, institutional and organizational bulletin boards, etc.

Placing of posters could well be a function of our sponsors and should be coordinated as far as distribution is concerned, not by the p.r. office but by someone like a part-time graduate student. I am not certain what it costs, but we might explore the cost of a limited and selective group of those little billboards on the "L" platform or in the buses.

2. This is optional, but if the budget can be stretched, and as a trial for future use as we go into other communities, I really would like to try a paid commercial on a major metropolitan radio program. This could be coded. A special (temporary) post office box number is a good, cheap, easy way. Another is to have inquiries directed to a special address, such as someone's office other than the director's.

3. We will need lots of pictures of everyone whose efforts in this program we are going to feature. This isn't as expensive as it sounds. One-column glossies cost 11¢ apiece at the photo lab; less, I think, in larger quantities.

4. We need vitas of all those who would fall under #3.

5. In the smaller but not the larger city, we must have our people ready to talk (five-minute spots) to service and other clubs and groups. We will have to operate a regular "Speakers Bureau," and this could be another place where junior staff could take over; however, I will be happy to help with preliminaries, since I know a lot of people and could suggest contacts.

F. AMENITIES
1. Special letterheads listing all sponsors. This would not be bond (at least for p.r. purposes); it would be inexpensive lightweight duplicating paper, and the letterheads would be used for the first sheet only. This makes for good feelings.

2. A meeting in the metropolitan area of all the public relations people for all the sponsors involved. Past experience has shown that they probably will not wish to become involved in the actual task of publicity/promotion; people in these jobs usually--especially in smaller schools--have pretty much of an overload. However, they will wish to be informed and

to be given a chance to contribute help and information on special items in their areas of particular
interest and expertise, where they have individual
warm relationships with people in the media.

3. <u>A meeting in the smaller city</u> of all the p.r.
people who might, as they deal with their various publics, need to have knowledge about the pilots. This is
a bigger group than you might think, and the people
from the cosponsoring agencies should be included as
well as those on our own campus.

4. <u>Another meeting in the smaller city</u>, this time
for people we can get together who might be valuable
in getting the word out—people from the North End,
from the women's movement, from civic organizations,
from the churches and social agencies, etc. We might
call this "The Advisory Committee on Information" or
some such. The purpose is to get many groups (and
opinion leaders in the various segments of the commu-
nity/area) involved with a personal interest in the
project.

5. <u>Open houses</u>, over several days and evenings, in
each location. We will need a good deal of informative
material, and possibly some exhibits, for this will be
an important function. One of its end results will be
to let all the people who have been active in various
phases of the project's preparatory states actually <u>do</u>
something visible; another will be on—spot news coverage as opposed to the prepared releases and the feature stories/appearances that will have preceded it.

6. <u>Press kits</u> will be prepared for use in connection with the promotion—publicity efforts, at the
"grand openings" or whatever, and for reference use by
the news media. The gathering in of all the kinds of
information useful in a press kit has an added value—
it helps provide a sort of guideline for making sure
we have covered all the bases, and that anything which
might even remotely be needed as media (or staff) information is right at hand in a convenient form. I
should think the press kits also might have some use
when and if we move from the pilots into additional
communities, as it would give our cooperating sponsors
in those communities an idea of the actual pro-
gram/project we are proposing.

It would be really nice to have the metropolitan

p.r. meeting involve luncheon or perhaps afternoon re-
freshments for the local group, since this may be late
afternoon, or evening, or both. However, this sort of
frill can be eliminated in the interests of economy,
even though it does have a definite plus factor in
stimulating informality and a relaxed and cooperative
atmosphere.

G. AND SO ON. . . .

1. A prime necessity for a good, all-out professional public relations effort, providing maximum information to a maximum target audience, is the allocation of <u>plenty of time</u>—time for the professional
staff to do its work; time when, without hurry, the
director and the others will be available for interviews and public appearances in both cities.

2. We also need some budget for this kind of a public relations effort. I will get our financial officer
to obtain some kind of a ballpark estimate. However,
we need to think in terms of temporary clerical
(typist; list maker; bright, perhaps local student in
a summer job) help; staff travel and per diem; duplicating and postage (including the letterheads and
other paper and envelopes); printing and design of the
brochures, flyers, posters; some equipment (rent or
borrow a good typewriter and a dictating apparatus).

This list is really not all that expensive (G-2),
and every effort will be made to keep costs down. My
salary and that of my associates are not on a revolv-
ing basis, so professional staff time is not an actual
added cost, but in fact is a university expense. Our
unit's duplicating room and the university's photo lab
provide excellent services at costs which cannot be
matched or approached elsewhere. We don't have any office rent to pay. Most of our equipment is right at our
fingertips and was paid for long ago.

To sum up this budget discussion, please allocate a
sizable block of time, enough money for temporary
help, production costs of p.r. materials, staff travel
and per diem (including such expenses as cabs, phones,
etc.).

It also is useful (sometimes necessary) to have
some sort of a small contingency cushion for the
emergency which somehow always occurs.

They are asked to contribute unreasonable work loads and to work at hours which conflict with their regular jobs or their family life.

OK. They don't have to do this. They quit.

You are the loser.

A volunteer usually has some dedication to the project beyond that of the paid staff members, for whom it is only another assignment. A large proportion of volunteers are fully as disciplined as professionals. You have lost that element of dedication, enthusiasm, and channeled energy.

A volunteer usually knows a lot of people whom neither you nor any member of your staff knows. You have lost that entrée into new areas of recruitment.

A volunteer who comes from a cosponsoring agency or organization may have more background on the history and development of the root idea behind this project than you have. You have lost that valuable source of information.

A volunteer—any volunteer—has gifts and capabilities not shared by you or others with whom you work. You could have made use of those gifts and capabilities.

To generalize, volunteers can add the most to the project if:

1. Time is taken to ascertain their particular interests and capabilities.
2. Responsibilities and assignments are given to them which take advantage of and build on these capabilities and interests. Be creative as you think of ways they can enhance the project and its p.r. effort.
3. Their work is monitored, rather than supervised. Do check at intervals— courteously and appreciatively. Do, if necessary (and how many times is it not necessary!), make suggestions and rap about the assignment. Do help and instruct, but with the utmost tact and interest in their interests.
4. They are given full credit at every step along the way. This is not an apple-for-the-teacher tactic. They deserve that credit; they have worked for it; they have given up their leisure time and expended their energy. It is due them and it should be honored.

PROFESSIONAL VOLUNTEERS

Happy circumstances often emerge wherein a friendly professional may be willing to help out for free or for a modest stipend. A program or other continuing education activity which you are trying to publicize may be dear to the heart of an editor, news director, reporter, or newscaster. It may be a pet project for someone in graphics, advertising, or printing.

Think about the possible payment of a token stipend to your friend in the media—and here, we are not talking about contracting out the promotion-publicity to an advertising agency or publicity agency. People in the media frequently are glad to take on individual p.r. jobs on a one-shot or continuing basis. This means moonlighting, but what with double-digit inflation, it can be a blessing all around.

I know of one community college—there probably are similar instances in all kinds of outreach settings—which has contracts for part-time year-round p.r. work with a good media person who has his own commercial public relations firm in the area.

Some of you may have people from the media right in your constituencies as friends, coworkers, fellow club members, adjunct faculty members, and so on. These people—writers, editors, reporters, newscasters, p.r. people, advertising people—may be willing to help you with your outreach p.r. as a public service or for a minimum amount of money.

Or even as unpaid volunteers.

Latch onto them. You have just found a gold mine.

Among other things, your friendly neighborhood editor or news director can help you with releases, mailing pieces, and poster copy. He or she can even—heaven forbid that he or she'd ever have to—prevent your mailing pieces from going out with errors or grammatical goofs.

Also, when you are in touch with people in the media, don't be afraid to ask for a little advice and a little help.

Don't ignore that word "little."

Ask for a *little* help.

Don't ask for too much.

Don't do it too often.

These are rushed, understaffed, busy people.

But the way to a reporter's or an editor's or a news director's heart sometimes can be found through sympathy on his part or hers for a self-admitted dumb cluck who has a job to do but doesn't know how to do it.

PHASE III

D DAY AND THE PRESS: FACILITIES AND MECHANICS

THE DAY YOU HAVE WORKED AND WAITED FOR

For weeks, months, even a year, you have been thinking about, preparing for, and maybe dreading it like the blazes.

What?

D day, of course. The day or days of the program that you've been publicizing and promoting.

Be of good cheer. D day isn't all that bad. There will be so much going on, and on so many levels, that the hours will rush past you into tomorrow. And, if you've been the early bird this book has tried to prod you into being—if your arrangements have been made and your work has been done, up to the smallest detail—D day will be a walk-through.

Depending upon the size, degree of sophistication, and news appeal of the project, D day may involve such activities and embellishments as the operation of a press room, the management of one or more press conferences, and the development of a press kit.

You will find step-by-step directions for these on pages 168–200.

SETTING UP

GET THERE EARLY

A factor which is basic to your p.r. efforts surrounding D day is to be on hand early—very early—at the site where the activity will take place or is centered.

If you're conducting the program on home turf—in the building where you work, maybe, or across the street—you will not have to worry about getting there early. You are already there. But being on home turf sometimes poses particular problems, more than those you may encounter in a strange place or otherwise away from your own backyard.

People will impinge on your concentration on this important effort. They will want things. Worse, when you can't conjure up an unmannerly response, they will hang around to chat.

As far as you can—and make sure that you can!—clear your calendar and conscience of all other projects, programs, commitments, and concerns until you get this one out of the way—even if you have to hide from all except your immediate staff, those assigned to this activity, and the press.

Be rude if you have to (and you may have to, particularly if there are graduate students or young coworkers pulling at your sleeve and clamoring for your attention). There is no one in the world more self-important than many inexperienced young people, and no activity is nearly as important as the one (probably minuscule in potential and priority) in which the neophyte is engaged.

Many public discussion and other continuing education programs are held away from home—at a hotel or a convention center, perhaps. Be there ahead of time—well ahead.

Get to the program site the afternoon before the gun goes off or the gavel goes down. No later, and earlier is better. Take your assistants with you.

Your budget person may raise Cain at the prospect of a carload or so of people spending an extra per diem out of the precious budget. Manage that person any way you can. Fight with the budget person. Ignore him or her. Wheedle.

There are *so* many reasons why this is necessary. If you ever fail to get to your program site the day before, you'll count these reasons off with sorrow and dismay: ITEM: My p.r. group walked into a conference location (a combined hotel and center) on the day *before* D day to hear ourselves being paged and paged and paged. We didn't get out of the lobby phone booths for several hours.

The reason was that news had broken out that the Reverend Jesse Jackson, one of our speakers, had received a threat on his life, and the media wanted to know—quite properly—if he was going to cancel out. Was the press conference scheduled for the next day called off? What precautions were being taken?

The scramble lasted several hours. We had to get a statement from Reverend Jackson's headquarters. We had to call back all members of the press who had inquired and leave messages for the others. We had to alter our arrangements considerably—move the press conference into an unannounced suite (we had couriers out who informed the individual members of the media of the new press conference location as they arrived at the previously designated place).

Without those extra hours what merely was a climax could have been a catastrophe.

ITEM: Another city, another hotel, another year. A news-generating United States senator was a major speaker. The evening before he was to arrive (and yes, we were there ahead of time, "wasting" a per diem), the city hotel workers' union went on strike. No restaurants, no maid service, very sketchy switchboard operation by willing but inept managerial types who didn't know how.

And that picket line!

The senator, honoring both management and labor, corroborated by phone that no, he could not cross the picket line. What a night that was! We moved his speech session to the auditorium of a nearby parochial school. We moved the press conference to the airport. The good people who came to the conference got a self-service buffet instead of the fine banquet the committee had planned.

But they both were good conferences, thanks to our early arrival.

In my experiences alone—and I wager that there isn't a p.r. person, in or out of continuing education, who can't match them, sad tale by sad tale—I have seen whole programs, confirmed and with contracts signed and all arrangements made months before, go through a kaleidoscopic change overnight as travel plans went askew, airports became snowed in or fogbound, or personal and professional emergencies arose.

I've also seen people called in off the bench to take the place of those detained.

I have seen plans hastily reworked to fit the changing conditions.

I have seen good programs emerge from what could have been wreckage—and only because we were on hand ahead of time.

Another reason why you must be on hand early concerns the matter of the "futures files" in the media offices. Remember that the media person who has been handling your releases and therefore is familiar with the project probably will not be the person who will cover the event.

A reporter or newscaster, however capable, who is green about your project walks into work and finds that the day's assignment is to get over to the conference center and handle your national symposium on blood diseases (or whatever).

The assignments editor may have a clip or so to give the reporter, or may not. The press kit you sent or hand-carried into the newsroom probably is lost somewhere on a rewrite desk, or has been cannibalized in the staff's process of doing features or news advances on it.

So here comes Hans or Maggie or whoever the reporter is, and he or she doesn't know much, if anything, about the activity you are promoting. A smart reporter will try to call or locate the news source, and that person is you. Be there, ready to help, where reporters can find you.

When you run a press room in connection with your event, you should set it up the night before D day, if at all possible. It is possible only if the conference center or hotel management is kind and understanding, and of course if there is not another event scheduled in that same room the evening before D day. If you can't manage a day-before setup of the press room, get in as early on D day as you can. (Details about a press room are on pages 168–180.)

BASIC D-DAY RULES

The basic D-day rules for the publicity-promotion people, yourself most of all, are three and only three in number.

These three are:

Be party-ready. (If you have to empty one ice tray after the first guest arrives, you are not party-ready.)

Be an early bird.

Check and double-check.

Oh, we could add a few others—"be flexible," for one. But the three are laws of that particular jungle which we call continuing education publicity and promotion.

Unless the whole evening before is a turmoil of crises, get to bed early. There will be time enough to socialize when the project is over. See that your helpers observe this rather simple but oft abused precaution.

On D day itself, regardless of what time the program is to start—i.e., morning, noon, or evening—get up early. Get your helpers up early. And get at it.

Be smart about nutrition and other things which will keep you going over this period of intensive activity: Eat a good breakfast. You don't know when you'll get another chance to eat. Sure, there's a conference luncheon; sure there's a banquet. Can't you eat the conference meals? Don't be silly. Another law of the p.r. jungle is that you are always—but always—called away to the phone, or to help an on-site reporter, or simply to take i.d. (names and other identification) for a photographer, right when everyone else sits down to eat.

If you are going to be really bright about taking every chance to keep going through a time of physical and mental strain, you will follow the advice of veteran p.r. persons:

Do not miss any—repeat, *any*—chance to eat (even if you are not hungry); to visit the rest room (even if . . .); or (if you are female) to have your hair done (even if it's holding up pretty well) or (if you are male) get a shave (even if your 5 o'clock shadow isn't showing yet).

I dare you to laugh. *You'll find out!*

So you're up; you've showered and dressed; you've eaten a good breakfast. Ready, set, let's go.

First, go back and review every detail of the program and every detail of the provisions for press coverage and press amenities.

1. *Check the press room.* Put a sign out front (page 175) and another sign on a table just inside the door, situated so as to be a partial barricade to easy entrance. This helps keep interlopers out.

    Is everything in place and connected (such as electric typewriters and telephones)?

    Are supplies and handout materials in place?

    Is the press room staffed? (It *must* be staffed, *at least a half day before the program starts.* See pages 172–175 for particulars about equipment, materials, and staffing.)

    If you've ordered beverages and snacks, like soft drinks and coffee and cookies or rolls, check out your order with catering.

2. *Check the press conference site.* Go look at the room where the conference will be held, using the Checklist on pages 182–185 (even if you've checked it earlier). Don't forget such important small things as the modesty skirt on the table where your speaker will sit.

 **Remember to mix up the chairs so the room will have that casual look; the schoolroom setup is deadly. Break chairs out of row arrangements into a casual, free-form half circle.**

---

3. With your aides, be back in the press conference room at least an hour before the press conference is scheduled to start.

4. *Synchronize press activities with the steering committee.* If there are persons from the steering committee and/or sponsoring agencies or organizations who are acting as hosts and who will meet the dignitary or headliner(s) and escort the star(s) to the press conference, double-check the hosts' schedules with them, and browbeat them into displaying the same early foot you are cultivating in yourself. If the personage who will be interviewed could arrive at any of several entrances to the building, post scouts.

5. *Check the press table* and the "Reserved" sign (see page 168) in the conference banquet hall.

6. *Check the room where the general session or the panels or workshops or class will be held.* Make certain that the tables for the working press are marked off and cordoned off, and that each guard and aide has been advised to keep interlopers out of the areas reserved for the working press.

7. *Now check with the program's registration desk crew.* Talk with each individual—don't leave anything to chance. Make very certain that *each person* on that crew is aware of the exact press arrangements, or complimentary press and admission tickets, or other amenities, and of the fact that you or your surrogate is there to help the press and that any person (however unlikely looking) who walks in and announces that he or she is a member of the working press should be referred to you (or your aide) without any delay whatsoever.

8. After the press conference, or if a press conference has not been scheduled, work your way back to the conference registration desk (whose crew has been provided with extra materials—press kits, speech copies, etc., stashed safely nearby for possible use if added starters in the press corps arrive).

   Ensure that all members of the press are greeted and assisted in finding seats, are provided with all materials, are helped in arranging interviews, and are cordially invited to social occasions.

9. An important duty of all staff members and members of all committees—including the steering committee and your task force—is to assist in making an on-the-spot evaluation of the activity. Assigning people to this task may not come to anyone's mind but yours, so check to see that it has been done.

The best way to make certain that all these bases are covered is to do it yourself. Yet sometimes a press conference hour will conflict with that "registration period" of about 1 to 2 hours immediately prior to the start of the program. You can't be at both places simultaneously, so assign a very bright, dedicated, well-briefed, and conscientious aide or associate as a floater around the registration area until you can hurry back from the press conference.

THE INEVITABLE EMERGENCY

There is an immutable law which some credit to Casey Stengel and some to another person (unknown to me) called "Murphy." Stengel's Law—or, if you insist, Murphy's Law—is:

Anything that can go wrong, will.

Nowhere does this hold more true than in the case of p.r.—particularly educational p.r. The reason is that many of our associates are conditioned to the rarefied atmosphere of the ivy-clad towers, where practicality is viewed as something gauche.

Oh, I count my bruises and the stitches on my brow, as do my fellows in this exasperating and exciting field of endeavor.

What will go wrong?

Who knows?

The only thing you can be certain of is that it *will* happen. An emergency will occur:

Someone you confidently trusted to carry out a chore didn't do it.

Someone invited the Governor to attend, and he does—expecting full press coverage of what he considers an important policy statement on an occasion which you (and the press) had considered not that newsworthy. No one told you the Governor was coming—no one told you that he'd even been invited!

Someone, without telling you, changed the location of the press room or the press conference. Worse, you learn when you get there that no space has been reserved as the press room or for the press conference or that a room so reserved has been preempted.

Your supplies are lost, and the mail room never saw them.

It will happen, all right.

Which is why you must be confident, prepared for all foreseeable emergencies, calm but swift to act in case of crises. And—if you can—manage a reassuring but not silly smile.

Don't panic, don't lose heart. It will, somehow, all be over tomorrow. There will come another day and another crisis, but next time coping will be that much easier, and your scar tissue will become, in time, armor.

As to the program itself—the one you've been promoting so long, the one in the hall or auditorium just behind the registration desk and across from the press room, where you've been fending—go in and hear the speeches or the lecture or attend the class or see the movie—if you want to.

If you don't want to, you still must stay nearby and keep yourself available and flexible, so that you can assist the members of the press and help them do well in this effort. It's your job.

Operate firmly on the basis of that attitude engendered by Stengel's (Murphy's) Law, and hold to it without swerving until the program is over—even if it's a conference which lasts 3 days or a symposium which lasts 5.

You can relax, but only after the program winds up. Then and only then you're entitled to a nap—with the phone off the hook, natch; or to take a day off; or even to have a drink of wine or sarsaparilla or whatever is your pleasure.

But don't expect any recognition or thanks from on high. As Captain Bligh said, "You don't knight a man for doing his duty." Or a p.r. peon.

And don't begrudge or resent it if you don't get accolades from above. The pro—and most anyone who has done a job in a professional manner—can, and should, take fierce pride in having done that job well. It is its own reward. (Not, of course, that you shouldn't also realize that the job could be done a little better next time.)

D-DAY OPERATIONS, ARRANGEMENTS, AND AMENITIES

PRESS BADGES

Members of the press should, of course, be supplied with conference kits and with conference badges, along with tickets or passes to all conference functions.

If you wish to differentiate members of the press from the others who are attending the program, you give them specially printed press badges; you can use a color for their name cards that is different from the color of the name cards of the others; or you can take a regular badge and mark it in some way with a gummed label (star, dot, whatever).

MEALS FOR THE PRESS

When working with your steering committee and, through it, with the caterers at your conference site, make provision for a press table at conference meals. Not all reporters who cover a major program will be able to break away from their jobs to attend those meals (see pages 179–180). Those who do attend the meals may wish to sit with members of the audience, rather than with their buddies from the working press, in order to get the "feel" of the occasion and participate in audience reaction.

A press table in dining rooms, however, is an important matter of courtesy and service. It should have a sign on it which says "Reserved for Working Press."

It should be fairly well up front, so that the reporters can see and hear everything that is going on.

It also should be situated fairly close to a door, in case reporters are called to the telephone or have to leave the banquet room early to file for a deadline or conduct an interview. These things happen. You may find it hard to reserve a press table at conference meals which has these two attributes—being close to the front and being close to a door. Look around a little. It may be easier than you think. A "door" does not have to be the main entrance. It can be a side door (even one leading to the outside), or the door through which the food is transported by waiters.

HOW TO RUN A PRESS ROOM

When a Press Room Is Justified

The average practitioner of p.r. for an educational or similar public program seldom will be called upon to organize and run a press room.

A press room becomes a must only under certain circumstances:

1. The activity is large and complex.
2. It lasts more than 1 day. (There are exceptions.)
3. It attracts more than a few reporters and newscasters.
4. It involves an intricate schedule of press conferences and interviews.
5. You have sizable amounts of handout materials for the news media (background information, advance copies of a speech, etc.).

The key points on the list above are 3 and 4.

There is no need for a press room unless you have an array of name speakers or specialists on topics which fairly sizzle with public interest. The press room approach is called for only when you have important speakers or performers coming in and out at various times (necessitating press conferences), and/or when you have a number of sessions, possibly conflicting or interlocking, on subjects of major concern to the news media.

You'll get an idea of when a press room is called for if we cite a few organizations whose programs regularly require such a service facility.

The annual meetings of the major health organizations—the American Medical Association, the American Dental Society, etc.—always have press rooms; so do the national conventions of the League of Women Voters and the Federated Women's Clubs; so do the meetings of the American Association for the Advancement of Science; so do any major meetings of national organizations (or programs which such organizations sponsor) which can be counted on to spawn a great deal of news and feature coverage. The average locally sponsored or statewide activity usually doesn't justify the time and expense of a press room, although if the meeting is important (and controversial) enough, this fact can be reversed.

Usually, you can operate from a desk near the registration table, and out of your room, office, briefcase, and a few cardboard boxes.

When we talk about "reporters" in the context of a press room, we of course mean those dealing in both print and broadcast media. We do not necessarily mean only reporters from daily or weekly newspapers or from local or area radio and TV. The "press" may very well be writers or commentators with special subject-matter interests who are associated with programs or magazines, journals, or columns dealing with such special topics.

A press room, particularly if your reporters are from out of town, is a convenience for both the reporters and the speakers, as well as for yourself.

It gives the reporters a working base. This is doubly important if your program is held at an auditorium, a coliseum, or any kind of hall or facility which is away—even as far as across the street—from the hotel in which the reporters are housed. It thus saves them from their two most precious commodities in the stress of big-event coverage—time and effort.

With a press room as headquarters, reporters can make telephone calls, they can write copy, they can pick up handouts and supplementary materials as these become available, and they can relax and talk shop.

In some instances, they also can use the press room as a site for informal interviews, although an interview is not always feasible in such crowded, cluttered, and usually noisy surroundings.

For the speakers, panelists, and other program participants in your activity, the press room is a place:

1. Where they can make contact with the p.r. staff.
2. Where they can leave their handout materials. So often a major speaker arrives with one or, at the most, two copies of his or her address in a briefcase, expecting the p.r. people to have it duplicated and distributed! Therefore, the publicist should have made advance arrangements to have the use of a copying machine (even on the weekend and in the evening, if the event takes place at those times).
3. Where, under the right circumstances, they can give informal statements or on-the-spot interviews to the press.

Given the reservations stated above regarding holding interviews in the press room itself, you may want to provide some sort of adjunct facility or "quiet room" for interviews.

"Quiet Room"

The "quiet room" can be someone's sleeping room (if the program is held in a hotel), or any unoccupied room where individual interviews can be held and where reporters can call their home offices *without being overheard by other reporters.*

Why is a "quiet room" necessary?

The privacy (or lack-of-privacy) factor.

The noise factor in the general press room and in corridors and corners of meeting rooms where catch-as-catch-can interviews often take place.

Even more important, the curiosity factor. Nothing attracts attention and a horde of disruptive observers faster than a TV camera or the sight of an (obvious) reporter-questioner with a notebook.

The potential of an exclusive. During a big and complex program activity, reporters often seek different sorts of information. At a health-related conference, for example, one reporter might want to talk about "crib death" and another about a possible breakthrough in the treatment of leukemia. Then, too, some reporters do their homework—i.e., prepare themselves for an assignment more diligently and more thoroughly than others. The sluggards should not be able to benefit easily by the superior dedication and hard work of their betters.

Press Room Location

Large conference facilities—in hotels or out of them—may have a year-round press room, which one conference group appropriates as another moves out. It usually is well located and well equipped. In addition, at least the local press will know where to find it easily, which is a plus.

But when you must use general-purpose space for a press room, be picky about the location.

Ideally, your principal press room (as distinguished from the "quiet room") should be near the core of the entry pattern for the activity—close to the registration desk, close to the temporary association office, close to the convention headquarters.

 **The press room should be easy to find.**

What if "they" won't give you the room next to the registration desk or any of those other preferred places? Opt for a space near the meeting rooms—the auditoriums and the break-out rooms where panels and discussions will be held. Away from the entry pattern possibly, but still in the general traffic flow.

Third choice, in an auditorium or in a conference center, would be an easy-to-find and easy-to-describe location elsewhere in the building. Examples: "next to the snack bar on the lower level"; "on the main floor, down the corridor just to the right as you come through the front entrance."

If the activity is in a hotel, you still should try for (1) an entry-pattern location, (2) a main-traffic-flow location, (3) an easy-to-find-and-describe location.

 **Wherever your press room is, be certain that the door can be locked and that only you and your staff have keys. Don't leave a key *for any reason* at the conference headquarters or at the registration desk. Looters are everywhere, particularly when it has been rumored that such goodies as press kits and speech copies are around. And staff members who are conscientious about their own part of the overall operation may be forgetful or lackadaisical about yours.**

There is a fourth, much less desirable location for the press room. This is the parlor of a suite, probably one attached to your own sleeping room. This poses many drawbacks and only a few advantages.

The drawbacks are (1) it probably will be inconvenient for both reporters and program "stars," and it may be hard to find; (2) it makes for uneasiness—even the least sensitive will feel that they are invading your privacy (and they are!); (3) you will be denied even the small amount of rest you otherwise might be able to steal during the pressure-cooker kind of p.r. activity we are describing.

Don't let anybody talk you into using your own *sleeping room*—just a sleeping room with no parlor whatsoever—for a press room. This is a situation intolerable both to the reporters and to the husbanding of your energy and efficiency in what (if the project is as big and as complex an activity as we're talking about) is a constant crisis situation.

Also, even if you have to talk shrilly and throw a temper tantrum, don't let "them"—those otherwise nice people who sometimes, in planning a program, turn into a venomous "them"—talk or pressure you into having your press room share the convention headquarters or the duplicating room.

The reporters won't be comfortable.

You won't be comfortable.

Your materials will be dissipated; in fact, they will disappear.

There will be no way to get to a telephone.

Nobody will take messages.

The typewriter you carried in, yourself, at the loss of who knows how many vertebrae will be usurped at all hours by other people, both staff members and strangers, despite any urgency you may have with regard to deadlines.

It simply . . . does . . . not . . . work.

Press Room Equipment

You now have persuaded, cajoled, or fought your way to obtaining an adequate press room, conveniently located for effective use.

You're halfway there, but only halfway there. You need supplies and equipment. Prepare to fight again.

All these things must be ordered and assured—*in writing*—3 to 6 months ahead of D day. Wheels move slowly, and orders take time to be filled. Also, sometimes a priority or reservation must be established.

Here is what you need, at a minimum, to equip a press room:

1. Several long tables, for use as worktables and on which to spread materials for scrutiny and use by the press.
2. At least three good typewriters. Two of them should be electric. Many

newspeople, and certainly your office staff, accustomed to using an electric typewriter, are "spoiled." For them, using a manual typewriter is almost a skill to be relearned over a period of time.

3. Two telephones, one of them authorized and equipped for long-distance use. Telephone directories (how often this is forgotten!).

4. A file cabinet with drawers *which will lock.* You keep the key.

5. Several straight chairs (for use by those who are typing or working at tables) and several comfortable chairs (for general use and the reading of materials and writing of notes).

6. Ashtrays.

7. Supplies and other materials:
   a. Pens and pencils.
   b. Tablets and memo pads (lined paper).
   c. Typing paper and scratch paper.
   d. Carbon paper.
   e. Typewriter ribbons to fit all typewriters in the room.
   f. Envelopes, usual business size.
   g. Manila envelopes in small and large sizes.
   h. Mailer envelopes, with padding (for photographs).
   i. Cardboard, cut into envelope sizes (for photographs).
   j. Staplers (and extra staples), paper clips, rubber bands, scotch tape, scissors, masking tape, typing correction fluids.
   k. Something—a counter or an additional long table—to use as a barricade which will help keep most of the press room off limits for browsers. There are people who register for programs, ostensibly for professional or business purposes, and then make a beeline for the press room in hopes of snagging free speech copies and reports so they can play golf or shop instead of attending the sessions. They are thieves. If you don't guard against them in this and other ways (such as by using the file cabinet with the lock), they will "liberate" materials which were intended for and needed by the working press.
   l. An automobile for exclusive use.
   m. Signs (as designated in this section).
   n. A blackboard and a bulletin board (chalk and thumbtacks).

8. The above are to be provided by the program sponsors (either the local hosts, the convention committee, or the national office) or through your purchase order, with subsequent billing to your project's account.

   You, however, will want to bring or send ahead basic reference works— *Editor and Publisher Yearbook* and *Broadcasting Year Book*, for instance—as listed in the "Bibliography" and the "Basic Bookshelf" (pages 96–100).

9. You also will need a special list, usually mounted on cardboard and in color for easy recognition among all that stuff which will be piled around. It should serve as an on-glance reference to the local news outlets, similar to the ones on pages 244–245.

Press Room Staff

An effective press room operation requires a staff of at least four people:

1. The person who is heading up the effort—probably you. This person can be known by whatever title he or she chooses or is given: director, coordinator, chairperson, supervisor, head, etc. It doesn't make any difference, except that it should indicate that the person is in charge and is responsible. The three groups of people with whom this individual is working—the press, program developers, and speakers or other "platform" participants—need this kind of assurance.

2. An assistant—someone who can deal capably with the people in all three groups and help keep the operation running. Your assistant can be a volunteer, a person from your own institution or agency (even your own office), or a person representing a cosponsoring agency or institution—so long as he or she is knowledgeable and knows the people and the territory.

3. A *very good* typist-receptionist who also can be depended upon to answer telephones (and deliver messages), direct traffic, and generally hold down the fort while you and your assistant are out tracking people down and caddying for the press. A press room operation involves an awful lot of matching up of press people with platform people for interviews and statements. All this takes a lot of time and effort, so an anchor person (the typist) is a must.

   The typist-cum-office secretary and anchor person must be a pro. Optimally, he or she will be your *own* secretary, assigned for the occasion. Your *own* secretary, in a press room operation, is worth his or her weight in emeralds. Your own secretary will have been in on the action from the beginning and will know the answers without having to dig them up or find you to supply them. Your own secretary can explain without hesitation, for example, just *why* we don't have an advance copy of the Vice President's speech.

4. A gopher. A person—maybe a college student or another individual of that age level—who can "go fer" this or that.

   The principal qualifications of this aide are energy, stamina (not always the same), enthusiasm, and the ability to drive a car. "Gopher" assignments include taking releases and other materials around to the local newsrooms and to the various places where people from the out-of-town press may be headquartered, taking mailings to the post office, and going out for supplies.

   If your gopher owns a car, this is great. Otherwise, you'll have to find one somewhere, even rent one. Free, high-prioritied, and unrestricted access to an automobile *at all times* is a necessary accessory in the operation of any press room.

   The gopher can be someone hired or assigned for the occasion on a one-time basis. However, if he or she has worked with you before or is from your regular operation, so much the better. Just so the gopher is energetic, has stamina and a high quotient of enthusiasm, and can drive a car. As we said.

 **These people must be assigned to you and only to you on a full-time basis, or forget it.**

Don't under any circumstances agree to "share" a typist with the conference office or registration desk.

Don't agree to "share" a member of the conference committee who also has interests and assignments of other kinds as your assistant.

Don't agree to "share" one of the minor functionaries, also with side assignments, as your gopher.

They'll be tied up with somebody else's chores, believe me, right when you need them.

Take fewer people if you must (however, fight this to the death), but be certain those people you do have are *full time with you.*

Operation of the Press Room

You are on-site early. Your press room has been set up.

You are ready to go into operation, having completed all advance preparations.

1. Signs are in place.
   a. Directional signs point the way to your door. They read "Press Room," and arrows indicate the route.
   b. There is a large sign at your door, even two signs (mounted on easels) if the traffic is from two directions. It says "Press Room."
   c. A few feet inside the press room door there is a counter or a long table (see page 172). On it is a sign which reads "Working Press Only May Enter Room Past This Spot." Enforce this edict. Remember what was said about the vandals who will steal all your materials.

      That ought to do it, as far as signs are concerned, unless (1) you are having a press conference, in which case you'll need a fourth sign which says "Press Conference," or (2) you don't have a press room (as in the case of a low-key, small-scale activity), in which case your table in the conference registration area will have a sign which says "Press Information," or (3) there are program-connected meals, in which case you will need to place upon a table a sign which says "Reserved for Working Press."

2. Equipment is in place.

   Everything outlined above under "Press Room Equipment" (pages 172–173) should be in its place and on hand a full day before the conference begins— especially the telephones and typewriters.

   This is sometimes difficult in a big convention hall or hotel where one or more meetings are completed a few hours before the next ones begin. In that case, muscle up as much priority as fits of temper and persuasion (in whichever order) can obtain for you, and get into your press room the very minute that you can.

The items which are difficult to obtain ahead of time are the telephones, the typewriters, and the file cabinet with a lock. Get them anyhow.

3. The job itself has no loose ends.
   a. If you have a "star" coming in and you will have a press conference, this should have been set up far in advance.
   b. Individual interviews also should have been set up in advance—sometimes an impossible feat, but try.
   c. You have delegated as much as possible of your operation to your helpers.

   This leaves you free to write releases as the news comes in and to make last-minute and on-the-spot arrangements as the press and dignitaries show up.

   Local TV people and local radio people usually do not let you know in advance what sorts of interviews and other opportunities for special coverage they desire—not until they get to the scene. Neither do press association people, unless your meeting is being covered by a specialist—a medical writer, an education writer, a music or art critic, etc.

   Distribute information in writing and in advance to the press and to the reception desk and the headquarters staff as to (1) the hours that the press room will be open and (2) the schedule of where you and your assistant— together or separate—can be found at all hours. (See the sample on page 177).

   It is important that regular press room hours be established and that at least one of your staff members be in the press room during the office hours announced—usually 9 A.M.–5 P.M. In most cases, this will be the secretary.

   You and your assistant probably will be on the run most of the time, as will the gopher. However, you should check in at regular intervals (personally or by phone) to get messages and to touch base. Whoever answers the press room phone should be able to say, "Ms. Parmalee will be back at this number at 4 P.M. May I have her call you or give her a message?" Or, "Ms. Parmalee can be reached at Extension 1516, where an interview is in progress." The same information should be supplied re the whereabouts of your assistant while he or she is running errands.

   As for the gopher, he or she should report in at regular times—such as every hour on the hour—and should be *in* the press room every minute you don't have him or her out on an errand.

4. You have a *press signup sheet* (a sample is on page 178) for the members of the press who cover the event. Reporters should sign in the minute they appear. The *press signup sheet* will be used to find members of the press when circumstances suddenly change (the "inevitable emergency," remember?) and to apprise them of changes which may affect their coverage. The sheet should be ruled off for name and title, affiliation, local address (hotel, if they are

D DAY PRESS INFORMATION SHEET

Jan Parmalee, Press Room Director
November 21

8 A.M. ....Breakfast in coffee shop

9 A.M. ....Open Press Room, 111 Lower Level

9 A.M.–10:30 A.M. ....In Press Room or on call through
                          Press Room, 111 Lower Level

10:30 A.M. ....Press Conference, U.S. Senator Mel-
                          vin Rumpus, chair, Select Committee
                          on Inner Space. Laurel Room, Upper
                          Level

11:30 A.M.–1 P.M. ....In Press Room, 111 Lower Level, or
                          on call through Press Room

1 P.M.–2 P.M...............Conference luncheon and program,
                          Trianon Room, Upper Level (at Press
                          Table)

2 P.M.–5 P.M...............Press Room, 111 Lower Level, or on
                          call through Press Room (possibly
                          sitting in, 3:30 P.M., interview by
                          Meg Morton, Evening Standard, with
                          Betty Friedan)

5 P.M.–6 P.M. ....Room 1916, West Wing

6 P.M.–10 P.M. ....Reception, Grand Ballroom Foyer;
                          dinner and program, Grand Ballroom

10 P.M. ....Invitational reception honoring
                          Senator Rumpus, Presidential Suite,
                          14th Floor

Can be reached for emergencies, at various times, in Room
1916, West Wing

Press Room Number———356–8819, ext. 11

REPORTERS' SIGN-IN SHEET
Health Education Conference

(please print!)

NAME	AFFILIATION	REGULAR ADDRESS AND PHONE	ADDRESS(ES) AND PHONES WHERE WE CAN REACH YOU DURING CONFERENCE

out-of-towners, home address if they live in town), and telephone numbers when they can be reached or where messages can be left—home, office, other. The reporters should sign up even if they are your buddies and you see them every day—otherwise a helper may miss them when those on the signup sheet are being called or located.

Press Room Amenities

See also "Press Room Equipment"—pages 172–173.

1. A blackboard and a bulletin board. You use these for reminders and messages to the press.
    Examples:

    "Senator Rumpus's plane has been delayed by fog at Cincinnati. He will be in about 7:30 P.M., and the press conference will be held at 8 P.M."

    "Betty Friedan's speech copy has just come in [9:30 A.M.], and we are having it duplicated. You should have it by 10:15 A.M. Leave word where you'll be, and we'll run it to you."

2. Comfortable chairs; restaurant guides; guides to the city—things a visitor (even from the press) might want to snatch a few minutes to see or do.

3. A place where reporters can leave their stuff—safely—at night or when they are out of the press room. Remember that file cabinet with the lock? It serves as such a repository. Each person covering, if a large press contingent is present, should be given his or her own reporter's folder with his or her name on it. A reporter can leave materials which he or she doesn't want to carry around in the reporter's folder. Some big meetings and conferences involve providing the press with great and exhausting armloads of valuable materials for current or future use. The press room staff can insert materials and messages in the individual folders as these come in, and each reporter can simply consult the folder at intervals to be brought up to date on the available materials and information.

4. Goodies. At a minimum, coffee and soft drinks should be delivered early in the morning and in the midafternoon. At a more hospitable level, snacks (rolls or donuts in the morning, cookies in the afternoon) build goodwill, except among dieters.

    Some organizations and agencies which sponsor programs that draw heavy press coverage provide light lunches in the press room during the noon break. This hospitality is welcomed because many newspeople are writing or calling in stories during that break; they don't have time to eat even at a snack bar before sessions resume. The usual pattern for light lunches is assorted sandwiches, relishes, coffee and soft drinks, and an easy dessert—brownies, cake, pie, or the like.

If sandwich lunches cannot be provided, be sure that the gopher is available to run out to get them for those working through the lunch break.

HOW TO PLAN, SET UP, AND RUN A PRESS CONFERENCE

FIRST CATCH YOUR RABBIT

An old recipe for rabbit stew began, "First catch your rabbit."

A bona fide "rabbit"—i.e., one or more "stars" in a particular area of activity or persons otherwise providing a large measure of assurance that they are newsworthy—is the basic ingredient of a successful press conference.

If—and only if—your program and the speakers or panelists are apt to create strong news or feature interest, consider holding a press conference.

PRESS CONFERENCE ADVANTAGES

There are several advantages in the press conference format:

1. It amplifies the probability of coverage.

    Many assignments editors and directors will assign a staff member to cover a press conference when they would not assign the staffer to cover your entire program or even the major parts of it.

    Why?

    The "main events" are very apt to be held at the hours when newsrooms have deadlines or are short of staff—e.g., dinner speeches or luncheon speeches (these overlap air time for both the broadcast media and deadlines for the daily print media). A press conference allows coverage within a comfortable time limit in respect to deadlines.

    The press conference gives those attending it an opportunity to pose questions and get answers outside the narrow limits of the speaker's formal presentation. It allows the press to invite the speaker(s) to enlarge on points which may get passing mention in a major presentation on what perhaps is a professional theme—points which are the news kernel within that presentation.

    It is a stratagem to get reporters and newscasters *to* your program; often it will get them involved in further coverage of the program or of your year-round efforts. This is because it gives you an appropriate setting and occasion in which to provide them with both information and an incentive for follow-through reporting. Good reporters like to have banks or backlogs of ideas for future news stories or coverage. A good press conference can draw newspeople into your area of promotion and build future coverage.

2. The speakers, panelists, and resource people—those featured in the press conference—welcome it, too.

   It gives them an opportunity to meet with the press and to offer amplification and interpretations of their formal remarks or of their attitudes and opinions on other matters of news value.

   It gets this part of their obligation to the program—dealing with the press—out of the way.

   Under the frenetic pressures of a program important enough to warrant a press conference, the major figures are being tugged and pulled in all directions. Although there sometimes are individual requests from the press to be honored or commitments to members of the press, most of the reporters can be handled—to the reporters' satisfaction and to the speaker's advantage—in one comparatively short session.

   (Example of an exception: A noted medical person might meet with the general press at a press conference and yet also schedule an individual meeting with, say, a writer for one of the medical journals or a person with a syndicated health program or column.)

PRESS CONFERENCE DISADVANTAGES

The press conference format also has disadvantages:

1. If you schedule press conferences for inappropriate or trivial reasons and/or with only minor, inarticulate, or uncooperative people as the so-called stars, you (and your sponsors) will get a black eye from the press that steak won't heal. Be certain your press conference is a plus, not a minus.

2. If your press conference is subject to major drawbacks—a bad location, a bad hour for coverage—it is detrimental to the overall coverage of your current and future programs. A bad location is one which is out of the way or difficult for the press to get to, and/or without parking nearby. A bad hour for a press conference is just before *or* far after the deadlines for the newspapers and/or broadcast stations which you hope will staff the press conferences.

   We repeat: Do not let your sponsors, your committee, or even your bosses talk or pressure you into having a press conference as a vanity fair or as a misguided salute or courtesy to a minor figure (or one who hasn't much to say or can't express himself or herself).

   Tell them they are lousing up the whole effort—and stick by your guns. They are.

   If you are scheduling a press conference (and you should search your soul very deeply before you get into this), you must first assure the speakers' commitment.

Send each "rabbit" a letter similar to the one opposite.

A very prominent speaker (such as a United States senator or a Cabinet officer) could be a trifle reluctant to bother his or her exalted self with a press conference in a smaller city.

Just to reassure this individual (and his or her press aide) include such paragraphs as these:

> Jonesboro is a good press center, and I think I can assure you good coverage. The community is the base for three television stations (representing each of the commercial networks) and for a public broadcasting television station. There are four lively radio stations.

> It also has two competitive daily newspapers, in addition to the college paper, and the news which originates here frequently makes the wire services.

The Timeframe on page 184 calls for you to write for speech copies and photographs 3 months in advance of the program or (when there are some blanks in the program—when topics have been decided upon but not speakers) as soon as you get the speakers' names.

Avoid Crashers

One of the problems you may have with your steering committee is that they will want to crash the press conference.

The answer is "*No.*"

They also will want at least selected students from their class or younger members of their club or firm to attend the press conference as a "learning experience."

Double "No."

A press conference is not a "learning experience." It is an exercise in public relations, a service to the media, and a way of getting mileage out of the program's publicity-promotion effort.

You let young members or staff from an organization or firm or students in journalism, political science, or any discipline come to a professionally structured press conference covered by professional reporters, and you have made a mess of it.

The students and other crashers will want to ask little questions about the state of whatever art your star speaker practices, and the time will be up before the pros have a chance to get in the questions which their editors instructed them to ask.

PRESS CONFERENCE SITE

The press conference site should be well lighted, naturally or artificially. It should be big enough to accommodate television crews, but not so huge that a small group of

OFFICE OF COMMUNITY SERVICES
The Freeland Foundation and Freeland College
Box 1819, Freeland, Massachusetts 01600

September 1, 1979

Dr. Mary M. Whipple
Room 1417 College Hall
The University of Upper Oregon
Upperville, Oregon 97880

Dear Dr. Whipple:

Professor Elliott Clark of our Department of Education
has informed me that you will be a major speaker at the
forthcoming conference on "Challenges in the Teaching
Process," to be held November 18-19 at the Copley
Square Conference Center, Boston.

I am coordinator of the publicity and press relations
for the conference. In this capacity, I should like
to obtain, as soon as possible, a copy of your most recent vita and a head-and-shoulders photograph suitable
for press use.

If you are preparing your remarks in advance, please
send me a copy of your presentation.

I need this material for use in press releases and
other accounts of the proceedings, and would like to
have it by October 15.

You will not have made your travel arrangements this
early, I know. However, please tell me whether or not
you can be available for a press conference at 10 A.M.
November 19, at a room to be selected in the Copley
Square Conference Center.

It will not be of long duration, and it will give you
plenty of time for a period to yourself before the
luncheon at 1 P.M.

It will be a pleasure, both professionally and personally, to work with you in November.

                              Cordially,

                              _____
                              Your name and title

reporters will be lost in it and the general impression will be "almost nobody came—why did I bother?" A too large press conference room makes both the speaker and the reporters uncomfortable.

Timeframe: Press Conference Arrangements*

6 months ahead	Make a decision as to whether a press conference is justified by the program, topic, or person to be featured.
3 months ahead	Catch your rabbit. Set a time and place. Pin down his or her agreement to participate in a press conference.
6 weeks ahead	Check out the facilities, including wall plugs.
6 weeks ahead	Send out a first notice to the media.
4 weeks ahead	Get handout materials† ready.
4 weeks ahead	Obtain helpers, and drill them.
3 weeks ahead	Issue a second alert (a press release with a note of invitation).

By this time, everything—but everything—should have been covered. Everything should be ready to go up to the day before D day.

1 day ahead	Drill the helpers a second time.
1 day ahead	Make calls or send telegrams as reminders.
evening before or	
Early D day	Make a last-minute check of facilities and amenities, again including wall plugs and lighting.
Press conference	Do your thing.

It should be easy to find (see pages 171–172 for criteria) and preferably near the press room.

The first thing to do in checking out a room where a press conference will be held is to look for wall plugs. The advance of technology has scaled those huge TV contraptions that took two men and a horse to wheel from place to place down to

---

*A mini-list for a middle-range activity.

†A press kit, if you are using one. Otherwise, a packet including a program of the activity, a vita of the "rabbit" with a photograph, and a speech copy if one is available in advance.

today's minicams. Minicams can be shouldered and operated like a tommy gun, and they can run on batteries.

So what's with the wall plugs?

You still need them. Some of the super-sized TV equipment may be brought in. Increasingly, reporters from all media backgrounds are using tape recorders in interview and press conference situations. Some radio stations prefer to plug in their mikes rather than use batteries. In either case, the devices are put on the table in front of the person who is being interviewed.

PRESS CONFERENCE DIRECTION

The hour for the press conference has arrived.

The members of the press have arrived.

The speaker has arrived—or the speakers, if a panel has been scheduled.

When you greet the speaker, you ask, "Do you want to open with a statement, or shall we immediately call for questions?"

The majority of people in the "star" category handle press conferences very well and usually start out with a statement. It often is a brief recap of the high points of the formal speech that they will deliver later in the day.

The speaker, if knowledgeable and a veteran at this kind of thing, comes in and walks around the room, exchanging introductions and shaking hands.

With a little direction from you—"Won't you take your place at the table, please?"—the "star" will be seated.

You, then, will say, "Ladies and gentlemen, this is Mr. [or Ms.] Bigwig. Our guest will open with a statement," or "Our guest will accept your questions."

When the guest concludes the opening statement, or when a speaker with no opening statement is seated and appears to be ready, you will ask, "Do any of you have questions?"

The questions are accepted as hands go up and you or the guest (if he or she takes this initiative without hesitation) points to one and then another. Someone may have been ignored. You say, "There is a reporter in the back row who has not had an opportunity to speak," and then point that reporter out to your guest speaker.

Watch the time carefully. You will have been standing in the back or at the side toward the back. When the half-hour mark arrives, drift to the front of the room and watch your speaker.

About that time, you should catch the guest speaker's eye and point significantly to your watch. If the speaker nods, that means he or she is ready to wrap it up. The speaker may shake his or her head if the questions are eager and interesting. In that case, relax and give it another 10 minutes.

When the time is up, come to the front of the room and stand beside the table where the guest is seated.

Ask, "One more question?" Accept that one more question and then say, "Thank you, Mr. Bigwig," or "Thank you, Dr. Whippel," or whatever.

That's it.

Reporters may crowd around as the speaker stands and starts to leave.

Most speakers handle this very well, talking and smiling as they walk toward the door. A good-humored speaker, when the hour is not pressing, may stay around and talk for a few minutes more. That is up to the speaker, *unless* the guest is due on some platform in the building at that very moment. In this case, you must be firm. "Sorry, people, but the Governor has a major address to give in 15 minutes, and we should allow her to have a moment to herself before she begins." Or whatever suits the occasion.

For some reason, and there is nothing except on-site "research" to back this up as far as I know, 30 minutes is the best time span for a press conference. Cut it off earlier if questions lag or the reporters start packing up their gear in preparation for departure.

But you'll find that 99 times out of 100, 30 minutes will work out all right.

USES AND ANATOMY OF A PRESS KIT

The press kit is an integral part of the services a publicist offers the media in connection with either a major program or an ongoing, year-round activity.

NOMENCLATURE: TITLE OF KIT

What we call here a "press kit" can be known by a number of related names. Some people call it a "press packet" or a "press folder." Other sponsors seem to want to get "media" or "information" into the name. I even have seen press kits labeled "reference packet."

Unless the word "reference" means a lot to your steering committee or is rooted in tradition at your institution or agency, please try to keep it out of the title of your press kit. In most newsrooms and publicity offices, a press kit is what it says—a packet of information for use by the working press. But a "reference packet" is an indexed booklet, intended for long- rather than short-term use.

Otherwise, the name of your press kit doesn't make a lot of difference, providing the meaning and the use of this collection of informational material are clear.

DESIGN OF A PRESS KIT

With some reservations, it is also not too important what kind of wrappings you give your press kit. You can use:

A folder with inner pockets

A bound booklet

A loose-leaf format

A large envelope

A zipped (usually leatherette) briefcase-envelope

Something of your own discovery or devising

You may find your answer to the "wrappings" question by checking out what is available and suitable for this purpose among the services and supplies in your agency's stores department or duplicating room.

A number of institutions, organizations, and agencies work up a standard press kit—both its cover and its basic ingredients—to which they can add additional items appropriate for each occasion or activity as it arises.

This is not a bad idea, and when we get to the packaging in more detail (pages 192–195), we'll get back to it.

There are both physical and psychological factors to take into account when you set about developing a press kit.

The *physical* considerations are:

The outward appearance of the press kit

The need for systematically obtaining or originating materials which will go into the press kit

The design of the contents so that they are of maximum help to those in the media

The *psychological* matters to remember include:

The press kit's image-building capacity

The usefulness of its contents to whatever segment(s) of the media you are serving

Is the second "psychological factor" a repetition of the third item in the "physical" group?

Not really.

Designing the contents so that they can be found readily for instant reference is not the same as making certain of the usefulness of the *information* you provide. To be useful, the information must be accurate and complete. This fact does not overlap the fact that the information included in the kit is printed on blue paper instead of on white paper or pink.

SPECIFICS OF PRESS KIT PREPARATION AND PRESENTATION

Let us now proceed to the specifics of press kit preparation and presentation.

How and when is a press kit used? How shall it be packaged? How many kits will you need? What items will be included in each kit?

Press Kits—When, Where, and Why Used

A press kit is not needed when you are publicizing a small program unless—by some infrequent chance—the activity has a news quotient high enough to pull a lot of coverage.

A press kit is useful in helping to publicize and promote a medium-sized program.

It is invaluable—a "must"—when a large and complex activity is being publicized and promoted.

A press kit is a basic ingredient in any recipe for a year-round public information effort.

What are some pluses which can be garnered through the use of a press kit?

It can be helpful to your p.r. effort when you have a project which is not elaborate enough to warrant staging press conferences or staffing a press room but which may deserve (and need) more publicity backup than is accrued through an invitation to the press to cover an event or the provision of a printed program and advance speech copies.

It also provides the media with:

Assistance in their coverage of your program or activity.

Background information about the event, its platform participants, and the sponsors.

A reference tool for their future use and file material which will come in handy at some (as yet unforeseen) moment.

It provides you (as the publicist) and the activity's sponsors with:

An opportunity to get a pitch across—to state facts and frame information in words and from viewpoints which present the case in a favorable light. But don't ever allow a concern with your particular interests to *cause you to bend the truth*!

An insurance factor contributing to the accuracy of the reporting when exact quotes are involved. If it's written down (in a speech copy or a statement) right there in front of the newsperson, he or she is more likely to lift it from its context rather than rely on notes, memory, or even a tape recording.

An increase in the apparent stature of the activity. A press kit in a newsroom or in a reporter's hands adds to the substance which the event assumes. The press now sees it as something solid instead of something which came to their attention on the basis of a mere verbal or even written exchange.

An addition to the archives, important when checking back (pages 42–44) in preparation for that "next time" which invariably comes.

Visibility for the sponsors.

How Distributed

Once you have prepared press kits, what do you do with them? How, when, and where do you distribute them?

You make physical use of the press kits, first, by walking them around:

In introducing yourself or your group to a member of the media who has just come into your community or region or who works in your field of interest (e.g., education, the sciences, health—anything related to the theme of your current or ongoing activity).

When you visit the newspeople in their offices as you begin the publicity-promotion effort for the single activity or group of activities (pages 42–44).

 **It always is a good thing to have something tangible to leave with the editors, news directors, and reporters with whom you talk.**

When you are going to operate away from "home base" and take a press tour of the area where your program will be held. By all means go armed with press kits. They will be a great comfort and an even greater help.

In this walkabout method of contact, the publicist can get acquainted with and provide necessary information for the newspeople without wearing out his or her welcome. When you have a press kit to leave behind, you don't have to make as heavy a pitch as might otherwise be necessary. You can, instead, verbally sketch your project and any unusual materials which you are providing.

At this point, before the editor–news director lets his or her eyes wander back to the work that was under way when you popped in, you can inform the busy person with whom you are talking, "It's all in there—just have someone call if there are any questions."

And be sure it *is* all "in there."

We have indicated that a press kit can be a valuable addition to a news office's files (valuable for both them and you).

Let us underscore that point.

A press kit is not easy to throw away. It is the kind of information package that people like to keep around—in a desk drawer, on a bookshelf, in the reference library or morgue.

And the newspeople remember it.

"I have something on that organization around here somewhere," they muse. And they act upon that supposition—when your institution or agency later returns to their notice.

If you can't deliver the press kits personally, use the U.S. mail or recruit on-the-spot assistance. Let's say that your home base is Chicago or Cincinnati and that the program you are publicizing will be held in Atlanta or Kansas City.

Walking your press kits around may not be practical. You'd have to make a special trip to Atlanta. Only a big-budget project could allow for that extra expense. There are two answers to this dilemma.

First answer: Bundle the press kits up, and send them to a trusted associate in Atlanta, or Kansas City—with *full instructions* for walking them around.

Second answer: Send the press kits out, individually addressed *by hand* and accompanied by a personal letter from you to the reporter or newscaster. How will you find out where to mail them, and to whom? Look up the newspeople in an area media directory (if one exists for that region), or in one of the other references whose effective uses are explained in the section on the "Basic Bookshelf." (pages 96–100). Also, the people who manage the facility where your program will be held may have local media rosters already made up to send or give to you (see pages 244–245).

 **You can get an early-bird head start on doing a publicity job in strange terrain by subscribing to the newspapers in that community; mail subscriptions are not a budget-breaking item.**

Reading the newspapers of the community where you will be operating, even temporarily, can help you understand the area and its various constituencies. It can introduce you to the editors and reporters. Peruse the newspapers carefully. Make notes on who writes what. Is there a calendar column? Does someone write with the most enthusiasm (even though he or she covers other matters as well) about education, or energy, or the world food crisis, or whatever your program concerns?

Jot names down on a master sheet so that you will know whom to approach when the time comes.

Do the same for radio and television. Can't get the station on your set? Perhaps not. But you can subscribe to the *TV Guide* for that area, or make a systematic study of the TV sections of the newspapers.

Ayer Directory (see the "Basic Bookshelf" section, pages 96–100) lists virtually every publication which originates in a community by state and town. Look it over when you are making out your media mailing and calling lists.

"Homework" and "head start," in this case, are synonymous.

Additional press kit distribution can be accomplished during a press party (a particularly desirable event if yours is a year-round effort). (See pages 226–229.)

You also should have a supply of press kits available in your conference's press room, if you staff one. At any rate, have plenty of press kits on hand, and pass them out during the event itself.

A Mini-Checklist for Press Kit Distribution

Walk them around.

Hand them out during a press tour.

Present them at a press party.

Mail them in large batches to an associate who will walk them around.

Mail them individually to editors and news directors and to writers and newscasters who have a particular interest in the activity's theme.

Distribute them at the event itself: at the press conference if you hold one; in your press room if you have one; and to individual members of the press as they show up to cover.

 **You will have made some last-minute additions to the materials (speeches which come in late, etc.), so be sure everyone gets a press kit on D day—even if each person got an earlier version as well.**

Mail kits and auxiliary materials, also, to outstanding columnists and others interested in writing or newscasting on the subject of your activity. They may or may not use the materials thus provided at the time of the program, but these may help you gain future and favorable notice.

Don't be stingy.

Once you have assembled the materials for press kits, most of the effort and expense is behind you. It does not cost a whole lot more to make up 50 press kits instead of 25, or 200 instead of 100.

Distribute them widely to members of the news media.

It is rare that a well-prepared press kit, even one which is highly pinpointed as to a specific program, does not gain for the program and/or its sponsors some print and air time.

Assembling the Kit—Packaging

In assembling a press kit, where do you start?

At the beginning, of course.

With the package (see physical and psychological factors, page 187).

Here are some matters to think about when you are grappling with the idea of the image you want the press kit to bolster:

Is the program a profit or nonprofit venture?

Who are the sponsors? Educational institutions? Nonprofit organizations? Industrial firms? Others?

What are the intended uses of the press kit? For a one-shot program or activity? For year-round reference? To introduce a new feature or element at your institution or in your group of sponsors? To tell a story? To welcome the press to your headquarters or campus? To provide useful information for backgrounding or for immediate release? Any identifiable combination of the above?

How much do you want to spend? How much *must* you spend to do the job? How much can you afford to spend?

It is obvious that you, as a publicist, face one kind of situation if you are working on behalf of a business concern or an agency funded *otherwise* than by taxpayers' money, and an entirely different set of conditions if you are working in a tax-supported institution or organization, or one which looks in major ways to the public for support.

The publicity staff for an industrial giant can order press kits which fairly reek of financial supersolvency and get nothing but plaudits. Oh, there may be complaints from one or two little old ladies who own three shares each of that precious stock.

The financial-industrial publicist can present to the media a really magnificent press kit: leather, real leather, perhaps; gold lettering; multicolored graphics (signed, of course) by notable artists and practitioners—the whole works.

But the publicist for a nonprofit and/or tax-supported organization or institution has a slightly more complicated job than does the industrial publicist who has only to commission extravagant products and lo! they appear in full gloss.

The appearance of the press kit, then, is a tricky matter.

If the project is a dignified and prestigious symposium on a scholarly subject, the package should be dignified—even austere.

If the program is a festival of the lively arts, you can give your fancy—or that of your graphic artist—an unlimited ticket. The package for such a program can be highly colorful and imaginative, even circusy and almost garish.

In whatever case, the package should be sturdy. You want members of the press to keep the kit in their files, don't you?

Your press kit should express the stature and excellence of its sponsoring institution(s) but at the same time convey a definite feeling of prudence and economy—and this holds true even if the project on which you are working is a profit-making venture!

 **Do not let your steering committee have a hand in the press kit's design or its contents. Steering committees have a way of turning a tool meant for a specific purpose into something which reflects their own interests and becomes much less helpful and useful to the press. Use your good judgment and follow the advice found in this book and elsewhere in p.r. annals as to the packaging, the number of copies you will have available, and the contents of the press kit.**

A nonprofit organization (particularly a tax-supported institution)—no matter how generously funded—should choose a modest press kit package which comes across with respectable (if slightly threadbare) dignity yet exudes the distinct aroma of excellence.

It should never prompt the viewer or recipient to gasp, "Where did they get *that* kind of money?"

Despite the admonitions above, a tax-supported institution is justified in and even commended for taking the big-dollar route if the program it is presenting is for high-level professional people who are paying large fees to attend, and if it is appropriate because of the situation at hand to use a general conference portfolio also as the press kit package.

And, to repeat, the outward appearance of a press kit can help or hinder your cause.

The packaging does not need to be elaborate, and it should be neither cutesy nor messy.

It can be as simple as an 8½ × 11 inch business envelope imprinted (or, less expensively, stamped neatly) with your organization's or institution's letter or logo, and with the current program's title, dates, and site printed, stamped, or typed upon it.

Imprinting can be handled by direct typing (if you are preparing only a couple of dozen press kits); by your printshop or duplicating room (if you are preparing hundreds); or even by the use of gummed labels, which are run off by your duplicating room staff or on a copying machine which is equipped for that kind of job.

Packages which can vie in price and practicality with manila envelopes are the so-called student portfolios, which are available in office supply stores.

These modest portfolios come in heavy stock and rainbow hues. You would, of course, select a single color for a single activity. This entails ordering ahead, since "student portfolios" are put out in boxes of assorted colors. Groups which use a number of such portfolios a year often buy the boxes of assorted colors and have a low-paid employee or a volunteer sort out the portfolios and package them for future use by color—a box of red, a box of blue, and so on.

The student folders have two inside pockets which are handy in presenting the materials you have selected for the members of the working press.

Student portfolios range in price from about 20 cents, give or take a penny, up to 30 or 40 cents apiece or even more, depending on the vendor and the quality of the stock. Large quantities can be bought at bulk prices.

Again, you can have gummed labels run off which identify your project, and you can place them or have them placed on covers and inner flaps. The end result does not look bad; it is practical; it is inexpensive; and it obviously is not the work of a gang of spendthrifts.

Many institutions, collegiate or otherwise, solve a multiplicity of kit concerns by having somewhat fancier folders custom-designed and printed up in great quantities for year-round use. A group of folders of uniform color and design is easily identified with a particular institution. The folders bear its crest and motto. The inner flaps are printed and tell some fine things about the agency. The folders are handsome. Because they are mass-produced, they are not exorbitantly expensive.

An imaginative staff will find many uses for such institutional packets.

They will be used:

At conferences and institutes sponsored by the institution to hold the materials for those taking part.

To carry instructions to a special faculty group—e.g., the group which teaches extramural classes or correspondence courses.

To hold expense blanks and advisory materials for guest speakers or other platform people.

For in-house meetings, symposia, and round tables. The institution's various citizens boards—advisory, according to discipline; alumni association; foundation—will find them useful.

In presentations by the field staff to their constituencies.

With gummed labels pasted inside so as not to mar the handsome covers, the multiuse folders can be very satisfactory press kits. The inside labels can always identify the specific project under way and supply the name, address, and phone number of the publicity and promotion chairperson (you).

One drawback to the use of uniform all-purpose kits which are identified with your institution is that multiuse of such kits can be confusing.

A reporter who regularly covers educational events, for example, could get frustrated in searching for a fact about your institution or agency during a rush. What happens? He or she is confronted with a veritable 5-foot shelf of folders, all of which look exactly alike. He or she may not have the time (or patience) to leaf through them to find the one needed at that moment. As a result, he or she may abandon the article about (or the favorable mention of) your agency which had been planned. That would be a shame.

To prevent such a mishap from occurring, it is wise to use the same kit *design* but perhaps have a different-*colored* cover for each of the different types of occasions on which the kits are used.

How Many Press Kits Will You Need?

On page 191, we advised you not to be stingy with the press kits. We repeat that advice, because:

You will need at least *three* times as many press kits as the number of media outlets to which you will distribute them, plus file copies (ten) and extras, for emergencies (twenty).

Why?

Because you may not see the same media representative from any one outlet more than once as you progress through the advance publicity-promotion campaign, through D day, and through the mop-up.

Let us take a target news outlet—say, a daily newspaper—and look at the pattern of press kit distribution.

1. The first copy of your press kit will go to some kind of editor or public-service manager.

    If he or she can let it go (press kits are not easy to throw away, remember?), this first press kit may be passed along to the rewrite specialist or to the reporter who is going to write an advance story based on its contents.

Even on that initial visit, you may distribute as many as a half-dozen kits to various people who can—you hope—use them.

These may include a Sunday editor, a columnist or two, an education writer, a critic (recipients can range from entertainment writers to cultural writers, and from book reviewers to travel writers, science writers, sports editors, feature editors, women's-page editors and others—as appropriate to your activity's theme).

2. Except in a very small newsroom, the press kits you originally take or send to that office will not reach the hands of the reporter or photographer who will cover the program "live" or work with you in other ways.

So we come to the next level—D day—and it becomes obvious that you will need another complete supply of press kits for the reporters who show up at your program.

Because it is not at all unusual, even in a medium-sized city, for a news outlet to send one reporter to your program's morning session, another one to the evening session, and still a third if the sessions continue.

And none of the three will have had their hands on—or possibly even have glimpsed—your press kit until they arrive on the scene, asking for information to improve their opportunity for good coverage.

Contents

The contents of a press kit should be tailored to the occasion. Seven basic ingredients should be found in any press kit of any kind of sponsor, without exception:

1. A program or schedule for the activity or event.
2. Thumbnail sketches of all platform participants and resource specialists.
3. A list, with identification, of all committee members and staff members, if this is not included in the program or schedule.
4. Background information (a folder or brochure, or copies of a typed or printed statement) on each major sponsor.
5. Pictures, if these are available, of the major chairpersons and speakers. Use good, sharp, black-and-white, head-and-shoulders studio photographs only. An exception can be made if the subject is a dancer, an athlete, a model, or some other kind of performer or specialist and a full-figure action shot is relevant. Note that we stipulated professional studio portraits when pictures are being used. It is hard enough to get white space and camera space for nonaction photographs in the news media without compounding the difficulty by furnishing them with pictures by amateurs—even "gifted amateurs." Put away that Brownie Starflash. It is fine for vacation pictures and for family use, but not for a publicity-promotion attempt.

THE SPRINGFIELD WORLD AFFAIRS CONFERENCE

Information for the Press

<u>Releases</u> have been mailed to you on the major speakers
(Senator Javits and the Indian Minister to the
United Nations, the Hon. N.P. Jain), on the
panelists, and on the conference committees. A
wrapup story is being mailed on or about Feb. 26 for
release (hopefully) on Thursday, Feb. 28 or Friday,
March 1, when the conference is about to begin. Feel
free to use any of the materials included in this
press kit.

<u>Press Conferences have been scheduled for</u>:
<u>Senator Jacob K. Javits</u> (R-New York)--4 P.M. March 1
(Friday), in the Century Room, Mezzanine, Ramada
Forum XXX, Springfield. <u>The Honorable N.P. Jain</u>,
Minister and Deputy Permanent Representative of
India to the United Nations-10 A.M. March 2 (Satur-
day), in the Century Room, Mezzanine, Ramada Forum
XXX, Springfield.

<u>Interviews</u> with the two major speakers (above) are
available <u>only</u> at their press conferences. If you
want to interview any of the panelists (Harold B.
Steele, President, Illinois Agricultural Association; Stanley L. Johnson, President, Illinois AFL-
CIO; Thomas F. Slattery, Manager, International Marketing, Illinois Department of Business and Economic
Development; Prof. Harold G. Halcrow, agricultural
economist, University of Illinois; Gerald Marks, Regional Director, U.S. Department of Commerce, or
Vincent J. Riley, Division Chief, International Relations, World Bank)--<u>please let us know</u> as soon as
possible, and we'll try to set up individual arrangements for you.

<u>Conference Coverage</u>-We will have credentials and tick-
ets for all conference sessions for all members of
the <u>working press</u> who will be covering the conference. They will be available from the publicity
coordinator, Helen Farlow, at the press conferences
and just before the gavel sounds at Ramada Forum XXX
for each conference session. If you have questions,
call or write her at 114 Illini Hall, University of
Illinois, Champaign, 61820 (217-333-0517). She will
be staying at Ramada Forum XXX, Springfield, starting Friday morning, March 1 (217-798-1530).

<u>Press Kits</u>, in addition to those mailed out in ad-
vance, will be available at the conference from
Helen Farlow.

Photography—as it relates to the publicist and his or her job—is dealt with more fully on pages 81–89.

6. Speech copies, if you have been diligent enough and fortunate enough to obtain them.

7. A quick facts sheet containing information for the press. (See examples on pages 177 and 179.) This will be a summary of what the newspeople need to know to facilitate their on-the-spot coverage of the event. The information will vary according to the nature of the activity. The essential facts are:

a. The subjects, hours, and places of any press conferences.

b. The location of the press room, if one is being provided.

c. The names, addresses, telephone numbers, and hours and dates available of the p.r. people (you and your press room staff—assistants, secretary, gophers, volunteers). This information should cover the times immediately preceding D day and also D day itself.

Other than the seven basic ingredients, your press kit may include:

8. A history of the event, if it is a "Sixth Annual," but particularly if there is an anniversary to be noted. Special anniversaries are the fifth, the tenth, fifteenth, and the twentieth. After the twentieth, go to 10-year intervals—thirtieth, fortieth, etc.

9. Full vitae of all the program "stars." The thumbnail sketches (see page 196) usually suffice, but sometimes a reporter wants to go into more detail.

10. A digest of the contents of each speech, with quotes.

11. Tickets and invitations to any conference-related meals, social occasions, or special functions.

12. Background information on the event (see "history," above). This could include its origin, its funding, how it came about, what need it is meeting—anything pertinent and/or interesting.

13. Copies of any position papers, white papers, or papers on philosophical-action stances to be discussed during the program. Always include these so the reporters will have as much information as anyone else when the discussion or debate begins.

14. A calendar of events, if yours is a year-round activity or the current program is a part of that activity.

15. A directory of facilities, if you have, at your institution, certain facilities and service offices of which the press might reasonably make use.

16. A listing of other activities in the same general area of interest as your current conference or other programs. A press kit for an annual conference for highway engineers, for example, could include a listing of off-campus graduate courses in engineering, or refresher courses (if any) for engineers, and other related events and services.

17. A brief glossary and a short listing of good (and easily obtainable and readable)

references, if the event at hand has specialized or technical aspects unfamiliar to a general-news reporter—and particularly if that event is of some importance and magnitude.

Is there a trick to arranging the contents of a press kit?

Yes.

Some sponsors—notably those of entertainment or "concert series" types of programs—put out elaborate press kits with a lot of glossy photos and a lot of sample news releases, as well as reprints of articles about the performers or speakers. You can skip the action glossies and the sample releases, but including reprints of articles about or by the platform people for your program can be a very good idea. Don't omit these materials if they can be made available.

A good way to make a newsperson's life easier and the press kit (especially the low-budget type) attractive is to have each item printed on a different tint of paper.

 **It takes a dedicated and unhurried editor to go painstakingly through ten to fifty or more white sheets of paper containing printed or typed information to find the kernel or item which he or she needs at that moment.**

Note that we said a different *tint*. Black print on dark shades (maroon, marine blue, forest green, etc.) is hard to read. Use the light tints—pale sand-beige; pale blues, pinks, yellows, greens, mauves. Easier to read. More attractive. Less pressure in the impact.

Also, keeping the widths the same 8½ inches, use different lengths of paper. When you stuff the press kits, stagger the different lengths so that the title line of each paper is right before your eyes.

When you are talking with an editor or reporter and are asked a question about your project, it makes your presentation more effective, besides easier, if you can point to the press kit and say, "It's right there—on that second sheet from the bottom, the pale green one."

AT THE LAST MINUTE

Keep your eye out for late-hour features which may not receive active coverage and which should be phoned in or delivered to the newsrooms in the program's final hours or immediately afterward.

These include:

1. Elections and appointments
2. Resolutions
3. Speech copies or stories which did not arrive in advance
4. Future plans or major decisions, apart from formal resolutions (which often have a high news content), which also may have news value and which maybe arrived at—or announced—as the program closes

   Don't leave (or get hard to find, for reporters may be trying to reach you) until all these tags and tatters are wrapped up and your desk and conscience are cleared.

PHASE IV

MOP UP

THERE ALWAYS IS A NEXT TIME

When you wind up a project, the immediate and eminently human reaction is, "Whew! Thank heaven that's over." And with some other challenge in view, it is a relief to be able to clean up the remainders of the project just completed.

 **Don't throw anything away.**

The project is *not* over. You don't *think* there will be, but there always will be a next time. Granted, you probably will not do the exact same thing again. Yet it is most probable that you will, sometime in the future, be faced with a project where the materials, formats, strategies, or people used in the just-ended program can be used again.

GOOD FILES

Good files save a lot of time and effort and can provide such handy, ready-made conveniences as Checklists and promotion plans.

ITEM: Both projects—the one you have just completed and the one which comes up later—are in some way addressed to the business community of your city or state.

You have, prudently:

1. Kept a *complete file* on the project just completed.
2. Developed a *good media mailing list* from which to work. Granted, you, your helpers, or both are going to have to check it out pretty thoroughly for changes in people, in addresses, and even in emphasis or format. But you have a head start on this sometimes tiresome but vital ingredient of your promotion campaign.
3. Stashed away, in that same file, the *names of the people in the media* with whom you've worked, and possibly some little comments to remind you of your approaches to them.

    You may, in your private notes, have characterized those who helped advance or cover the earlier program in ways such as these:

Nice guy.

Interested mostly in views of the future and predictions of business trends.

Sourpuss.

Good writer but doesn't want to dig—give a complete background.

4. Kept copies of *routine releases*, which you also may be able to make use of as patterns.
5. Kept the *background material* on cosponsors which you worked up for the press kits and which undoubtedly can be updated with almost no effort and used again.

Additionally, that precious file should include, all in multiples:

Copies of all agendas

Memorandums and notes on task force and steering committee meetings

Correspondence, to you and from you all in multiples

Budgets, bills, receipts, records of estimates and of costing out

Photographs, logos, posters, brochures, flyers, graphics, all recruitment instruments

Clippings, tapes

Lists of friends along the way—good vendors, etc.

Press kits, facts sheets, information packets

Tear sheets of ads, copy for PSAs and for scripts

Summaries, reports, proceedings, transcripts, evaluations, and full notes on gut reactions

The file from "last time" is a treasure.

Five years may pass before you or a successor makes use of it, but *the time will come.*

Keep your hands on the file from "last time." Don't trust someone else or the person's successor or secretary not to throw it out. Beware, particularly, of those neatniks who boast that they are not "paper savers."

 **Keep duplicates or triplicates of everything.**

The copying machines will have served their purpose on the day that a colleague comes in and pleads for this or that file or set of materials.

And, without doubt, the day your caller has to have a certain set of releases "right now" will be the day when there is a blizzard outside and the coyping machines have gone kaplunk.

Keeping duplicates of everything also is a penny saver. It costs money to throw things away and then have to use funds, staff time, and materials to develop them a second time, or a third!

Speech copies are particularly important, especially if you take the time to have someone keep cross-reference lists. When you or your supervisor wants to make a report or speech or write an article on, for example, the continuing education unit, the speeches and articles you have in various files, all touching on the CEU, again can be a treasure.

TAKING SCORE

If you are so tired of the project just completed that you can't face another hour of thinking about it, put a tickler on your calendar and make yourself get back to it no later than 2 weeks from now—while it still is fresh in your mind.

Codes

Your use of codes should show who attended the program.

If your program was addressed to three kinds of audiences, and if you used colored registration cards to differentiate among them, all you have to do is count the blue cards (for librarians), the tan cards (for teachers), and the yellow cards (for community leaders), and you'll know where your audience came from.

A List of Easy Ways of Coding and Tracking

1. Have different-colored registration cards or announcement pages with tear-offs for each of your target groups—for example, green for engineers, blue for architects, pink for landscape architects, beige for environmentalists, and so on.

2. Individualize the return addresses given in each of your promotion attempts— announcements or brochures, advertisements, releases, etc.—so they can easily be separated according to the publication or broadcast. A paid advertisement in four separate publications can indicate that inquiries and registrations be sent to your office address. In each case the room number can be changed slightly. For example, an advertisement in the *Detroit News* might give 114-DP Administration Building as the address to which replies should be directed; responses triggered by an ad in *Architectural Digest* could be sent to 114-AD Administration Building, and so on. In other words, the letters indicating the initials of the specific publication can be added to your regular address and whoever receives the responses from all such promotion attempts can track them easily and identify those which generate the most response per advertising/promotion dollar by sorting out all responses according to the initials.

3. Have each target group, according to the promotional means used, send responses to 114-A Administration Bldg., for alumni; 114-B, same building, for those whose names have been purchased through a mail house; 114-C for those on mail lists developed by the program's sponsors from among their mailing lists of clubs, churches, industries, and so on.

4. If finances permit, get a different post office box for each of your forms of promotion and/or target groups. P. O. Box 332 could be the return address for paid advertisements in professional journals; 118 for news releases and public-service announcements; 112 for paid advertisements in the general-circulation press—you can be as specific or as general as seems to be appropriate.

5. Again, if finances permit, you may want to subscribe to a clipping service. Some large mail houses have these, as do a number of other sponsors. Shop around for your best buy in the area—and check references with people you know.

If your promotional materials were coded by return address for those seeking additional information and registration materials, the basic strategy will help you determine which approaches to prospective participants were effective. Your paid advertisement in *The Chronicle* might have asked prospective registrants to write to Room 135, Administration Building, while your article in the education section of a local newspaper might have asked them to respond to Room 111, Union Building.

Easy to track your responses?

Right.

Or, you might have asked prospective respondents to address cards and letters to a certain post office box, rented for that purpose, or call a special telephone number.

This makes for a simple evaluation of your promotion strategies.

Your coded materials can reveal a lot of other things:

Which media (and which people *in* the media) are most friendly to your endeavors.

What really was the honest, unhyped news value of the activity in question. What made it news.

The demography of the promotion effort. Where did the people come from? Who were they?

Most importantly, which outreach effort drew to your program the people you *wanted* to reach.

Example: An annual series of a public discussion conference in a suburban area, with a galaxy of sponsors which included several educational institutions, was suspended and probably will be abandoned because a survey of the questions on the registration cards and those on the evaluation instruments showed that it was *not* reaching the people it was intended to attract.

Those who registered were largely academicians and students from the sponsoring institutions. They definitely were people who should have been attracted to and registered for that particular program. But there was no comparable interest and participation evidenced by the community leaders and opinion makers in that suburban area (outside of academic)—the prime target group for the forum.

Clipping Services

Analyze the results of your clipping activities, whether you did your own clipping, had staff members or volunteers do it, or were able to afford the very specific and excellent commercial services available.

Who used what?

How did they edit, rewrite, or alter it?

What hints does the use given your materials offer for future promotion efforts? How could you have beefed up the parts they liked? Could you have provided the omitted material in a form which would have fostered or facilitated its use?

For example, could you have:

Written tighter?

Used more quotes?

Included more photographs in your packets and with your releases?

Provided better background material?

Gut Reactions

Earlier, we advised those of you who were so tired of the completed project that your eyes were glazing over and your stomachs were queasy to put it away for a while and *then* review it. As with all dogmatic statements, there are exceptions. Here is one exception: *Do not* delay the first assessment of the success or failure of the program and how your promotion effort contributed to that result.

The one kind of assessment you can't put into the closet for a week or two is that important one based on gut reactions and informal feedback.

This is one you need to look at and talk about while all impressions are clear in your mind. The same evening, the next day—these are not too soon.

At a meeting on the heels of the completion of the project, each person should be asked to give his or her reactions to the program and should be quizzed pretty thoroughly about his or her answers.

Call it a debriefing. Sample questions:

Why do you feel that way?

What made you like that portion of the program better than the other?

And—most important—what people did you talk with during and after the program?

What did they say?

How did they seem to feel—happy, so-so, disappointed?

This is a good meeting to tape and to have a backup steno take notes on.

The immediate gut reactions will be surprisingly candid.

They may give you a second surprise when you review them 6 weeks or 6 months later, and they can give an added dimension to the planning and promotion process when you set out to structure and promote another activity.

Facing Reality

All the fine means for taking score—coded outreach, evaluation instruments, a poring over clippings, and the review of informal feedback and gut reactions—can be both helpful and extremely tricky.

Depending upon the general mood of the staff and committee after the ball is over, they can experience euphoria or fall into a dismal dump.

Neither of these extremes is going to help you with future publicity efforts or help you analyze the effect of what you have or have not accomplished in the present case.

At this point, you turn to a detailed Checklist for internal assessment—one like that on pages 207–208. This excellent "example of typical program data to be collected for a detailed marketing activity review in a continuing education setting" (his quote) was developed by Larry R. Bramblett of the University of Georgia.

You will want to revise it according to the particular context in which you operate programs, but it is a realistic and honest framework. In using it, you should expand it under each of the headings and subheadings to include every individual outlet in which you advertised. Your news release and PSA impacts can be more generalized—you can list these by category, rather than individually.

Your elaboration of the ingredients in the program's magic mix, under the disbursement and return headings provided by Bramblett, is the framework for your financial summation.

In this summation, also use the chart on costing it out which appears on pages 103–105.

In accordance with the parameters of these two Checklists, you should be able to be very, very specific about how you spend money, on what, for what, and the return received in the numbers of enrollments or registrations.

It goes without saying that you should keep a running tally, full of even the minutest details, as estimates are received, bids are let out, and bills are returned.

(From sad experience, sadly and foolishly repeated, I can testify that it is *not* the path of efficiency to throw all financial papers into a big box and get back to them later. "Seventeen boxes of paper clips? What in the world did we do with *them*?")

Many institutions and organizations even have a departmental financial officer who keeps these records and arranges them in orderly patterns. That person also sometimes receives the bills directly. If you have a "money man" or "money woman" in your shop, you should request (nag, if you must) copies of all such records for *your* present checkpoints and your future assessments, and you should keep *your* own running accounts as you go along. Saves shocks later on.

Marketing Audit

Program Component	Disbursement	Return
Title of program		
Content area of program		
Program topics		
Program length		
Program level		
Program format		
New or former program		
Promotion Component		
Direct-mail response		
Cost of direct mail		
Responses from TV		
Cost of TV advertising		
Newspaper response		
Cost of newspaper advertising		
Radio response		
Cost of radio advertising		
Institutional representation contacts response		
Cost of institutional representation		

	Disbursement	Return

Sales promotion response
   Cost of sales promotion

Publicity response
   Cost of publicity

Place Component
Contract amount

Grant amount

Participant fee collected

Direct costs of program

Indirect costs of program

General Target Market Characteristics
Cosponsored program

General-audience program

Geographic distribution of participants

And in checking costs against the "Costing It Out" list and Bramblett's formula for analysis—whether or not with assistance or the opposite on the part of a financial officer—you and your staff and task force (possibly also the steering committee should take part) must certainly make comprehensive notes on the efficiency and effectiveness of every disbursement.

What worked?

What bombed?

What went (unexpectedly) wrong?

What went (unexpectedly) right?

When you do it again, what would you keep "as is"?

When you do it again, what would you change, omit, add, consider? How?

And be sure to add in the intangibles, such as the apparent mood and pitch of interest of all concerned—sponsors, speakers or instructors, and participants.

EVALUATION INSTRUMENTS

As an Aid in Taking Score

Evaluation instruments, as they are called in the hallowed halls of educational institutions and the busy back rooms of industry, are a fad whose time has come.

They are a fad of which you should make use. They offer one of several approaches you can use to find out why *some* of the people attending your program or enrolled in your courses took part in the activity.

Note that I say *some* of the people.

Getting *Your* Question Answered

The stumbling block may be that the questionnaire your steering committee plans to use does not include your question—the one to which you need answers.

To get *your* question included, you may have to be both ingenious and tenacious.

Many larger institutions, and some which are not so large, have people who are specialists in drawing up evaluation instruments. They teach or practice (or both) the art of assessing the efficacy of a program or course by the answers they receive on questionnaires which are distributed to the participants.

Usually, the questions are based on ordered answers. For example:

How did you find this session?
Poor ☐ Good ☐ Very Good ☐ Excellent ☐

Or, "Please rank on a scale of 1 through 10, with 1 being very poor or worthless and 10 being superior, the presentation by the morning panel."

The question you will want inserted in the questionnaire does not fit into either of these patterns, and that fact will be a roadblock in the path of your getting it inserted into the questionnaire.

However, the answers to it should benefit both your staff and the others involved in audience-centered program development.

Here, paraphrased for the sake of emphasis from the evaluation instrument shown on pages 210–211, is the question you want inserted:

Where and how did you hear about this program? Please be specific.

You may want to indicate a choice source, such as a news feature or feature release in a certain newspaper, magazine, or journal, or an announcement or talk show over a certain radio or TV station, or you may want to determine whether it was a brochure, a flyer, a poster, an announcement at some organizational meeting, word of mouth via an acquaintance or a friend (how did the *friend* hear about it?), or "other."

Now that is quite a bit to try to get into a questionnaire that somebody has been ordered to keep short. Try anyway. It may not be easy, because the evaluation instrument writer will have preconceived ideas about his or her product and also may be hard to locate, for the program development specialist and other members of the committee (i.e., the prime movers of the conference or course) often are not the same people who will draw up the evaluation instrument.

<u>Evaluation</u>

SCIENCE WRITERS WORKSHOP

Held on Wednesday, November 8

Illini Union

To Participants:

The planners of this workshop consider participant reactions very important. Please fill out this form, slip it into the enclosed envelope, and mail it to my office. Your opinions will be very helpful to us in planning subsequent workshops.
Thanks very much.

_____

1. Please rank the following parts of the seminar, using the scale from 1 to 5 below.

	Ineffective				Very Effective
a. Location	1	2	3	4	5
b. Length	1	2	3	4	5
c. Topics					
(1) Coal & Good Soil	1	2	3	4	5
(2) Beginning with Basics	1	2	3	4	5
(3) Interdisciplinary Re- search Developments	1	2	3	4	5
(4) Refuse & Residue	1	2	3	4	5
(5) Environmental Muta- genesis & Carcinogen- esis	1	2	3	4	5
(6) Sulfur Pollution Mortality	1	2	3	4	5
d. Handout Material Prepared	1	2	3	4	5
e. Opportunity to Meet Indi- vidual Faculty Members	1	2	3	4	5

2. What was the single <u>most</u> effective aspect of the

seminar? _____

_____

3. What was the single <u>least</u> effective aspect? _____

_____

_____

4. Would you come to another seminar dealing with
   similar science-related topics?

   _____ NO   _____ YES

   a. If so, what topics would you like covered?

      (1) _____

      (2) _____

      (3) _____

   b. If so, would you or your employer be willing to
      pay a registration fee to cover a portion of
      the costs? How much?

      (1) $25 or less__;   (2) $26-50__;   (3) $51-75__

5. What changes, if any, should be made in the

   manner of presenting information? _____

   _____

   _____

6. How could the University of Illinois at
   Urbana-Champaign help you further in your

   science writing responsibilities? _____

   _____

   _____

7. How did you find out about this workshop?
   Please be specific.

   _____

   _____

8. Please provide other comments. _____

   _____

   _____

So, first you find the evaluation specialist. Then you have to convince the specialist to put your question in the evaluation instrument and also to insert the specific suggestions by which you will code the answers to your question.

To do this with effect and assurance requires that you understand the current interest in evaluation instruments.

They can be of sterling worth. However, some program development and program coordination people, often backed up by specialists whose products and pronouncements have attained almost oracular mystiques, are carrying the fad to absurd lengths.

Some zealous demon evaluators add a couple of other instruments to the original and justified questionnaire.

There are programs carried on which suggest (or demand) that the participants or students (in whichever category) fill out three or more questionnaires—for this is what the instruments are, no more, no less—in the course of the event.

1. The first may zero in on the participant's expectations.
2. The second, on his or her reactions at, say, the end of the first cluster of activities.
3. The third, on his or her feelings about the program as it closes—i.e., Did you get what you expected? Which parts of the program were best on a scale of 1 to 10?

An additional appraisal may be scheduled as a 6-week, 6-month, or even year-long follow-up to determine what program information each person is using or had found valuable when he or she carried it back into professional, personal, or educational settings or activities.

Pitfalls of Evaluation Instruments

Evaluation instruments, questionnaires, or whatever they are called, have some merit. Carefully worded, judiciously structured for impartiality and avoidance of bias, they can be helpful in toting up the effectiveness of the activity and provide a basis for planning and premeasuring the effectiveness of future activities.

But the people who draw up these questionnaires very often are deeply involved with the activity and deeply concerned about getting good marks on its worth. Whether they themselves realize it or not (and usually their motives are of the best), their perspectives are apt to be slanted, and the questionnaires they draw up are apt to reflect that slant.

Let's look at a questionnaire being developed to discover the "marketing" techniques being used to best profit at a sample of institutions offering continuing education programs. The developers, who would have their own theories about "marketing" and its most potent strategies, will perhaps unwittingly word their questions to mirror their bias. Their questionnaire will provide very little feedback for the administrator or other respondent who feels that "marketing," in this connection, is an improper and nonreflective word. Yet whatever the answers, the marketing-approach advocates will take them as a justification of their view of the problem. If the questions are phrased somewhat differently, with "publicity" or "promotion" as an umbrella term in place of "marketing," the responses could prove an entirely different set of points.

So this, to underscore the point, becomes a problem when there is an overdependence on evaluation instruments:

Too often, they are structured and phrased to reflect the special interests of the persons who draw them up and who are conducting the program.

Let's start a list of possible pitfalls in the use of such questionnaires:

1. They are written so that the results inevitably are slanted or reflect a bias.
2. Certain kinds of people fill out questionnaires, while others do not. They simply like to answer questions.
3. Often, people who fill out such instruments are apt to tell you what they think you want to hear.
4. On the other hand, persons with antagonistic attitudes are more apt to answer questionnaires than people who feel good about their experience.
5. A person with some involvement and concern in a program will, again possibly in all innocence, manipulate any answers or percentages to prove his or her point. The end analysis of data obtained through the instrument is at least as important as the instrument's wording and structure.

Privacy Factor: Legitimate Questions Versus Nosiness

There is another minus value in many evaluation instruments. It usually lies in the fact that questions can infringe upon people's privacy—and they resent it. The example on pages 214–215, for instance, is entirely too detailed, with questions even on introductions.

Some conference center staffs and other sponsors have rather elaborate enrollment forms which ask not only for such specifics as name, title, and institution but also for others like job, salary range, age range, and supervisor's name.

Rebels against answering these questions are chided with the sort of things as "These are not used for personal purposes. They are used for purposes of program evaluation and attraction, and for research on the users of our services."

That's all very well and good. But lots of people refuse to reply to some of the more prying questions.

Those types of questions could tell any nosy person that I, for instance, work at the University of Illinois, that I do this and that, that my title is Head of Information Services for Continuing Education and Public Service.

I do not object to anyone's knowing these facts.

Staff Development Program

Levis Faculty Center
Friday, September 23, 1977

EVALUATION/NEXT STEPS

TOTAL CONFERENCE EVALUATION

As a part of the Staff Development's effort to increase the effectiveness of this and future programs, we would appreciate your reactions to this program and your suggestions for future programs. It is important that everyone complete this form so that the reactions of the entire group will be reflected.

1. Please evaluate the worth of the various segments of the conference. (Circle one number on each 1-5 scale) (low) (high)

   a. Introductions of New People   1 2 3 4 5

   b. A View From the Top   1 2 3 4 5

   c. Section Heads--The Year Ahead   1 2 3 4 5

   d. Fiscal 1979 Funding   1 2 3 4 5

   e. Director Search Committee Report   1 2 3 4 5

   f. Update from 1976   1 2 3 4 5

   g. Career Development [answer]   1 2 3 4 5
   h. Grantsmanship[only the one] [you attended]   1 2 3 4 5

   i. Improving Office Organization   1 2 3 4 5

   j. Lunch   1 2 3 4 5

   k. Summary/Evaluation/ Next Steps   1 2 3 4 5

   l. Staff Development Program as a whole   1 2 3 4 5

Which Session was most valuable?

_____

Why? _____

Which was least valuable?_____

Why?_____

What changes would you have made?_____

_____

CONCURRENT SESSION EVALUATION

Session you attended _____

Please evaluate your experience of this session on the following dimensions (circle one number on each 1-5 scale).   (low)   (high)

a. The session was clear and to the point   1 2 3 4 5

b. The session promoted interest and discussion   1 2 3 4 5

c. The speaker demonstrated thorough understanding of subject   1 2 3 4 5

d. I liked the balance between information presented and time allowed for discussion and questions.   1 2 3 4 5

e. In general, I rate this session: 1 2 3 4 5

The level of the material presented was (check one):

       _____over my head

       _____at my level

       _____too basic for me

The seating arrangement promoted participation.

       _____yes

       _____no

       _____had no bearing

COMMENTS:

(over, please)

NEXT STEPS

Would you like to see other Staff Development _____Yes
Programs?   _____No

Where would you like   _____ Allerton
these programs?   _____ Levis
                            _____ Union
                            _____118a Illini Hall
                            _____ Other_____

When?   Time of Year?   Day of the Week?
_____Morning   _____Fall   _____Monday
_____Afternoon   _____Winter   _____Tuesday
_____All day (8-5)   _____Spring   _____Wednesday
_____Evenings   _____Summer   _____Thursday
_____Weekend   _____Friday
                                                    _____Saturday
                                                    _____Sunday

Length of program

_____ Series of 1 or 2 hour sessions
_____ ½ day sessions
_____ All day sessions (8-5)

In what format would you like to see these topics presented?
_____formal presentations
_____group discussions
_____lecture-discussions
_____work group sessions
_____luncheon meetings

What specific topic areas would you like to see as future
Staff Development Programs?

_____
_____
_____

We've tried to evaluate this program and seek you suggestions for future ones without being long-winded about it.
We hope we've succeeded. It there is anything that we
haven't covered that you'd like to comment on, please do
so in the space below.

The Staff Development Committee

Dick Beck
Linda Bock
Barbara Jain
Charles Kozoll
Judy Riggs
Ron Sears
Pola Triandis
Jim Votruba

Where I ra'ar back and refuse to answer is when they go on to try to ascertain my sex (They could guess it by my name, but some others' names are tricky—my own daughter is named Jeffrey and nicknamed Jef). One question would, if answered honestly, give them my age, and I would not like that; I agree with Oscar Wilde: "A woman who will tell her age will tell anything." Other questions would give them my salary and my home address and telephone number, and I certainly can do without those porno and crank phone calls, even if they are made long-distance, which adds a flattering factor.

The profile that prying questions can provide is just too complete and too easily identified as that of not a statistic but one particular person. Research, this is not. It is nosiness.

Subjective Responses

Your truest judgment of whether the program succeeded or bombed lies in subjective responses as gained during the activity itself. Talk to people at intermissions and at the close of the activity. Talk with them at any meals associated with the activity. Notice their nonverbal attitudes; their smiles, frowns, angry scowls, and blah expressions. If they come out chatting happily or vividly among themselves, it probably went off well.

Remember, it isn't always necessary for people to *get something out* of a program in the sense of a solid chunk of knowledge for it to have benefited them. Enjoyment—a good time in a good setting with interesting presentations and a pleasant, even exciting group to be with—this in itself is a valuable educational experience.

 **To obtain a good, albeit subjective, idea of the activity, it is necessary to learn the reactions of a cross section of the participants in the mix.**

During the program, make *very* certain the committee and staff are firmly instructed to *spread out.* It is the instinct of a committee and staff, after having worked long and hard on an activity which may or may not bomb, to huddle, as in their cave with wolves prowling outside, in a sort of peer-support group, craving for protection.

This may be soothing to the committee and staff, but it certainly wrecks the concept of subjective assessment.

Refuse to have a "staff table" at the meals. If there is a hospitality suite, take precautions to keep it a hospitality suite and not a place where the committee and staff can cluster and hide.

Make rules. Assign tables. Assign areas for floating during intermissions. Everything should be written down and distributed and discussed before the program comes off, probably at the final full staff and committee meeting before the event. Each person must get a memorandum in his or her name. Like this:

"Mr. Gordon is assigned to table 7 for the luncheon and table 12 for the banquet. During various intermissions, he is to talk with people from Southwestern Kansas Technical Institute, and with those from the Better Business Bureau."

You should ask the chairperson, coordinator, or project director (or do it yourself, if you wear one of these hats) to suggest some appropriate questions to throw into the conversation as the occasion arises.

"Are you enjoying the program? Why did it attract you? Where did you hear about it? Is it what you expected? What do you like best? Least?"

Of course, if your *only* mission is that of a publicity-promotion honcho, the answer you will be interested in hearing is the answer to the question "Where did you hear about it?"

The most frequent answer probably will be "My neighbor [boss, wife, friend] heard about it and told me." This, unless the neighbor or other contact is sitting nearby, is a dead end. Because the question now comes down to: "Where did the neighbor hear about it? Did we send her a brochure? Did she see a poster? Read about it in the newspaper? Hear a public-service announcement on the radio on the way to work?"

Such frustrations are frequent, but at least you've got a tag on one form of recruiting, and the best of all: word of mouth. Peer influence.

MIND YOUR MANNERS: MAKE YOUR THANK-YOUS

People have been helpful to your publicity-promotion campaign.

You probably said "thank you" to them at the time of their help, or on D day as the activity wound down.

It is time now to say "thank you" again to every one of them.

Write them notes, and send copies to their bosses.

Your helpers, even if they work in the office next to you, will appreciate the attention and the courtesy.

Your task force members, in and out of your own shop, will entertain similar feelings.

PAYOLA

In thanking members of the media, a little payola is not out of place. It must be permissible payola, of course. Just something to add a little emphasis to the note, something which you hope will remind them in a pleasant way of your institution and its recent program.

Buy them a lunch, on a one-to-one basis, and *do not* talk business.

Send them a little gadget or ornament which says something about your institution or organization. This could be a book or a trinket tray embossed with a seal, logo, and name of your group. In many ceramic engineering departments, gadgets or ornaments are made up by students in their spare time for use at an "engineering open house" or for a sale to increase departmental scholarship funds. Other institutions stock them through the college or agency bookstore or alumni association. Associations and industries have similar mementos. Look around. You will see a number of suitable things. Small, obviously modest in cost, nothing elaborate. Just a "thank you" and a reminder—something in the "more than a card" category.

Giving some sort of small remembrance, a token, is mannerly and appropriate. It is not mannerly—nor is it appropriate—to send a gift which the reporter or newscaster you are honoring could feel might put him or her under any sort of obligation. So be polite, be appreciative, but also exercise extreme care and keep your good taste working overtime.

PHASE V

ET CETERA

ADAPTING THE PUBLICITY MIX TO YOUR ORGANIZATION'S NEEDS

The formulas which work for educationally sponsored programs and activities work equally well for activities sponsored by profit and nonprofit organizations.

They are what chefs call "master recipes" in that they are basic, usually uncomplicated, and infinitely adaptable.

Think of a tetrazzini, if you will, or a fondue, or a soufflé. Anything which actually is a way with food instead of a single entity in your cooking repertoire.

On another level, think of a sonnet. All poems which can claim the name have essentially the same skeletal structure.

It is like that when you publicize and promote a program.

Follow the charts, follow the guidelines, follow the Checklists, take advantage of the hints.

And if you do, you will have it made, whether your p.r. effort is for a social agency, a governmental or privately supported institution, a service club, a civic organization, a business, an action organization, a charitable effort—whatever.

Count your blessings, as advised, acquire a "Basic Bookshelf" as advised (or locate one with easy access), and get started. You can do it as well as anyone, and your sponsor or the group with which you are affiliated will profit.

The same holds true if the items you are offering to the waiting public are not programs or activities which are wrapped up in a few days but instead are long-term program commitments such as formal and informal classes, both credit and noncredit; study by correspondence, tapes, TV, newspaper, or combinations of these—what is increasingly being called "guided individual study"; or membership in an organization which involves people in study-action types of situations (e.g., League of Women Voters).

The variation for a long-term commitment is that it is a series of soft taps instead of one 6-week thrust to which you have led up through several months of advance work.

It is the sort of thing that repetition makes work. You should plan on one big membership or enrollment push at the start of each season, followed by the kinds of reminders made possible in the section, which follows, on the year-round publicity program.

Publicizing opportunities for long-term commitment involves milking every situation for its last drop of benefit. Analyze, adapt, and take it from there. You will be surprised what a little ingenuity and effort can evoke in the way of favorable publicity—publicity which will show results.

Particularly in the noncourse situation, keep the personal approaches to prospective participants as active as possible; go back and read the short section on the laying on of hands (pages 89–95). And take every bit of advice contained herein.

THE YEAR-ROUND PUBLICITY ASSIGNMENT

A person who is assigned the job of publicizing and promoting an institution or agency with a cluster and multiplicity of things going on of various sorts and at various levels all the time has to be a juggler.

This juggler must:

Set (and enforce!) priorities.

Be stern and be consistent about the allocation of staff time.

Be judicious about emphasis and selectivity.

Be absolutely honest to the point of bluntness—and beyond—with all who are concerned. (Of *course* Mr. Lenahan thinks his program for traffic engineers is a momentous event; of *course* Ms. Vernon thinks her humanities classes in the suburbs should occupy all your attention for the next month; of *course* the program development staff is all wrapped up in the grass-roots energy discussion—and they think you should be, too.) Set them straight. Tell them where they are in the scheme of things. Don't let one person's (or group's) insistence that you go all out for their comparatively minor activity be the one trip too often to the well—the trip which wears out your welcome with the media.

At the same time—and it is difficult but necessary—you must keep an edge of flexibility which will enable you to recognize the great stuff when it comes (unexpectedly, almost always) along and instantly regroup and realign priorities and efforts to give it the p.r. support it deserves and must have.

It is a rough row to hoe.

It requires a real organizational talent, but this is a talent which can be developed.

WORKING TIMEFRAMES

It often helps keep the ducks in a row if you work up some sort of a chart. A chart can help you keep on schedule without neglecting either the major or the minor matters at hand. The sample, on pages 222–225, was developed in our own shop. It enables you to work out your priorities on a yearly basis and check on the status of any given project when needed.

YEAR-ROUND CALENDAR

A similar help—and this is a *must!*—is a year-round wall calendar that gives you the whole year at a glance and that is big enough to scribble on. Get the *very biggest* one you can. It may save your sanity when things start to pile up.

But before you start scribbling, spread the calendar out on a conference table, if you have one, or on the floor, if you don't.

1. Write in, first, *the dates for every annual event you have to publicize.*
2. Now write in the dates of any occasional or one-time-only events or programs you know about in advance. Examples: Bus tours to a nearby museum because of a special exhibit? A "futures" symposium with outside funding?
3. Leave plenty of space for later additions for events or programs which will be developed and which you will publicize.
4. Put in any personal commitments that will affect your work calendar.

    Staff meetings and such fall into this category. Those who serve on boards, commissions, or committees with fixed schedules of meetings will want to note those dates.

    Vacation? Wedding anniversary and (maybe this year) a cruise? Home for Christmas? The party bus to Ann Arbor for the Michigan game?

    Get them all in.

You will be able to see at a glance:

CALENDAR

Program	Week of Aug. 21	Week of Aug. 28	Week of Sept. 4
Marching Band Festival	Write and mail first release; write second release; write and mail PSA	Arrange for talk shows with WCIA, WAND, WILL, WICD; picture, maybe Dale with trophies	Mail second release; include info on judges, parade routes, entry deadlines
Engineering Open House	Write and mail third release—committees, new stuff, trivia	D day wrap-up: schedule, sites of shows, exhibits	
Extramural Classes	Write and mail first release, PSAs	Write and mail hometowners, spec. subject matter	D day wrap-up repeating registration info
Science Writing Workshop			
Shakespeare Symposium		Write and mail first release; have Joyce prepare mailing list	
Divorce Aftermath Counselor Workshop	Send announcement to professional journals		Special media mailing lists—don't forget church press
"Government by Budget" Spin-off —Springfield			

Note: We always leave the sheet with an empty panel or two for scribbles and for notes to ourselves like "Don't use Jake for photographer again—too uncooperative" or "Remember to send Janet a note and maybe ask her to lunch the next time I'm in Washington" or "Kill Brandt the moment this thing is wrapped up." Unless you are tidier than most people who practice or dabble in p.r., neither your entries nor ours will be neatly typed. The panels will be full of scribbles and scratch-outs in all colors of ink and a mess—but an operative mess.

Week of Sept. 11	Week of Sept. 18	Week of Sept. 25	Week of Oct. 2
Write and mail third release, include all bands, order of march, order of show, contest	D day		
Classes start; hometown reminders—"registration still open"		Feature story on new WATS line	
	Letters of invitation to editors, press in Science Writers Association		Telephone pals, major media not heard from; coming or not?
Check with Humanities Council on grant details; write and mail second release	Posters go up	Write and mail third release include names of plays to be discussed	D day
Set up talk shows —Chicago, St. Louis, local	Write for speech copies		Write and mail first release
		Call Maggie at *Times-Register* Dave Coleman at WICD	

(continued)

Program	Week of Oct. 9	Week of Oct. 16	Week of Oct. 23
Marching Band Festival			
Engineering Open House			
Extramural Classes			
Science Writing Workshop	Send out all background material and kits	Hometowners, D day	Evaluation; check for clippings, tapings
Shakespeare Symposium			
Divorce Aftermath Counselor Workshop	Write other releases; write and mail PSAs	Check press conference details; letters to press re coverage; mail second release	D day
"Government by Budget" Spin-off —Springfield	First release —barebones	Give final brochure copy to printer	Send calendar notices to agencies, League of Women Voters, newspapers

When your work load is heaviest

When you'll have to hire extra help, perhaps

When you will have to refuse all outside invitations or assignments because of your peak loads

When the decks probably will be clear enough that you can go sit on the beach or (if need be) get some work caught up in advance like the early bird you have become, so that the peak loads won't peak all that high

And organize all things accordingly.

Week of Oct. 30	Week of Nov. 6	Week of Nov. 13	Week of Nov. 20

Set up meeting
with Charles, Tom,
Jim, to investigate
funding for
possible repeat

Write and mail second release, include brochure; special letters of invitation to community leaders, editors	Check speakers, travel arrangements and hotel facilities	Wrap-up release; D day	

To get the very most out of this year-round calendar, use different-colored crayons or inks for the events you are publicizing and for your personal commitments. Don't throw away either the outdated calendar or the outdated countdown timeframes. Keep a file of them somewhere. You will need them as references in planning for effective expenditures of time, staff, effort, and budget on the year-long or more temporarily focused work plans.

HOW TO HOLD A PRESS PARTY

A press party is an embellishment in the p.r. effort, one which often serves some useful purpose. A press party should not be embarked upon in a frivolous, haphazard spirit. Instead, it should be carefully worked out, planned, and carried through, in order to become an additional component of the publicity-promotion plan and not a distracting ornament.

When Appropriate

A press party is appropriate in a number of circumstances, which include but are not exclusive to the following:

1. To introduce a person who may serve as a resource to the press in the future—your new director, chairperson, president, dean, public relations officer, or whomever.
2. To promote a program or a product or a coming attraction. A plus provided by a press party with such a goal is that reporters may have a chance to talk with a personage, star, or author who is announcing a forthcoming activity or service; introducing an entertainment event, benefit, or book; or unveiling a line of merchandise. It also allows you and your associates to be useful to the press in an informal way, based on a simple invitation: "Come have a cup with us while we tell you about it."

    I think you can see how, in many cases, a press party held for this kind of reason can turn into a prettied-up group interview. It is common, particularly in large cities, to hold a press party in tandem with a press conference, particularly when it is held to honor a theatrical or political personage, or indeed anyone with a high quotient as a newsmaker.
3. To assist the press in covering an event by providing an informal occasion for backgrounding or briefing, or to serve as a social element in a hectic, workaday setting. Many firms, organizations, and institutions have hospitality suites during conferences and conventions where they are represented. These often are the sites of one-shot invitational affairs ("Please come to suite 1804 to meet with the Tri-Conference people from 5 to 7 P.M. on Thursday.") or, they may in fact be the locations for open houses, where hospitality is served up to all the conference-goers on an everyday basis.
4. To honor one of your own. If a colleague wins an award, writes a book, or in some other way brings honor to himself or herself and thereby to the group, it always is appropriate to invite the press to whatever celebration you hold to signal this happy circumstance.
5. To introduce the year's plan of activity, outline its highlights, and provide the press with information on all the events and on the personalities involved. Those organizations, institutions, and agencies which have year-round p.r. calendars

may logically consider having a press party—on an annual or semiannual basis—for this reason. A press party of this sort can be helpful both to the press (saves them time and effort later on) and to the leadership in your group. It is a very good place, indeed, to have press packets and information kits ready to distribute, with perhaps an opportunity to point out certain items of special interest.

6. To say "thank you." Of course, it always is nice to say "thank you," and having a press party is one way to do this in a graceful and hospitable way. This is particularly true if you, and the press working with you, have just completed the grueling task of providing coverage for a major program or event. "Thanks. You helped a lot. Now let's get together socially to unwind." It is a pleasant gesture, usually well received.

Invitations

Invitations are a first step. Don't be choosy or elitist. Invite all members of the working press. You may find that some of your leaders have biases and prejudices and like to play favorites. This is another instance in which you must be firm. Everyone—but everyone—should and must be included. No matter if you don't approve of some campaign that "such and such a paper" or "that horrible station" is waging. No matter if you think Jake Nieman or Molly Picard is a gossip columnist below your notice. Invite them anyhow. People, media, and roles have ways of changing. But good manners do not change, and being elitist in a p.r. situation is very bad manners, indeed.

Personalize your invitations whenever this is possible within the bounds of reality. If one member of your group is a friend, a neighbor, or in some ways a friendly acquaintance of one of the newspeople, have your associate call the friend and say, "Marian, I'd particularly like you to come and meet some of the people I work with." Or, if whatever you are planning for the occasion being scheduled, for the year ahead, or for the personality involved is of particular interest to someone in the news media, call that person and point this out as a way of seconding the invitation.

How Organized

Except for the "thank you" occasion described in number 6, above—and even then, not often—a press party should be as carefully planned and executed as any other ingredient that a p.r. person puts into a specific mix.

Dates should be meticulously cleared to omit all possible conflicts.

A site should be selected which is convenient and generally well situated. You don't (except under circumstances so unusual as to be once-in-a-lifetime) invite the working press in a medium-to-large community out to the hinterlands for a press party. Move your group and your party into a convenient club or hotel or city apartment, if you want to have a good attendance. There are exceptions, as there are to any rule. These exceptions, however, are few. The press will come out to a party in a fairly inconvenient place if the person being featured or honored is a celebrity of the first stature—the President of the United States or the center of a national, not local, raging controversy. The press also may come out to a party which is in a site so unusual that they've been dying to see it for years. A historic site never before open to inspection, such as the only Frank Lloyd Wright house in the area, might attract a group of specialists. In the old days, the annual press outing at the Kennedy compound in Hyannisport always was completely attended. But as a rule, let us repeat, a downtown area near the various media newsrooms is the best place.

Wherever you hold a press party, be certain that the setting is attractive. Have flowers, little bowls of goodies. Make it look pretty and hospitable.

What time of day should you hold your press party? Usually the cocktail hour is the best time, particularly if you are holding it in connection with a conference or convention. Commercial and other sponsors sometimes block out time in a conference for a press breakfast or press luncheon. At a food writers' conference, a few years ago, one educational—not commercial—agency had an iced milk breakfast. It was pretty good, too, and the event won them not only press attendance but also national coverage. A press breakfast was held a few years ago to brief the members of the visiting press covering the anniversary of legislation for the land-grant colleges and universities. A luncheon is less well received than a late-afternoon party simply because at lunch you are competing against numerous deadlines. In general, hold to the cocktail hour.

How should you staff your press party? As carefully as you would a press room or press conference. Get all your more articulate and attractive task force members to come, and also as many members of your leadership as you possibly can recruit. The full-scale press party should, because it is in itself a showcase for your agency, institution, or organization, be a "must" on the calendars of your top brass.

Make certain that your people are well identified. Name badges with a color that is different from the color of the guests' badges; a carnation on the shoulder or in the lapel. Some sort of instant identification.

Have all your people well instructed. They are not to get into little huddles and talk shop. They are not to socialize with their professional buddies. No, this is a press party, and it is held for a purpose—to help and provide a background for help from the press. They must mingle, be cordial, provide materials and explanations of materials, and in general act as hostesses and hosts.

In the unhappy chance that the spot for the press party is remote from the various news centers or is hard to find, be sure and call a couple of weeks before the party to offer rides to those who might want them. And then call back with exact arrangements a day or two before.

Always tell them—the members of the working press—that you would welcome them alone and that you also would be happy to welcome a guest or spouse.

Let Your Hospitality Show

It is not hospitable (or very smart) to invite people to a press party and have them arrive only to find a pallid bowl of who knows what kind of punch and a rapidly congealing cheese dip with some crackers.

For early-day entertaining, such as at a morning coffee hour or a luncheon, have enough snacks of some substance to hold your guests until the next regularly scheduled meal. At the cocktail party, you should have, in addition to some oddments and nibbles (the ubiquitous peanuts, pretzels, and cheese bits), what I call a "stopper"—i.e., a food offering which can serve the dual purpose of satisfying the appetites whetted by drinks and salty tidbits and telling the guests that the party's over (in a tactful, friendly way). There is nothing worse, as a party closing, than having the bartender start packing up and the waiters and waitresses start carrying out trays and decorations. Both rude and tacky.

A Fillip

If you want your party to linger in happy memory for your guests, an unusual component is not amiss. It can be in the form of entertainment—a roving barbershop quartet, perhaps, or a juggler—anything that can provide additional enjoyment without detracting entirely from useful conversation. A souvenir, given upon arrival or departure, usually is well received if it is clever yet unpretentious. At best, your souvenir should be something comparatively indestructible, something which your guests will want to keep on their desks or among their knickknacks as a conversation piece.

PUBLICITY BEGINS AT HOME: NEWS NEED NOT BE "BIG"

On pages 38–40 we discussed the question "What is news?" and gave a group of items which should be considered. There, however, we focused on events that are an agency or organization's annual biggies, the really big programs or activities which merit the all-out publicity push.

Here we want to emphasize the kinds of closer-to-home news events that occur on smaller scales during the year and usually within your own organization, be it a church group, a business firm, a civic or service club, a school district, a college or university, and so on.

                    Timeframe for a Press Party

Two months to six
weeks in advance.........Clear the dates, secure a site, de-
                         cide on the format, order invita-
                         tions, hire any help (bartenders,
                         waiters, entertainers), order edi-
                         bles, potables, decorations, and
                         invitations.

Four weeks ahead.........Address and mail invitations. Ask
                         for replies by a date at least two
                         weeks ahead of the party.

As soon as your in-
vitations have had
time to arrive via
the U.S. mail ....Make first follow-up calls to
                         people of your acquaintance and/or
                         those with special interests in the
                         area, event, or person you are pro-
                         moting.

Two weeks ahead..........Backup calls--"Would you like to
                         bring a guest?" "Do you have a
                         ride?"

One week ahead ....Check all details of site, food, ar-
                         rangements, entertainment, hired
                         help, assignments (if any) for in-
                         dividual members of your group.
                         Correct any omissions. Have some-
                         one check by phone all who have been
                         invited but who have not indicated
                         that they will or will not attend.

One day ahead ....Recheck all arrangements above
                         with particular attention to the
                         presence and assignments of members
                         of your group. Be certain all your
                         hosts and hostesses will arrive
                         early and stay throughout, until
                         the last guest has departed.

The day of the
press party..............Be on site at least two hours ahead
                         (once you are certain that every-
                         thing is in order, go out and get
                         some coffee, or change into your
                         party clothes). But do make this
                         final check.

                         With everything arranged before-
                         hand, go to your press party--
                         and have a good time!

For not all publicity which can be of benefit is connected with special events, programs, or clusters of activities. Some of the most effective publicity you may put out can be generated from the everyday matters which go on in your shop and all too often go unheralded.

The sample Checklist that follows was developed for use by a police training agency. With small and easily made alterations, it can be helpful as a starting point for any business, institution, or organization.

The sample list does not include at least one major thing: "Anniversaries." An anniversary of almost anything can, if handled right, be legitimate news. Staying with the police training agency example, it can be the anniversary of the agency's establishment, or the anniversary of its first basic course. The chief administrator could be quoted in a retrospective and prospective release: he or she could talk about changes in societal attitudes which necessitated changes in police training tactics; look to some plans for the future, with regard to both instruction and facilities (Are they getting a new crime lab?); and sum up the progress of the organization in terms of how many officers have been trained, how many former students have achieved honors or high rank (with examples), and how the program has grown.

Publicity Possibilities for a Police Training Institute

Faculty
> Appointments to the staff
> Assignments to the staff
> Changes in assignments
> Honors or promotions
> Articles and books
> Appearances around the state and nation—speeches

Basic Police Training Courses
> Winners of class honors
> Class officers
> Unusual students
> Distinguished visitors to a course
> Guest faculty
> "Graduation" speakers

Other Courses
> Course announcements—especially of off-campus courses
> New course or courses
> Guest faculty

Student or faculty recognition (honors, awards, appointments to prestigious boards, etc.)

Distinguished visitors to a course

Unusual students

Noteworthy features

General

Special events

Anything out in the state

Distinguished visitors

Guest faculty (such as for a span of time)

Organizational matters—e.g., locations of satellite facilities

Grants received

Reports—e.g., views of the future

OTHER EXAMPLES OF NEWS-GENERATING FACTS

It *is* news, if only in his neighborhood "shopper" or in the little town where his mother lives, if Gary Schuster gets promoted.

It *is* news if a company opens up a new employee cafeteria which provides a "skinny table" for peer reinforcement for people trying to diet, or it *can* be news if you give the story to:

Area papers' news desks.

The newspapers' feature sections.

Food-service, dietary, and general-interest media.

The hometown and associational media of your food-service manager(s).

General-interest talk shows. My goodness, you could even put your company doctor on to talk about obesity's being a number 1 (or whatever) killer and an enemy of internal efficiency. And what you are doing about it, under his or her advice.

There are three traits involved in year-round, everyday publicity work which will enhance your institution or organization, and they are traits which you can develop:

Be inquisitive.

Be imaginative.

Be analytical.

Analyze and keep analyzing the actions and procedures and developments you may have been shrugging off as "routine." There is no such thing as "routine." *Almost anything can be news or feature material somewhere.*

Why bother?

A good image is beyond price, and your organization deserves a good image (or else it ought to go out of business and probably will).

A good image is *cumulative.* You do not win it in one grand, creative effort. Not at all. You earn it, bit by bit and piece by piece, as people hear and read nice things about your organization. Did someone say it is the little things that count?

It is.

A Case Study

Take, for example, the appointment of a new person to a middle-management position in your firm, institution, or organization. The appointee is a good, solid, well-trained, demonstrably effective young person, but there is nothing unusual about him or her.

No?

Don't you believe it.

You are going to get some mileage out of this appointment; some additional bits and pieces for that good image you are helping to build.

Analyze the new employee's vita, and make a list:

List A
1. Birthplace.
2. All places where the new employee lived during the growing years.
3. The place where the parents live. The college the new employee attended. Graduate school?
4. The family's former home, if you're bringing the family in from another city.
5. The new employee's hobbies, outside interests (including sports), and other skills, and perhaps prizes, membership in organizations, and affiliations.
6. The spouse. The new employee's spouse may also be news. Check on career and hobby interests, membership in organizations, affiliations, the hometown of the parents, the college and graduate school attended—all the points you checked for the new employee.

With list A, you are now ready to make up list B—your media mailing list.

List B
1. Hometown media—print and broadcast—for the person's:
   a. Birthplace.
   b. Present place of residence (and place in the immediate past, if he or she is moving from another town).
   c. All former places of residence.

 **Do not forget the neighborhood outlets—usually weeklies, radio, and giveaway shoppers.**

2. Education-associated media
    a. Alumni magazine(s)—college, university, trade school, whatever.
    b. The special newsletter of the college within the university which the newcomer attended. His or her law school or business school or almost any academic agency within an institution will have an alumni newsletter.
3. Organization-associated media
    a. Union affiliation.
    b. Church affiliation.
    c. Social sorority or fraternity affiliation.
    d. Journals of honorary and professional associations (for example, Phi Beta Kappa, The Society of the Sigma Xi, the state bar association).
    e. Special-interest journals and magazines, depending upon the organizations to which the employee, if of the male persuasion, may belong—a service club (Rotary, Kiwanis, Toastmasters, etc.) or a fraternal group (such as Elks, Moose, Lions); possibly a veterans' organization; perhaps a lodge, such as Masons or Shriners.

If the "new boy on the block" is a woman, she may be affiliated with a number of organizations that have newsletters—League of Women Voters, Federated Women's Clubs, Altrusa, Hadassah, American Association of University Women.

She, too, may have interests in lodge work, unions, etc., comparable to those suggested for male employees.

People of either sex with strong hobby interests often belong to national, state, or local organizations that have newsletters which would welcome a "people and places" note.

And don't forget your own organization's newsletters.

True, you will have better luck getting an item in local print media if you are in a medium-sized or smaller community instead of a metropolitan area. On the other hand, don't ignore or neglect to service your large metropolitan media. You may strike a special-interest chord or luck out in some other way.

Now write your release. Get in all the major points. Also get in a quote from the new employee's supervisor as to where his or her place will be in the firm and what special talents and insights the employee will bring to the organization. A *short* quote—not more than two or three sentences.

You will then mail the release, with a current head-and-shoulders photograph, to print media (no picture, of course, to broadcast media).

 **It will help here if you send (or take) your items to specific business-page editors and columnists. Don't forget special-interest pages, columns, and newscasters.**

A local sportscaster or sportswriter very probably could make use of information such as:

"John W. Faulkner, who as a top-seeded college tennis player in the early 1960s fought his way several times to the NETA semifinals and once beat Arthur Ashe 6-4, 6-0, 6-3 in tournament play, is moving to Midland to take a managerial position with the Standard Service Outlet."

A similar bit would be appropriate for a woman who has achieved some notice in sports, a career, a hobby, or volunteer work.

"Diane Kerber, who has spearheaded the over-the-top March of Dimes campaign in Metrocity for the past 5 years, has accepted the directorship of Midland's United Fund."

We've been talking a lot about print media. Your sportscaster could use a feature spot with a tennis player and your talk-program interviewer a spot on achievers and plans for the super fund raiser. This is true regardless of the sex of the sports star and the agency director.

The purpose of all this is not necessarily to make the individual look good (although such a job introduction will bring a new employee before the public, facilitate his or her orientation, and provide him or her with credibility in dealing with others on an immediate basis), but to add favorable mention of your organization to the cumulative image.

Once you start this, you've got to do it every time, so decide on the *level* at which you're going to operate.

Top management? President, chancellor, dean, or director? Department head? Full professor? Middle management? Introductory-level management (assistant professor)? Supervisor (instructor)? Officers of volunteer organizations?

However, keep your options open so as not to miss a really good news idea and image-building bet from the lower ranks of your organization, e.g., the new mail room employee who was a hero in the last big Peruvian earthquake disaster, or the new math instructor at Lincoln U. whose solution of the XYZ problem in linear algebra now promises to spearhead a revolution in computer technology. Your excuse for writing about these people, even though they are below your usual "cutoff rank" in the organization, is that they have done things which are important, and therefore their connections with us will make our organization look good via the halo effect.

When you start, you have got to do something (and make arrangements and give assurances that you will do it) for the folks of equal stature who are already on the staff.

Otherwise, the effort will work against the new person—and you—and create instant dislike, envy, and friction. "Who," they will ask, "does he think *he* is?"

How to do all this?

There are interesting things about everybody.

Dissect the current staff's vitae like you did that of the newcomer.

Discuss their interests and hobbies. Given time and honest effort, you can get the job done, and make everyone happy.

While we are on the subject of using personnel in the year-round p.r. effort, there is a service not to be neglected: Supply short, narrative biographies of *only*the members of your *top* leadership (and the other few real *stars* in your group) to the appropriate commercial and professional media. Accompany these with head-and-shoulders photographs of the people. Include a note—"for your files and possible future reference"—and the *date.*

The note with a biography and a photograph also should include something like this: "Please substitute these current materials on Mr. John Faulkner, president of the 18th National Bank of Midville, for earlier information which may be in your files." Add, for future contact, your name, title, address, and telephone number as information officer.

Insist on an *up-to-date* head-and-shoulders photograph. Be firm about "up-to-date." Don't let her foist off a photograph on you with a hairdo which went out with bobby socks or even miniskirts, and don't accept a likeness of him that must go back to the date he got his Eagle Scout badge.

Send the materials to the locals, to the business/professional media, and—if your organization is large enough to warrant this, or if you think your materials are interesting and important enough (Be honest!)—to the nearest press association bureaus.

Update these materials at a certain time each year, or when an individual gets a promotion or change of responsibility, whichever comes first.

If and when you send the updated bios and pictures, include a memo: "This is updated for your files, and for reference should you wish at some time to ask President Faulkner to comment on news developments within our organization's area of interest. For press assistance: Josie Marcus [and give your title; department; firm, institution, or organization; address; and telephone number]."

PROVIDING ACCESS TO YOUR PROFESSIONAL ASSISTANCE

A great help in your year-round publicity effort will be still another Checklist (see pages 238–239). It should tell your coworkers exactly what services you are prepared to offer which will assist them and their staffs in obtaining appropriate year-round publicity.

WHEN YOU HELP LOCAL AMATEUR PRACTITIONERS

As you get more and more involved—and proficient—in publicizing continuing education programs, you are going to find that more and more people come to you for help.

In an educational setting, these may be student or departmental groups who want publicity for a simple little undertaking—e.g., one involving a visiting speaker (unimportant, except to them), or a national or regional or even state officer of their association.

In other settings, the same kinds of situations may arise, or the supplicants may want publicity for a program such as might be mounted by Kiwanis or the League of Women Voters or the Family Service Bureau.

They will want to inform the local public so that interested persons can attend; motivate members of their own constituencies to take part; and—not all that incidentally—gain an ego stroke for themselves and/or the sponsor they represent.

You want to be helpful, but you don't have the time or energy or interest to get involved in an activity which is not even in your bailiwick.

If the people who come to you for help are particular friends or have some connection with the job you are regularly assigned to do, you may allow yourself to be seduced into doing their work for them.

That is dumb—from your standpoint and theirs.

From yours: There go your noon hours, or an evening, or a weekend.

From theirs: There goes an opportunity for time to learn by doing.

You will be much smarter—and possibly better thought of on all sides—if you are able to hand them, already prepared, a simple sheet (never a folder—that makes it look too hard!) listing the local outlets with which they may wish to be in contact.

Unless there is a whiz-bang feature involved, something that makes you think or say "Wow!" when they tell you about it, advise them to concentrate in their own backyards. If it has a "Wow!" element, advise them to forget the do-it-yourself approach and find a pro.

In a metropolitan area, the "backyard" limits probably will mean their neighborhood. Even in a middle-sized city, there will be no need to go beyond a countywide area.

 As you get into bigger towns, with the sophisticated "star" radio and TV talk shows and interview programs, you will find that many such shows have not only a host but also a contact. Therefore, list both names (star and contact) for the use of your ambitious amateurs, and warn your friends to go to the *contact*—not to the star, who often doesn't know who's on base until he or she gets to the studio that day.

INFORMATION SERVICES

The Information Services Office has responsibility for the publicity, promotion, and public
relations for all activities related to continuing
education and public service.

This office provides the following:

1. Publicity, Promotion, Public Relations

These vary according to the type of program and
its requirements.

The Information Services effort may be as simple as a one-page release to a limited mailing.

It may be a major undertaking which involves
several releases, the inducement of live coverage
by the media, the placement of key figures on talk
shows, or the insertion of public-service announcements in the broadcast media.

It even may require one or more press conferences, the development of press kits, and arrangements for tours and interviews, as well as use of a
variety of other strategies and instruments directed toward supplying information and gathering
favorable recognition for the project, its sponsoring agencies, and the institution.

2. Editorial Services

The Information Services staff is available to
help members of the continuing education staff and
faculty associated with continuing education and
public-service projects with their editorial
needs.

These involve acting as liaison between other
staff members and print shops-mail rooms, checking

You are not, of course, going to try to condense all the directions and hints in this book on publicizing and promoting continuing education programs into a handout sheet, now, are you? All you need to tell your anxious amateurs is where to direct their bare-bones releases. And advise them to *buy* this book!

brochures, program announcements, and other types of copy for accuracy and for print-shop style, and helping with the writing and revision of articles or other types of materials intended for publication and concerned in any way with continuing education at the University of Illinois.

In some instances, (a) when time allows and (b) when the subject being treated merits the effort and hours which would be involved, the Information Services staff ghosts articles and assists with books and other publications planned by staff and associated faculty which bear on continuing education. In other instances, a partial rewrite or help and advice on rewriting may be all that is needed.

3. <u>Counseling</u>

The Information Services staff can provide advice and assistance, sometimes helpful and, sadly, sometimes not so helpful on such matters as:

Photographic needs, availability, and use; media outlets where releases, articles, advertisements, photographs, etc., might be welcome and effective in view of the subject matter and approaches involved

If a program is being developed, in which speakers or leaders are of a character or have a position and title which would be a "plus" in drawing participants and media coverage

The locations of media outlets and of people in the media who might be helpful in a given project and/or area of interest

Other miscellaneous matters associated with public information, promotion, publicity, and related subjects and services

So within the purely local, middle-sized-city-neighborhood publicity target area, your handout sheet should look like the above example.

Another example of this kind of service, taken from a New Orleans establishment, follows. It is an excerpt from a much longer memorandum used for publicity

(This is a service of the Information Services
Office, Division of
University Extension)

September 1

SELECTED LOCAL PUBLICITY POSSIBILITIES

These types of publicity outlets require fairly
standard information:
   --Type of event and participants (speaker,
     soloist, etc.)
   --Sponsor
   --Date
   --Time
   --Place
   --Admission cost (if any)
   --Where to obtain more information
This can be stated concisely. It does not even need
to be in narrative or expository form. The facts will
be sufficient.

But it must reach the particular publicity outlet
by mail at least a week in advance. Public-service announcements, weekly newspapers, and print community
calendars may require as much as a month's lead time
and metropolitan outlets may require as much as three
months.

RADIO STATIONS
   1. XXXX (000 AM, country-western), XXXA (00.5, ABC)
send c/o Community Calendar, two weeks in advance, 1211
Skyline Dr., Toledo, OH 45600. To appear on "Today in
Toledo," 15-minute pretaped shows primarily concerned
with community issues (aired Saturdays, 9:45 A.M.
(XXXX) and 10:15 A.M. (XXXA), contact producer Jim
Votruba at 325-4545.
   2. WYYY (1000 AM, middle-of-the-road, CBS)--send
c/o Town Crier, WYYY, 610 S. Neil Road, Toledo, OH
45600. For major fund-raising events, public service
announcer Jim Skalberg will record a 30-second spot to
precede the project. Larry Barston schedules guests
for his talk-open phone show, "Let's Rap," aired
9:30-11:30 A.M. weekdays. Call him at least two weeks
in advance at 325-5800. Mike Patoff hosts a 15-minute
interview, "Current Comment," concerned with local issues, at 6:30 P.M. Tuesdays, Wednesdays, and Thursdays.
Contact him at the same number.

3. <u>WZZZ</u> (580 AM, 90.9 FM, classical, University Station, NPR)—send c/o Cultural Calendar, 100 Main Hall, Toledo, OH 45600. WZZZ does not use meeting announcements. For more extensive coverage, call Randy Blue in the News Department, 333-3000.

4. <u>WTTT</u> (103.9 FM, easy listening, ABC)—send c/o Public Service Announcements, 505 Truman St., Toledo, OH 45600.

TELEVISION STATIONS

1. <u>WAAA</u> (Channel 17, Toledo, ABC)—send notices c/o Community Calendar, WAAA, South Side Dr., Toledo, OH 45600. Mary Capel and Rick Northbow host a live interview program, "Looking in," aired at 9:30-10 A.M. The time can be shared with another group. For events meriting coverage on the local news, contact Northbow at 428-4848.

2. <u>WBBB</u> (Channel 3, Toledo, CBS)—send c/o Public Service Announcements, WBBB, Television Tower, Toledo, OH 45600. "Second Cup" is a 5-minute taped interview with Jerry Powell aired at 7:45 A.M. Contact Powell several weeks in advance at 352-8181. He also hosts interviews during breaks in the "Early Movie" aired 3-5 P.M. daily. To appear on "Night Cap," a call-in show with guest panelists aired Monday night, 11:30-12:30 A.M., call the News Department three weeks in advance. For coverage on local news, call Ann Anderson in the News Department.

3. WCCC (Channel 15, NBC)—send c/o "Now in Toledo," WCCC, Main and Grace Streets, Toledo, OH 45600. Michelle Mosley hosts a 5-minute taped interview aired at 8:25 A.M. weekdays, and a "Saturday Show" at 5 P.M. Saturdays, a 30-minute pretaped interview or panel presentation. If an event merits a news story, write (far ahead) or call Max Neill, c/o News Room.

4. WDDD (Channel 12, educational station, PBS)—send c/o "Coming Events," WDDD-TV, 110 W. Douglas St., Toledo, OH 45600. "Candid Comment" is a live special-interest program with open phone lines, hosted by Mary Leszczak, Carl Fisher, or Tony Powell and aired 6:30-7 P.M. weekdays. The program welcomes those with something of interest today concerning local college-community affairs and also out-of-town guests of note. Contact hosts at 352-2124. The station has no news department but does prepare special programs on issues of wide concern. Contact Program Manager Milton Ross at the station.

NEWSPAPERS

    1. The Toledo Citizen—Send the notice c/o <u>Citizen Calendar</u>, 1717 Race St., Toledo, OH 45600. Send press releases c/o the News Desk at least two days in advance. To arrange photo coverage, make suggestions, ask for feature stories, or report news tips, call Bob Sittig or the News Desk, 352-1800. A morning paper.

    2. The News-Clarion—Send press releases one week in advance to Barbara Firmine, 48 Douglas Rd., Toledo OH. To suggest feature articles, contact the City Desk, 352-1111. <u>The News-Clarion</u> does not have a community calendar, but it does use the Piute University calendar. An evening paper, except for morning editions Saturday-Sunday.

    3. The Daily Piute—The <u>Piute</u> is the student newspaper, published every morning except Sunday during the regular school year, once a week during the summer session.

    The official <u>University Calendar</u> appears in the <u>Piute</u> on Thursdays. Fill out a form in the Office of Campus Programs and Services, 110 Student Services Building, or send a notice c/o Calendar, 110 S.S.B. by 5 P.M. on the Thursday before the Thursday the notice will appear. A <u>Piute</u> "<u>Daily Piute</u> Notice" (different from and more detailed than the University Calendar, as well as more flexible both in format and content) should be brought in or mailed to the <u>Piute</u>, 620 E. Wollard St., Toledo, OH before noon in order to appear in the next day's edition. For a news or feature article, call either the news or feature editor, 333-5689. Coverage in <u>The Piute Weekly</u>, a feature magazine-type supplement in Saturday's <u>Piute</u>, is arranged by the editor of the <u>Weekly</u>, at the same address and telephone number.

    4. The Student Advocate—As its name implies, it is issue-oriented. A free biweekly published on Fridays, its copy deadline is a week before the date of issue. Send notices to the <u>Advocate</u> Editor, 118 Student Services Building.

ADDITIONAL OUTLETS

    1. The City Shopper, a throwaway advertising sheet, is published each Wednesday. Notices and free

personal ads must be received at least a week ahead by
the Shopper, 110 W. Main St., Toledo. Please do not
telephone the Shopper, as it is not staffed to handle
telephone calls.

   2. The Town Crier (a giveaway at local hotels, restaurants, and other locations) is a monthly magazine-
type publication full of information about realtors,
goings-on-about-town, restaurants, theaters, etc.
Send in your materials before the fifteenth of each
month to Katie Gillchrist, 52 Douglas Rd., Toledo. Do
not call.

   3. Exhibit Cases--Piute University Library, call
Sarah Black, 333-4100; Student Services Building Gal-
lery, call Ginny Lawler, 385-2121. The First National
Bank and the University National Bank both have space
allocated to art exhibits (usually one-person shows)
and similar displays. Call the bank in question; the
operator will refer you to the person currently handling exhibits. First National, 352-1811; University,
352-1818.

   4. Bulletin Boards--The University Calendar (see
The Daily Piute) also is posted on the campus bulletin
boards.

   Posters also can be placed on the campus bulletin
boards, but you first must (a) get permission by
filling out a form at the Space Office, 31 Physical
Plant Building, and then (b) put the poster up yourself or have an associate do it.

   Most banks, grocery stores, and other agencies and
businesses have bulletin boards where your moderately
sized posters can be placed. However, again you must
hand-carry, get permission (the cashier usually can
give it), and put them up yourself.

   5. Releases--The Campus Office of Public Information, 15 Burris Building, will distribute fifteen
copies of a press release to a list of local outlets if
the release deals with a university program of wide
interest and has been planned by a university-
registered organization or agency. Call Art Ellis,
333-1085, for details and assistance.

Department of
Public Relations

University Place
New Orleans, La. 70140
(504) 529-7111

FOR: An Informational Aid to Local Media

FROM: Marilyn Barnett, Director of Public Relations

NEW ORLEANS MEDIA

THE TIMES-PICAYUNE
3800 Howard Avenue
New Orleans, LA 70140

Telephone
Area Code 504

Ed Tunstall, Editor	586-3625
Fritz Harsdorff, Associate Editor, News	586-3680
Vincent Randazzo, City Editor	586-3680
Emanuel Alessandra, Business Editor	586-3678
Jesse Johnston, Financial Writer	586-3678
Wiley Masters, State Editor	586-3680
Podine Schoenberger, Medical and Science Editor	586-3690
Mary Lou Atkinson, Women's Editor	586-3656
Bob Roesler, Sports Editor	586-3610

THE STATES-ITEM
3800 Howard Avenue
New Orleans, LA 70140

Telephone
Area Code 504

Walter G. Cowan, Editor	586-3515
Charles A. Ferguson, Associate Editor	586-3516
William Madden, City Editor	586-3560
Jeanette Hardy, Editor, Lagniappe	
(Saturday Entertainment Section)	586-3560
Peter Finney, Sports Editor	586-3580
Bruce Eggler, Entertainment Editor	586-3566

ASSOCIATED PRESS
3800 Howard Avenue
New Orleans, LA 70140

Gary Clark, Bureau Chief   821-3946

UNITED PRESS INTERNATIONAL
1440 Canal-Suite 811
New Orleans, LA 70112

Joey Reaves, Bureau Chief   581-6371
Send press releases to News Desk

GRIS GRIS (Weekly)
1232 Decatur Street
New Orleans, LA 70116

Don Lee Keith, Associate Editor   525-2336
Martin Covert, Listings Editor
Marileen Maher, New Orleans Bureau Chief

LOUISIANA WEEKLY
(Voice of New Orleans Black Community)
640 South Rampart Street
New Orleans, LA 70113

C. C. Dejoie, Jr., Publisher and Editor   524-5563
Tex Stephens, Public Relations
R. L. Stockard, Sports Editor

ORLEANS GUIDE (A suburban publication)
8001 Chef Menteur Highway
New Orleans, LA 70126

Ken Salzer, Editor   241-6353

WDSU—TV (NBC Affiliate—Channel 6)
520 Royal Street
New Orleans, LA 70130

Steve Currie, Program Manager   588—9378
Doug Ramsey, News Director
Greg Fox, Sports Director
Warren Bell, News Anchor
Marcia Kavanaugh, News Anchor (& entertainment)

WVUE—TV (ABC Affiliate—Channel 8)
1025 South Jefferson Davis Parkway
P.O. Box 13847
New Orleans, LA 70185

Don Wilburn, Program Director   486—6161
Jim Kemp, Managing News Editor
Alec Gifford, News Director
Buddy Diliberto, Sports Director
Margie Luebke, Producer, "Good Morning, New Orleans"

WWL—TV (CBS Affiliate—Channel 4)
1024 North Rampart Street
New Orleans, LA 70116

Philip Johnson, News Director   529—4444
Jim Boyer, Managing News Editor
Hap Glaudi, Sports Director
Dick Akin, Promotion Director
Bob Krieger, Sports
Jim Henderson, Sports

WYES TELEVISION (PBS Affiliate—Channel 12)
916 Navarre Avenue
New Orleans, LA 70124

William Hart, General Manager   486—5511

WBOK RADIO (AM—1230 KHz)
3301½ Tulane Avenue
New Orleans, LA 70119

Bobby Earl, Program Director   827—1522

WGSO RADIO (AM—1280 KHz)
Canal LaSalle Building—8th Floor
P. O. Box 2000
New Orleans, LA 70116

Ed Clancy, News Director   581—1280
Wayne Mack, Sports Director/Evening Talk Show Host
Michael Sommers, Morning Talk Show
Mickey Crossin, Sports Coordinator
Eric Tracy, The Eric Tracy Show

WNOE RADIO (AM—1060 KHz)
529 Bienville Street
New Orleans, LA 70130
AM
Mark Sommers, Program Director   529—1212
David Kushler, News Director
Ted Jones, News Staff
FM
Bobby Reno, Program Director
David Kushler, News Director

WRNO (FM—99.5 MHz)
3400 N. Causeway
Metairie, LA 70002

Joe Costello, Owner & General Manager   837—2424
Michael Costello, Program Director

GREATER NEW ORLEANS CHAMBER OF COMMERCE
301 Camp Street
P. O. Box 30240
New Orleans, LA 70130

Linda Hayden, Director of Communications   524—1131

GREATER NEW ORLEANS TOURIST AND CONVENTION COMMISSION
334 Royal Street
New Orleans, LA 70130

Jack Kiefner, Director of Public Relations   522—8772 purposes by the Fairmont Hotel. Note the comments and marks to guide the visiting or amateur publicist. The hotel staff's public relations specialists have marked with asterisks the persons they think will be more interested than others in the visitor's particular program.

The lists of aids to amateurs given on pages 240–243 are suitable for use in a small or moderate-sized community or area and can be adapted to reflect the resources in each particular area.

However, a larger metropolitan community and effort will require a whole different set of information and instructions—the rules change as the city size changes. (See the New Orleans Fairmont Hotel example.) A more sophisticated technique is dealt with on pages 244–245.

It will take a couple of days of investigation by you and your aides to compile your original set of suggestions; it then should be updated about four times a year. In this mobile society, the cast of characters changes frequently, and you don't want to steer your friends and your associates to people who no longer work at a given office.

This effort will be very much worth your time. You will be doing a solid service, on the one hand, and, on the other, through this tactic you will be able to keep people off your back so that you can do the work you are being paid to do.

THE HEALTHY GHOST

The ability to write good, clear English with comparative ease is an attribute which leads (or tempts) many people into being professional or amateur publicists. Even in an organizational setting, they will find it easier to do it themselves rather than wait for a slow-writing colleague to get ideas down on paper.

You may be one of this ilk.

As a consequence, you may find yourself called upon to ghostwrite reports, speeches, articles, even books.

Don't do it unless you want to—or unless the person asking you to ghostwrite is the "Big Boss." The *very* "Big Boss."

But you may find that you actually enjoy it. It can be a game of skill—you are playing strictly against yourself, of course, as many good golfers do—but it also can be an ego trip.

How can you put another person's thoughts into fine, clear, simple words—and at the same time make it *sound* like that person?

It's a trick, of course, as most writing skills are. But it is a trick which can be practiced, and practiced, and practiced. And, at last, perfected.

There are two parts to the trick, and both of them are based on your careful, analytical reading of things that person has written and your listening with the same careful analysis when that person talks. They are:

1. *Strive to get the cadence of the person's speech patterns.* Everyone speaks in cadence. Some people speak in short, crisp sentences, and wouldn't it be nice if more of them did? Sad to say, such people seldom need a ghost. Others turn to convoluted patterns and multisyllabic word choices. When you write for one of these, you've got to structure the sentences so they are short but give the listener (and your speaker or "author") the feel of accustomed patterns.

2. *Always include a scattering of the person's favorite words and phrases.* Everyone has favorite words and phrases. (*Warning:* These sometimes change with time, while speech patterns seldom do.) There are fashions in speech—in words and phrases—which have nothing to do with jargon, even that rampant in the occupational and professional fields. Avoid them like the plague! A word or phrase comes into fashion, has its day, and vanishes into who knows where? It simply floats out of the common vocabulary.

A man I used to ghost for had a number of words which he really preferred. He never said "yes" or "no." He said "affirmative" or "negative." He used the word "merit" a lot. That kind of ponderous speech style, if you keep a vocabulary list for your speakers/authors, is very easy to catch.

Another for whom I have ghosted liked the word "excellent," so of course we let him use it wherever it was appropriate. He also liked "achieve," and we gave him that, too.

Don't be afraid of ghosting. You can do it if you use those two approaches—cadence and favorite words.

Just be certain that you keep the speech or reading material you are producing simple enough so that it will be easy for people to understand yet have enough complexity to fit your speaker's patterns and make him or her comfortable with it.

THE CATALOG AS A PROMOTION PIECE

College and university catalogs are among the most badly written pieces of prose in existence. This state of affairs must have been built, year upon year, in the days when they let professors describe their own courses for catalog use, and the professors strove to impress other professors with their full powers of profundity.

Any time you can do anything to brighten up a catalog, do so. Illustrations, sketches, a little white space here and there, some simple wording to replace the double-talk, and some subheads. *Lots* of subheads.

Get hold of some of the better catalogs put out by the extension–continuing education units of some of the larger institutions with professional continuing education publicists—University of California, Los Angeles; University of California, Berkeley; New York University. Study them for ideas. If your pundits try to buck you with their specialized jargon, say to them, "If you will put what you are trying to tell me into the words you would use in telling it to a very bright seventh grader, I can make the people 'out there' who are intelligent and educated, but too busy to bother translating, read through it and even possibly register or enroll."

INTERNAL RELATIONSHIPS

A publicist, more perhaps than other practitioners of other particular arts or crafts, needs to keep the people around him or her happy—most of the time.

The rest of the time the publicist should be so completely professional in approaching and dealing with all associates, whether they are in or out of his or her institution or organization, that it is a matter of no importance whether they are happy or not. The publicist is doing the job in a thoroughly capable way. So get out of the way and let the pro do it.

The same rules and hints which apply to keeping cosponsors and members of a publicity-promotion task force happy (pages 138–149) hold true in your internal relationships.

However, to skim over a few particular points:

1. Be completely straightforward, honest, and dependable in your dealings with associates.
2. Be mannerly in all things. Even if, to make a professional point, you have to indulge yourself in a temper tantrum, never allow it to include personalities.
3. Always give full credit.
4. Do the best professional job you know (or can learn) how to do. Be proud of your capabilities. Without being boastful or a braggart, acknowledge them. Be secure in your work. Feel good about it. The others, then, will have confidence and feel good about it, too.
5. Whenever you can, give them (any "them") something to read. As a security blanket, you know. Something tangible. A report. A brochure. A release. A catalog. Some rough notes. Some smooth notes.

We could go on, but it all boils down to "do your best job at all times" and "mind your manners."

In fact, the whole book does.

So go do it.

(A WORD IN CLOSING)
YET ANOTHER DIALOGUE BETWEEN YOU AND THE AUTHOR
(WITH A VOICE FROM THE REAR)

Well, how did it go?

It's over. That's the best I can say for it.

You mean you didn't get along all right?

Oh, sure. And I learned a lot. And people were nice.

Most people are. Did the Checklists and guidelines help?

A couple of people even said "Thank you." Sure they helped.

That's good.

But it certainly took a lot of time and effort.

Par for the course.

And at least I'm through with it.

Until the next time.

Oh, no! Not a *next* time!

There always is one—a next time, I mean. I already told you that.

Help!

(Voice from the rear: "They didn't lay a glove on me.")

GLOSSARY

Advertisement   Paid publicity.

Agate line   A unit of measurement used to compute the size and cost of advertisements, one column wide and ¹⁄₁₄ inch deep.

Animation   A method of filming a series of drawings in sequence to simulate motion. Think "Mickey Mouse."

Art   In publicity and promotion, the usual definitions of "art," as in "artistic," do not apply. Here, "art" refers to any form of illustration—photographs, lettering, drawings, graphs, slides, and so on.

Audio   Words, music, sound effects on television and radio shows and in commercials. Anything you hear, rather than read or see.

Author's alterations   Changes in copy made by the author after type has been set. The author, company, or publisher must pay for "AAs" because they are not corrections of printer's mistakes.

Banner   A bold newspaper headline covering most or all of the full width of the page.

Binding   The process of fastening the sections of a book, brochure, or pamphlet together.

B/W   An indication that the material is to be printed in black on white paper or, as in photography or television, that the image is black and white rather than an off-tone (e.g., sepia) color.

Bleed   In publicity and promotion, "bleed" has nothing to do with "blood." Instead, "bleed" means color that runs off the edges of a page, whether it be background color or illustrative color, and which fills one or more margins or borders.

Body copy   The main text in an advertisement, book, article, brochure, poster, etc.

Body type   Type used for the main body of a book, as distinguished from the headings.

Box   Printed matter within rules or borders.

Brand   A name or graphic symbol which identifies a particular manufacturer's product and differentiates it from similar products.

Broadcast media   Television and radio.

Brochure   A booklet, bound either with special stock or with a self-cover, used for promotion. Can be simple or elaborate. Also, the word often is used as an umbrella term for any kind of pamphlet or flyer.

Calendar notice   Full but brief information about an activity to be included in a schedule of events which is published or broadcast.

Camera-ready   Refers to illustrative and written material that is ready for photographic reproduction. The proportions must be exact so that it can be enlarged or reduced as necessary.

Caption   The words accompanying an illustration. Can also be called a cutline. In the offices of some publications, the caption is a single line consisting of a word or a few words, directly over or under an illustration, while the cutline is the expanded text which gives a fuller explanation of what the illustration is meant to convey.

Car Cards   Advertisements placed in buses, subway cars, and trains.

Circulation   The number of copies per issue that a publication distributes.

Classified advertising   Small-space ads in a newspaper or magazine with no illustration and a simple headline, arranged in various classifications and in a special section of the publication. Often called "want ads."

Closing date   Deadline. The absolute cutoff date by which material must be ready or a task accomplished.

Cold type   Printing methods that do not involve traditional molten metal type. Include chemical and photographic processes, transfer type, and hand lettering.

Column width   Not a standard measurement, simply a measurement of the width of a column of a particular publication.

Composer   A typewriter that appears to set type because it spaces letters like a typesetter and can justify (even up) both left and right margins. A wide variety of typefaces is available.

Contact print   A print on photo paper which is made from the negative and which is the exact same size of the negative. Usually an entire roll of film is printed in this manner for easy selection of negatives to be enlarged. The prints usually come out on sheets of proof paper, and so the sheets are called contact sheets, or proof sheets.

Contrast   The degree of difference between the lightest and darkest tones in a photograph, drawing, or other type of illustration.

Copy   All written material that appears in an advertisement, news release, article, script, etc., or is to be set in type.

Copy editing   Correcting and improving copy.

Copy fitting   Making measurements which determine the space required for copy, the amount of copy to be written for an allotted space, the size of type to accommodate an amount of copy in an allotted space. This is a made-up word which means exactly what it says—that is, making the copy fit into the space which is available.

Copy reading   Reading copy for errors and marking it for the printer or typist with proofreading symbols.

Coverage   The number of consumers who are exposed to a message, or the geographic area reached by a particular medium. The news media use this word to indicate their assignments of reporters to a certain story, the amount of time and space they give to that story, etc. A publicity person will invite the media "to cover"; a reporter will say, "I covered so-and-so"; and the media assignment people will say, "We will provide coverage" for such and such an event or development.

Crop   To mark photographs or other illustrations to show which section should be reproduced and which cut off or otherwise eliminated. Usually indicates trimming off the extraneous material or the untidy edges and borders.

Cutline   The text accompanying an illustration. (See also **Caption**.)

Demography   The study of the characteristics of consumers, such as average and median age, income, educational and professional levels, number of children.

Direct voice   Television copy spoken on screen, whether "live" or prerecorded in some manner for later broadcast.

Display advertising   Print advertisements which feature headlines, illustrations, or other display elements and are placed in editorial (not classified) sections.

Display type   Type larger than body type.

Dummy   A mock-up of the proposed finished page or product (book, brochure, magazine, etc.) to present for the approval of the editors and similar persons who have to provide approval, and to guide the compositor when making up the advertisements or the pages. Proofs or other indications of all the components which will go into the finished product (text, illustrations, captions, headlines) are drawn in or pasted into position in the desired page arrangement.

Element   This has nothing to do with the components of a given thing or operation, nor with climate. In public relations and office work, it is the name for the little gimmick (usually in the form of a globe about the size of a large walnut) which is inserted in a typewriter with changeable type and which contains upon its surface a set of the characters for one type size and typeface.

Facts sheet   This is a statement of information, usually one page long, which gives those who need it, such as committee members or members of the working press, the "who-what-where-when-why-how" of a given organization, agency, program, etc., in an easy-to-read and easy-to-understand form.

Filler   Optional material to be included if there is a little broadcast time or print space left over. It can be an announcement, a brief news or feature story, or merely a sentence or two which states an interesting fact or passes along an interesting quotation. In print, you see fillers at the bottoms of columns where it is obvious that the article(s) above ran just a little short.

Flatbed press   A printing press that makes its impression directly from type or plates locked into a flat form, pressure is applied from a rotating cylinder.

Font   When used in reference to printing and graphics, "font" can be defined in two ways. First, generally speaking, a font is a set of type of one style, or a set of similar typographic material. Second, more specifically, a font is an assortment of type of one size and style; it includes all letters of the alphabet and other characters.

Format   The size, design, and shape of a publication; can also refer to typographic requirements.

Foundry type   The p.r. practitioner seldom will come across this term, as it is part of a rather specialized graphics-printing vocabulary. However, in case you meet it somewhere, it refers to type which is fancy or to be used in fancy layouts and patterns, and which usually is found in display advertisements or special page or brochure or book layouts.

Four-track recorder   Machine that records sound in two channels (stereo) on both sides of the tape, thus splitting the tape into four tracks, e.g., cassette tapes.

Front Man   A person (male or female) who is the "up-front" representative or spokesperson for an agency, organization, business, or institution.

Galley Proof   Long proof sheets from type for the author to correct and approve.

Glossy   A photograph printed on shiny, hard-finished paper.

Group interview   Several reporters interviewing one or more people at the same time. Can be spontaneous or prearranged. When prearranged, it is a less formal "little brother" of a press conference.

Halftone   An illustration made by photographing a picture through a screen. The picture is reduced to a dot pattern for reproduction. A fine screen is used to make magazine-quality halftones, and a coarser one is used to make newspaper-quality halftones.

Headline   A clue, in large print, to the material in the article. It is used to attract attention and convey the main idea.

Hot type   Type cast from molten metal.

House organ   A publication circulated primarily within a company, organization, or agency. It can range from an in-house duplicated page to a slick magazine.

Insert   An extra section or page loosely inserted in a book or brochure after it has been bound, or in a newspaper. In writing and preparing copy for print, additions and substitutions of copy often are made as inserts and are fastened to the original copy for the editor's or typist's use. "Insert A, page 32" is an example of an informational notation.

Insertion date   The specific calendar date when an advertisement is scheduled to appear.

IPS (inches per second)   Refers to the speed at which tape is run and means exactly what the words infer, that is, the number of inches of tape which run through a machine in 1 second.

Job order   A form used "in house" to initiate work on a project and follow it through all its production steps. An order blank for work to be done.

Kicker   A brief subhead either below or above a headline. In a feature story, the punch lines at the close—often a surprise or humorous ending.

Layout   A pattern or diagram to show what the printed product should look like. The placement of items on a page or art board, or the schedule of items in a brochure, magazine, or other publication.

Lead   The first paragraph or so of a news release; should be concise and include the most important details.

Leading   The space between lines of type.

Letterfold   The instruction that a sheet is to be folded in thirds widthwise, like a letter.

Letterpress   A printing method in which an inked raised surface is used to transfer ink to paper. The oldest printing method.

Libel   A written, printed, or otherwise nonverbal insulting or defamatory statement, including signs, pictures, effigies, etc., which tends to cause harm to someone's personal, business, or professional standing or good name, or which defames the dead or makes known someone's personal defects. Slander is much the same, except that it deals with the spoken or verbal sort of defamation.

Lithographic conversion   The process of adapting a plate (printing surface) made for letterpress use so it can be prepared for offset printing or lithography.

Lithography   A printing method involving chemical or photographic processes, based on the principle that oil and water don't mix.

Logo   A symbol used to identify a particular company, organization, or institution, like the Red Cross.

Lowercase   Not capital letters.

Makeup   The arrangement of all the elements on a page or in a publication.

Market   The potential purchasers or users of goods or services, or the area covered by a campaign, publication, or broadcast station.

Marketing Research   Research conducted to gather information about a group which will be used to give and/or sell members of it goods and services in the most efficient and/or profitable way. Service to a client and his or her needs. (See other references in the text and in the "Bibliography.")

Mark up   To put composition instructions on copy, art, and a layout.

Media   Print and broadcast channels of communication—e.g., magazines, newspapers, radio, and television. This word often is misused to indicate a variety of borderline combinations of informational or communications methods. Be careful.

Moiré   A wavy visual effect caused by improperly rescreening a halftone print.

Montage   A composite picture formed by combining several separate pictures, or several pictures with art. The elements often are selected so that there is an unconventional mix of sizes and positioning.

Negative   The image obtained from the original in the photographic process, with the light and dark values reversed.

News release   Informational news or feature material written in a professional style for distribution to the print and broadcast media.

Offset   See **Lithography**.

Optical alignment   Moving certain letters, such as "T" or "Y," slightly into the left margin so they will appear to be flush with the margin. Otherwise, the letters would look unevenly placed in relation to the rest of the type.

OCR (optical character recognition)   Refers to a machine that can read special typewritten characters and convert them to tape, in effect "setting type" and bypassing the usual typesetting operation.

Outdoor advertising   Advertising on billboards, posters, or signs placed outdoors.

Overset   What is left over when more type is set than there is space to accommodate. The leftover type often is saved for future use.

Paste-up   An arrangement of everything that is going on a page. All the items are assembled in final form so that the page is ready to be photographed or made into a plate.

Phototypesetting   A method in which a machine chooses and assembles type characters via taped instructions.

Pica   A unit of type measurement—⅙ inch, or 12 points.

Pilot   A trial run or sample effort, usually intended as a model for replication and/or export.

Platform person   Anyone who appears before a group or during an activity or program and/or speaks to the group or during the activity, such as a person who makes a formal introduction, a speaker or panelist, a moderator, a session chair, a respondent, etc.

Point   A unit of type measurement, 1/72 inch.

Positive halftone   A photographic print with light and dark values which correspond to the contrasts we actually see. (In other words, the opposite of a negative.)

Press conference   A called and invitational session in which a person or persons in some way deemed to be newsworthy meet reporters from the news media for a question-answer session of limited length.

Press kit   A folder of information about an organization, event, or individual to aid an editor, director, or reporter covering an event, or to be placed in media "morgues" or libraries for future reference. It can contain all kinds of background materials—biographies, photographs, articles, schedules, information on sponsors and program participants, copies of speeches, and so on.

Press room   Sometimes, as in a large conference center, a permanent facility for the use of the working press. At other times, a press room is set up on a temporary basis for the convenience of the working press and the publicity people connected with an institution, activity, or event, it is available for the duration of an individual activity or event.

Proof   An impression of set copy to be examined (depending on the circumstances) by the proofreader, author, editor, etc.

Proofreading   Reading copy that has been typed or typeset, to find any errors and indicate any necessary corrections.

Public-service announcement   A short, concise message of a noncommercial nature used on radio or television to announce and/or promote an activity or cause.

Quire   A collection of twenty-five sheets of paper of the same size and quality.

Ream   A collection of 500 sheets of paper of the same size and quality.

Reproduction (repro) proof   A final proof in the printing process of a quality suitable for photographic reproduction.

Rotary press   A press capable of printing a high volume of material at high speeds because the printing surface and the impression surface both are curved.

Rough   A preliminary sketch or draft of a proposed layout, or a first draft of any written material. A rough provides an idea of the item—not a finished, polished product.

Run   The number of copies to be printed at a time. Sometimes called a press run. Also, the length of time or number of times that an item will be printed or broadcast. "Full run" would mean that all editions of a TV, radio, or newspaper item or ad will run for a week or other span of time.

Script   Written material read by performers or announcers over the broadcast media. Type which resembles handwriting rather than conventional print, because it slants and is run together.

Short spot   A brief broadcast interview or statement, usually promoting an event or cause. Normally runs 4 minutes, 10 seconds, if not sponsored; 3 minutes, 10 seconds, if sponsored.

Sidebar   A feature story that is peripheral to a major news story. While not news by itself, it adds depth and interest to the major story it accompanies. When Pope John Paul I was elected, sidebars detailed his childhood and career.

Silk screen   A process of making prints by forcing ink through silk cloth, nylon, or stainless steel mesh onto which a stencil design has been mounted.

Slander   See **Libel**.

Slug   An identifying word for a news release or article that appears on each page to help the typesetter or typist keep track of all pages in sequence. A murder story might be slugged "slay" or by the name of the victim. Some shops call this a tag line. Also, a slug sometimes is a piece of lead with no letter on it, used to separate elements on a printed sheet.

Speakers Bureau   A group of persons who agree (as assigned or invited) to make appearances and speak on behalf of a cause or activity, or on another single topic or cluster of topics. In some cases, a college or other organization may have a listing of speakers from its ranks which will include the topics they wish to speak on, the fee charged (if any), and information on their backgrounds. Commercial speakers bureaus, which in effect are booking agencies, exist in many cities to make engagements for paid "name" speakers with groups or organizations.

Steering committee   A group established to formulate policy and set directives for a major effort, such as running a campaign or planning a conference.

Stet (let it stand)   Noted when copy marked for deletion is to be put back in its original form.

Stringer   A reporter or photographer who is retained by a newspaper, station, or magazine to work "as needed" in a given area that does not generate enough major news to warrant maintaining a full-time correspondent there.

Task force   A committee charged with accomplishing a particular goal, such as establishing a scholarship fund or determining a name for a new public facility. In this book, we have used "task force" or "p.r. task force" as an easy, effort-saving term for those working as a team on publicity and promotion for an activity.

Tear sheet   A whole page from a publication, normally given to an advertiser as proof that his or her ad was placed as specified. When it is given to the advertiser in advance of the insertion date, the advertiser can make corrections.

Telecast   A television broadcast.

Text   The main body of an article or other form of written, printed, or scripted material. Also, a book for instructional use, i.e., a textbook.

Theme   A general subject, topic, or idea.

Trademark   A symbol registered with the U.S. Patent Office and used exclusively by a concern to identify its products or publications.

Transfer type   Type "embedded" in a plastic sheet. It is removed by rubbing it with a special instrument onto a poster or other paper. If the transferring is done well, the type can look like set type.

Typeface   A name of a design of type. Among popular body typefaces are Goudy, Garamond, and Baskerville, known for easy readability.

Type family   A font with a distinctive feature—such as italics, boldface, lightface, back slant; being expanded or wide, condensed, open—or a combination of features.

Type series   Within a typeface, the various sizes of types available. The usual range is from 6 points (1/12 inch) to 72 points (1 inch). Smaller and larger sizes than these exist for many typefaces.

Typo   Short for "typographical error," a mistake made by a typist or typesetter.

Typographer   A specialist who selects type for a given production. Often a page designer, sometimes a designer of typefaces, sometimes even a graphics specialist. The word is a flexible one, and outside the strict boundaries of the printing world it can be used in several ways.

UHF (ultrahigh frequency)   A limited-range secondary television broadcast band.

VHF (very high frequency)   The original television broadcast band, featuring national, international, or local programming on Channels 2–13.

Video   All the visual elements of a television program or commercial.

VDT (video display terminal)   A tool that enables one to type copy into a computer via a keyboard and correct it while it is on a screen.

Video tape   Magnetic tape containing both recorded video and audio portions for immediate replay.

Voice-over   The voice of a narrator who is off-screen. The narrator reads copy "over" a scene.

White space   An area without type or illustrations. This term in public relations and newspaper work and printshops usually refers to the areas of space left over and available for printed matter such as news, news features, and news photos after a publication has indicated via a layout the space which will be taken up by ads. In this context, it is sometimes known as the "news hole."

Wrong font   A letter or character that is not the specified size or face.

Wrap-up story, article, release   A final approach in the news media which "wraps up" the p.r. effort regarding an event or institution by including all possible information in detail. Goes out just before the start of the activity being publicized.

BIBLIOGRAPHY
The Basic Bookshelf*

The Associated Press Stylebook and Libel Manual. The Associated Press, 50 Rockefeller Plaza, New York, NY 10020. Paperback, 1977, 276 pages, $2.75.
  (Dictionary-type listing of newspaper styles for capitalization, abbreviations, punctuation, spelling, numerals, and usage. Good information on libel. Make this your style "bible.")
Ayer Directory of Publications. Ayer Press, 210 W. Washington Square, Philadelphia, PA 19106. Published annually, $54.
Bacon's Publicity Checker. Bacon's Publishing Company, 14 E. Jackson Blvd., Chicago, IL 60604. Published annually, two-volume set for $95. Volume 1—magazines; Volume 2—dailies and weeklies.
Broadcasting Yearbook. Broadcasting Publications, Inc., Broadcasting-Telecasting Building, 1735 DeSales St., N.W., Washington, D.C. 20036. Published annually, $37.50 ($32.50 if payment enclosed).
Editor and Publisher International Year Book. Editor and Publisher, 850 Third Ave., New York, NY 10022. Published annually, $30.
Regional and/or State Media Directories. Call your state press association for these volumes. (See pages 126–129 for a listing.)
Telephone Directories. Call your local telephone company office to obtain the directories for the communities you deal with. You may be able to arrange to be put on a list to receive the directories you need as they are published each year without reordering.

*See text, pp. 96–100.

Other Sources

Barban, Arnold, and Dunn, S. Watson. *Advertising: Its Role in Modern Marketing.* The Dryden Press, Inc., 901 N. Elm St., Hinsdale, IL 60521. 4th edition, 1978, 740 pages, $16.95.
  (There are thorough sections on background for advertising and promotion, planning the campaign, creating the message, the media of advertising and promotion, and special purposes and special publics. These provide an excellent basis from which to start your own program.)
Bernstein, Theodore M. *The Careful Writer: A Modern Guide to English Usage.* 1965, $7.95 paperback, $14.95 cloth. *Watch Your Language.* 1958, paperback, $3.95. Atheneum Press, 122 E. 42d St., New York, NY 10017.
  (Bernstein has an easy style, useful for the beginner. He's an authority on usage and syntax, a good arbiter of points in this area. *Watch Your Language* is divided into two major sections, "Words that Need Watching" and "Syntax Sinners," with often-misused words, phrases, and constructions alphabetized for easy reference.)
Burke, John D. *Advertising in the Marketplace.* McGraw-Hill Book Company, 1221 Avenue of the Americas, New York, NY 10020. 1967, 440 pages, $15.55, school price $12.44.
  (Units on advertising media, research and budgets, and creating practical advertising provide a good background. A good book for beginners.)

The New Columbia Encyclopedia. Columbia University Press, 562 W. 113th St., New York, NY 10025. 1975, 3,052 pages, $79.50.
   (An extremely useful one-volume encyclopedia with a well-deserved reputation for excellence. Many writers consider it a "must have" in their reference collection.)
The Congressional Directory. Superintendent of Documents, U.S. Government Printing Office, Washington, D.C. 20402. Published annually. Cloth, $8.50; cloth indexed, $12.95; paperback, $6.50.
   (Key information on Congress, including biographies, departments, and addresses of members of Congress and their committee assignments; biographies of major officials; names and addresses of officials in the judicial, executive, and legislative branches; names and addresses of press representatives; brief descriptions of departments and agencies; district boundaries. Your state may publish a similar volume; check with your local librarian or government office.)
Darrow, Richard W.; Forrestal, Dan J.; and Cookman, Aubrey O. *The Dartnell Public Relations Handbook.* The Dartnell Corporation, 4660 N. Ravenswood Ave., Chicago, IL 60640. January 1979 was the target publication date; $39.50.
   (A classic, expounding on public relations today, internal communications, external public relations, and p.r. tools and the media. Excellent examples and information throughout. A comprehensive appendix, including a tie-in calendar for public relations, principles of clear writing, and a "Watchlist" of words and expressions to avoid.)
Flesch, Rudolph. *The Art of Readable Writing.* 1974, $10.95. *The Art of Clear Thinking.* 1951, $10.95. *Look It Up: A Desk Book of American Spelling and Style.* 1977, $10.95. *Say What You Mean.* 1972, $10.95. Harper & Row, Publishers, Incorporated, 10 E. 53d St., New York, NY 10022.
   (Common sense, practicality, humor, and wit are Flesch's trademarks. His words are invaluable guides to good communication and, as a plus, are enjoyable to read. Several books, including *How to Be Brief*, are out of print; if you can latch onto any of them, at a library, perhaps, do—they still sparkle.)
Gebbie House Magazine Directory. National Research Bureau, 424 N. Third St., Burlington, IA 52601. Published annually, $48.
   (Information on 3,500 internal and external house organs of more than 3,500 United States and Canadian companies, government agencies, clubs, and other groups. *Gebbie House Magazine Directory* is Volume 5 of the *Working Press of the Nation* group. Volumes 1 through 4 are, respectively, *Newspaper and Allied Services Directory, Magazine and Editorial Directory, Radio and TV Directory,* and *Feature Writer and Syndicate Directory.* The first three volumes may be obtained for $126; all five for $161. If the volumes are purchased separately, each is $48.)
Greenfield, Stanley R. *National Directory of Addresses and Telephone Numbers.* Bantam Books, Inc., 666 Fifth Ave., New York, NY 10019. 1977, $9.95.
   (Includes the 50,000 most wanted telephone numbers and addresses in the United States. Categories are business and finance; government, politics, and diplomacy; transportation and hotels; associations and unions; communications and media; business services; etc. Great idea!)
Hanson, Glenn. *How to Take the Fits Out of Copyfitting.* The Mul-T-Rul Company, Fort Morgan, CO 80701. 1967, 115 pages, paperback, $7.95.
   (If you want to calculate how much copy will fit into a predetermined space, how much space copy will require in a given type size, and how much to crop pictures to fit, this little handbook will show you an easy way, using the Mul-T-Rul, a slide rule designed especially for those purposes. A Mul-T-Rul is included with the book.)
Information Please Almanac. Information Please Publishing, Inc., 57 W. 57th St., New York, NY 10019. Published annually. Paperback, $3.95.
   (A compendium of a wealth of reference material, including easy-to-locate material on colleges, news events, vital statistics, history, geography, awards, science, and more.)

Lem, Dean. *Graphics Master 2.* Dean Lem Associates, P.O. Box 46086, Los Angeles, CA 90046. 1977, 36 pages, $37.50.

(A workbook containing basic working information for each phase of graphic production. Includes concise technical guidelines and graphic tools. Quite sophisticated material.)

Lesly, Philip. *Lesly's Public Relations Handbook.* Prentice-Hall, Inc., Englewood Cliffs, NJ 07632. 2d edition, 1978, 663 pages, $29.95.

(If you can buy only one book on general public relations, let this one be it.)

A Manual of Style. The University of Chicago Press, 5801 S. Ellis, Chicago, IL 60628. 12th edition, 1969, $13.95.

[The "bible" of scholarly and research style. Not practical for literary and/or newspaper style. Academicians (rightfully) swear by it.]

Metz, William. *Newswriting: From Lead to "30."* Prentice-Hall, Inc., Englewood Cliffs, NJ 07632. 1977, 388 pages, $11.95.

(A good basic book on newswriting; it also gives a good idea of how a newspaper is run.)

Morris, William, and Morris, Mary, eds. *Harper Dictionary of Contemporary Usage.* Harper & Row, Publishers, Incorporated, 10 E. 53d St. New York, NY 10022. $15.

(Identifies words most commonly misused, and answers questions about usage, grammar, punctuation, etc.)

New York Times Manual of Style and Usage. Quadrangle/New York Times Book Co., 10 E. 53d St., New York, NY 10022. 4th printing, 1976, 231 pages, $10.

(Contains interesting editorial philosophy besides setting forth "The Times" stance on usage.)

Pocket Pal—A Graphic Arts Production Handbook. International Paper Company, 220 E. 42d St., New York, NY 10017. 11th edition, 1974, 191 pages, paperback, $1.50.

(An excellent introduction to the graphic arts, it explains the new printing processes, all steps of production, paper qualities. A very low price for such for such valuable, well-presented material.)

Politella, Dario, ed. *The Directory of the College Student Press in America.* Oxbridge Communications, Inc., 1345 Avenue of the Americas, New York, NY 10019. 4th edition, 1977–78, 632 pages, $25.

[Less comprehensive listings of the college student press are found in *Ayer* and *Editor and Publisher* (see the "Basic Bookshelf")]

Roget's International Thesaurus. Thomas Y. Crowell Company, 10 E. 53d St., New York, NY 10022. 4th edition, 1977, $10.50, $11.95 thumb-indexed.

(A classic reference, helps you find just the word you're looking for. A great source of synonyms when you realize you're getting repetitive.)

Shaw, Harry, ed. *Dictionary of Problem Words and Expressions.* McGraw-Hill Book Company, 1221 Avenue of the Americas, New York, NY 10020. 1975, $10.95.

(A valuable reference aid to improving your writing and keeping out of word trouble.)

Smeyak, Paul G. *Broadcast News Writing.* Grid, Inc., 4666 Indianaola Ave., Columbus, OH 43214. 1977, 202 pages, paperback, $7.95.

(This book will help you write your public-service announcements concisely and avoid common pitfalls. Good for beginners.)

The Statistical Abstract of the United States. U.S. Department of Commerce, Bureau of the Census. Superintendent of Documents, U.S. Government Printing Office, Washington, D.C. 20402. Published annually. Cloth, $11; also comes in paperback.

(A virtual gold mine of United States trends and statistics in numerous categories. Just a sample of the various topics included: income and expenditures, education, welfare and public aid, elections, geography, health, manufactures, the labor force.)

Stone, Bob. *Successful Direct Marketing Methods.* Crain Books Division, Crain Communications, Inc., 740 Rush St., Chicago, IL 60611. 1975, 334 pages, $19.95.

(Successful direct marketing is the right product, the right media, the right prosposition, the right tests, and the right analysis for the purpose of eliciting a *direct response.* By studying Stone's superb evaluations, checklists, guides, and examples, and by benefiting from his vast experience, you can be on your way to filling your programs in the most efficient manner. Learn from the mistakes and successes of others. This book is for the *experienced* practitioner.)

Strunk, William, Jr., and White, E. B. *The Elements of Style.* The Macmillan Company, 866 Third Ave., New York, NY 10022. 1972, 85 pages, paperback, $1.95.

(A very graceful little book, a delight to read. Helpful to the prose stylist.)

Turnbull, Arthur T., and Baird, Russell N., *The Graphics of Communication.* Holt, Rinehart and Winston, Inc., 383 Madison Ave., New York, NY 10017. 3d edition, 1975, 462 pages, $12.95.

(Valuable sections are "Verbal and Visual Elements of Communication," "Preparing Verbal and Visual Copy for Production," "Design Principles and Advertising Layout," "Planning and Designing Other Printed Literature," and "Paper: Selecting, Folding, Binding, Finishing." Intermediate level.)

Ulanoff, Stanley M. *Advertising in America* Communication. Arts Books, Hastings House, Publishers, Inc., 10 E. 40th St., New York, NY 10016. 1977, 492 pages, $8.95 paperback, $19.95 cloth.

(The sections called "Work of Advertising" and "Media" are informative, the former stressing the preparation involved, and the latter the many outlets available—transit advertising and Sunday supplements, for example. Experienced practitioners will find it useful.)

INDEX